Dog Days,
Raven Nights

Yale

UNIVERSITY

PRESS

New Haven and London

Dog Days, Raven Nights

John M. Marzluff and Colleen Marzluff

Original Linocut Illustrations by Evon Zerbetz

Foreword by Bernd Heinrich

Published with assistance from the Kingsley Trust Association Publication Fund
established by the Scroll and Key Society of Yale College.

Yale University Press books may be purchased in quantity for educational, business,
or promotional use. For information, please e-mail sales.press@yale.edu (U.S. office)
or sales@yaleup.co.uk (U.K. office).

Designed by Nancy Ovedovitz and set in Bulmer and Poppl Laudatio types by
Keystone Typesetting, Inc. Printed in the United States of America.

Library of Congress Cataloging-in-Publication Data
Marzluff, John M.
Dog days, raven nights / John M. Marzluff and Colleen Marzluff ; original linocut
illustrations by Evon Zerbetz ; foreword by Bernd Heinrich.
p. cm.
Includes bibliographical references and index.
ISBN 978-0-300-16711-5 (cloth : alk. paper)
1. Corvus corax—Behavior. 2. Corvus corax—Psychology. 3. Corvus corax—Research—
Maine. 4. Social behavior in animals. 5. Marzluff, John M. 6. Marzluff, Colleen. 7. Dogs.
I. Marzluff, Colleen. II. Title.
QL696.P2367M356 2011
598.8′64—dc22
2010037009

A catalogue record for this book is available from the British Library.

This paper meets the requirements of ANSI/NISO Z39.48-1992 (Permanence of Paper).

10   9   8   7   6   5   4   3   2   1

For Topper, Sitka, Brodie, Kenai, Sky, Buster, and Granite, forever together as a team over the "rainbow bridge." They carried heavy loads with quick feet and happy hearts.

And

For Zoe and Danika, who are shaped in part by our experiences.

Contents

CONTENTS

Foreword

Bernd Heinrich

There are few endeavors fraught with more tension, expectations, joys, and sometimes disappointments than a young researcher starting his or her career, or an older one fearing that his is petering out and suddenly finding a new direction. They generate dreams and spawn adventures that affect lifetimes and that will later be remembered, savored, and finally appreciated. You never know at the beginning what your labors will bring, but you knew back then that you *have* to go the mile or suffer the anticipated pain of possible regret. I believe John and Colleen Marzluff knew that when they left Arizona to join me in Maine at Camp Believe It. We were all captivated by an extremely charismatic bird, the raven, and working in the romantic backdrop of the Maine woods with colorful characters, human and other, living there. What we experienced is, I think, a surprise to all of us. It was at least for me far beyond expectations. It turned into the adventure of a lifetime that went beyond the discoveries we made and that revealed unexpected secrets in the lifestyle of a mysterious animal.

I have been a closet ornithologist probably since I was eight years old, but in my university positions, I had been a practicing insect physiologist. I had "made" my career on the study of the behavior and ecology of bees with reference to their evolution and their energy economy and the physiological mechanisms of exercise and body temperature regulation. But since childhood I have had a love affair with corvid birds and at various times have enjoyed the intimate companionship of free-flying but hand-raised tame crows, jays, magpies, and ravens. The idea that I could make scientific discoveries from these birds was beyond my ken since I presumed everything worth knowing had already been discovered.

By the 1980s I was starting to run out of steam with my insect work; I had answered the questions I had set out to solve and felt I had mined the major nuggets from my field. I could not see any looming enigma but sensed that there were many small, perhaps mostly repetitive, questions instead, most of which I felt could be solved by rote. But in fall 1984, I was attracted to a moose carcass in the woods near my camp by the noisy calls of ravens, calls I had never heard before. Having worked with bees who recruit colony mates to rich food resources, I was instantly intrigued, because ravens "shouldn't" give away the location of a rich food resource. Ravens are not social like bees. I knew of the raven pair that had nested for at least a decade in a pine tree at the nearby Hills Pond, but I had never heard these calls. Here, in part because of my ignorance as well as my knowledge of social behavior, I knew there was something extremely interesting going on. Could there be sharing behavior by proximally selfish individuals? This would not be a problem like my insect work, where at this point I usually already had a good hypothesis of what was going on at the beginning. Here I didn't have a clue. This mystery was to me irresistible, and I jumped in with everything I had.

It turned into an adventure, and it was the most physically demanding one I have ever encountered. Recently I had run ultramarathons but having had enough of them, I now had energy to burn while seeing the bright light of a potential exciting discovery ahead. After spending part of every week at my camp for four winters, then spending a sabbatical year there (with my tame raven Jack), I felt I had finally found an answer to the enigma. It was pieced together from a large patchwork of observations, "experiments," and inferences from theory and comparative behavior. It was sufficient for a publication. Ordinarily that would have been the end of it. Except there remained the troubling question: although the "yell" calls given at food did attract others, they could not account for the large numbers of ravens that usually arrived as a group from one direction in the dawn or even predawn. These ravens were nonterritorial vagrant birds that came from communal roosts. But how were they recruited from there, and from how far and by whom? Did the carcass discoverer do the equivalent of the waggle dance that bees did in the hive? Impossible! Here was another looming enigma, but one I doubted that could, practically, be solved.

Serendipitously, Con Slobodchikoff (an insect behaviorist interested in social behavior) invited me to a symposium he had organized in Flagstaff, Arizona. I presume he had asked me because of my work with bumblebees, since that was all I was known for. Instead I talked about my raven work because it involved recruitment, and I knew so little and felt there was much to learn; I needed a sounding board with the corvid researchers based there at Northern Arizona University. There I met John Marzluff. He had attended my talk and had apparently also mined out his area of research, the social biology of Pinyon Jays. Like me, he was captivated by corvids and excited by a good question. I stayed with John and Colleen Marzluff at their home, and I was much captivated by their interest, energy, and enthusiasm. I knew that if anyone could or would solve the recruitment problem it would be they. I think we were so enthused that we were able to "think big"—to talk of making a huge aviary where we would simulate wild conditions suitable to experiments of recruitment from a communal roost. This would be a big project, one I could not do alone especially as I was based in Vermont, where I was tied to teaching duties at the University of Vermont. The logical place to mount this project was in Maine, at my camp, Camp Believe It, where I owned the land and where we could chop down a patch of forest to build an aviary, since the only way to continue was with experiments with captive birds. This project required a huge commitment and a constant presence; John and Colleen, as postdoctoral researchers could and needed to be there with the birds full time. They had now a "perfect" question to try to solve, and it would be theirs.

One of the marks of good research is, I think, that it can be somewhat predictable but not too much so. As John describes in the pages that follow, we built a huge aviary (the late Eberhard Gwinner, a pioneer raven researcher in Germany, declared it the biggest he had ever seen when he came to visit). The aviary had a large central compartment from which radiated two long corridors ending in smaller side aviaries. We could house a territorial pair of ravens in one side aviary and could hide food with them or in the undefended side aviary for the captive young ravens to find. We made roosting sheds where the birds had perches under protective roofs for use at night. We equipped these communal roost sheds with viewing platforms in the back so that we could observe the birds through one-way mirrored windows. We thus hoped to determine how the food-discovering birds were able to recruit others into and down the long aviary corridors to the food hidden in side aviaries. Unfortunately, this, which I felt was *the* prime experiment of the project, proved to be impractical in the aviary setting. This should not have been too surprising to us as we knew that the aviary context was not guaranteed to be the best platform for seeing natural behavior of all kinds, although it was the only context in which to critically observe and test behaviors. In previous projects, I often ended up doing experiments other than the ones I had originally proposed. This was usually good because it meant that I had to be open to what the results suggested, not tied to my expectations. John and Colleen, by being enterprising and innovative, made the same discovery.

Despite our inability to witness recruitment from the roost within the confines of the aviary, it proved to be an extraordinary tool and a tremendous success. The wild-caught ravens, the shyest and most secretive birds I knew, tamed down quickly, far beyond what I expected, and they could then be observed up close and intimately, while at the same time we could manipulate conditions and, more important, also know the experiences of the individually marked birds. None of this would have been possible without the aviary setting. It was a golden opportunity to conduct many tests, something we did not anticipate at the beginning of our research. I was taken aback when John and Colleen started to "test" what I thought I already "knew." In retrospect, I should have known better. Almost every experiment led to another one that would divulge something new and unexpected, something that would not have been thought of or conceived were it not for the experiment that preceded it. I was pleasantly surprised and impressed with the cleverness of their experiments and how they revealed the intentions and motivations (mind) of the raven.

Previously I had worked only with wild ravens. I had enjoyed the help and company of numerous volunteers, people who were in it for the adventure but not the science per se, but John and Colleen and I had come together from different scientific directions, and so we complemented each other both in the work and with stimulating discussions. I, having studied insect behavior, had been concerned with the mechanics and function of that behavior; there was never any thought in my mind of an insect acting out of a proximate motivation *to consciously* do something for a purpose. Similarly, I felt the ravens recruited "to" overpower the defenders of food bonanzas as a shorthand, meaning there was adaptive significance to that behavior, which we could demonstrate with a benefit. I did not mean to imply any specific intention whatsoever. The yell calls could simply be a reflex of hungry birds to some stimulus associated with a situation where there was food and where there was a possibility that the presence of others might aid in gaining or maintaining access to it. Indeed, to me the *significance* of the raven recruitment was as a system of sharing based on selfishness. It was proximally based on the selfishness of nonterritorial birds and was ultimately a tactic functioning to circumvent the selfishness of others. To the contrary, however, some people presumed instead that I was proposing that ravens were kind-hearted selfless creatures willing to give up for the benefit of others. I felt it was nearly impossible to know what the proximate psychological reason for ravens to recruit was. John and Colleen, having previously worked with jays and squirrels, and not being dyed-in-the-wool believers that intentions are a taboo topic, were more open to and interested in the proximate reasons for the ravens' sharing. For this level of investigation, the aviary was ideal testing ground, and the new lever that they applied to the problem was the objectively derived dominance relationships among groups of birds. Ironically, because of the work with the ravens enclosed in the aviary I was later converted; I was led to experiments of perhaps the most proximate reasons of all—not just reflex responses to otherwise arbitrary stimuli, but also behavior in response to what was happening in their heads, such as "insight" and "intelligence." At this point the raven baton has now been passed on, primarily to another postdoc, Thomas Bugnyar, who came to Vermont from Austria, also with his family, and who stayed for three years to work with other groups of tame ravens in another aviary and who is now a professor at the University of Vienna.

The three years that John, Colleen, and I worked together to solve a raven mystery is recounted here in *Dog Days, Raven Nights*. As I read their accounting of our time together, I came to understand and appreciate much more about their personal adventure and unique experiences, not only with ravens but also with the dogs that shared their lives. The good times and often challenging times are laid bare. My love of a good joke and the feel of Maine culture and some of my closest friends since childhood are revealed with fresh eyes. The discoveries and the frustrations of a newly minted Ph.D. and a seasoned professor, the dynamic of a husband-and-wife research team, unique insights into the summer world of blackflies and the winter world of ravens and raven handling, as well as that of dogs and dog mushing, are here recounted. As I reminisce about that time, two decades ago, I see it as one of the great adventures of my life. It is brought back here in often-vivid detail, detail that at the time vacillated between the seeming routine and the still mostly hidden but sublime.

Preface

In 1988 we packed our belongings, bid farewell to the familiar, and headed with our two dogs, Sitka and Topper, from Arizona to a far corner of the northeastern United States. We were embarking on a three-year study of the winter ecology of ravens. The experience taught us much about biology and even more about rural lifestyles, strong friendships, career paths, dogsledding, and each other. Here we weave these themes together as we experienced life in a small cabin in the lightly settled mountains of western Maine. Ours is not a story of wilderness. It is a celebration of scientific research in a remote setting that fully involves, and critically depends on, the local people.

We wrote this book to share our perceptions and discoveries with a wide audience. We hope to motivate young scientists, who like us are following an unknown and tortuous career path, to persevere. We offer this motivation from the viewpoint of a young married couple who worked together to learn. In addition, we aim to teach the interested layperson about an often-misunderstood bird, the common raven, from our unique and personal view of their mysterious lives. For those who love dogs or are fascinated by working dogs and arctic travel, we introduce you to the work ethic of modern sled dogs and allow you to learn with us how to integrate a life-long companion into your work and recreation. Finally, as outsiders who were immediately and warmly welcomed into a large, extended Maine family, we share with you our understanding of rural life and character. The people of Maine who shared their lives with us are among the most resilient and resourceful people we have ever known. In today's uncertain world, they have much to teach.

Our perspective draws on our years in Maine from 1988 to 1991 and on the two decades since then, after we returned to our native western United States. Our story of those years remains a fresh and accurate picture of a recently married couple just out of graduate school, seeking permanent employment, before children. In writing this book, we draw on the extensive personal journal that Colleen kept and on John's detailed research notes. We clarified impressions and blurry details during a visit to our former abode in August 2008.

Much of the basic biological knowledge that we gained has been published in the scientific literature, and some of the adventure and discovery of our work has been published for the layperson in the books written by our partner in this research, Bernd Heinrich. Here we build on these past efforts by more fully exploring the daily insights we gained into the lives of captive and wild ravens. Our view as young, recently married scientists with an uncertain future and undeveloped connection to the people of Maine complements Heinrich's view as a well-established, single scientist and Mainer. We hope our fresh eyes provide new insights into ravens, the adventure that is field science, and partnerships.

In this book we explore three distinct partnerships: student-mentor, husband-wife, and human-dog. Each has taught us much. The student-mentor relationship is creative but tense, and we illustrate how both of these aspects made us better scientists. The husband-wife relationship is supportive but stressful in tight quarters and demanding work conditions. This personal relationship allowed us to succeed and grow. The human-dog relationship is simply fantastic. Our dogs lightened our workload and our lives by hauling supplies and providing a social, recreational, and humorous outlet.

We write in our personal voice so that you can more fully share our excitement, successes, and failures. To aid in knowing who the "I" is, we include each other in our opening statements and preface transitions to John's voice with a raven icon and to Colleen's voice with a dog icon.

Our adventure and this book would not have been possible without the support of our families, friends, and colleagues who came to visit to see what we were doing and to lend a hand. Tom, Zetta, Jenn, Hilary, Josh, Brodie, Sky, and Jocko Wojcik shared their home and lives with us, making our stay in Maine possible and enjoyable. Henry and Leona DiSotto, Billy and Butch Adams, and their extended family supported us as one of their own. They also were quick to help with our construction, observation, and raven-raising projects. Dave Lidstone was steadfast in his field support and enthusiasm for learning about nature. Stan and Jim Roth, Jim Parker, Rick Ashton, Harry Wycoff, and Wendy and Steve Freschette gave freely of their time to aid our field research. Bernd Heinrich encouraged and supported our research, mentored us as developing scientists, and provided the research and logistical network that was the basis for our work. Although we did not always see eye to eye on the daily grind of science, we remain respectful friends and valued colleagues. Bernd read the entire manuscript of this book and provided thoughtful, timely, and stimulating comments. The U.S. National Science Foundation supported our original raven research and the School of Forest Resources, University of Washington, provided the intellectual and physical space needed to write. Evon Zerbetz enlivened our work with her beautiful linocut illustrations. She sees ravens for all their fun, mischievous, and wonderful selves. Our current students and postdocs, Barbara Clucas, Heather Cornell, Jack DeLap, Laura Farwell, Ben Shyrock, Lauren Seckel, and Steven Walters, as well as Clara Burnett and Joanne Bartkoski, constructively critiqued our manuscripts. Jack DeLap did double duty, also illustrating appendix 1 with a scientist's eye and artist's skill. Eliza Childs edited our manuscript with a New Englander's eye. Jean Thomson Black at Yale University Press encouraged and improved our writing and thinking, literally helping us to see the book in our story.

JOHN AND COLLEEN MARZLUFF

Maltby, Washington

Cast Of Characters, Lay of the Land

Our story refers to many people, places, dogs, and ravens. To help readers keep track of our friends and land, we here provide a brief overview. The landscape we traversed in pursuit of ravens and their roosts, as well as in dog races, is mapped. Landmarks to which we often refer are placed on the map for quick reference. We illustrate the groups of ravens we captured, held in the aviary, and eventually released to the wild during three years of research in appendix 1.

People

Russ Balda, professor at Northern Arizona University, pioneered research into the mental abilities of corvids. He advised John's graduate work and employed Colleen as a research technician.

Frank and Don Castonguay, father and son butchers in North Livermore, Maine, supplied an offal lot of what the ravens ate.

Dwight Cram and *Mike Pratt,* state of Maine game and fish wardens, relayed the locations of road-killed animals for raven research and pitched in with construction and field work when needed.

Margaret Cook, a school teacher and sled racer from Boston, bred Siberian Huskies (kennel name Teeco) and mentored Colleen.

Henry and Lee DiSotto, husband and wife who lived in Jay, Maine, adopted John and Colleen into their extended family. They and Lee's three sons, *Butch (Vernon) Adams, Billy (Clifford) Adams,* and *Jimmy (Floyd) Adams* were indispensable research assistants and ambassadors to the Maine culture. Butch was an electrician married to *Nancy,* and together they had two daughters, *Monica and Lindsey.* Billy was a shoe pattern maker married to *Lili,* and they had a son, *Aaron,* and a daughter, *Kathleen.* Billy was deeply involved in all aspects of the raven project, including raising a brood of young ravens in 1989.

Peggy Grant, an early and influential Siberian Husky breeder, owned Marlytuk kennels.

Eberhard (Ebo) Gwinner, a raven expert from Germany, visited Maine.

Ed Hathaway, student of John's in Arizona, close friend of John and Colleen, and Boston native, spent extended stays in Maine helping us finish the aviary and aiding research.

Bernd Heinrich, professor of biology at the University of Vermont, initiated the raven project in western Maine where he was raised. He owned Camp Believe It atop York Hill. *Hilda,* his mother, lived nearby in Jay, Maine. Bernd, who was recently divorced, was often accompanied on raven research trips and visits to Maine by his young son, *Stuart,* and his nephew, *Charlie.*

Dave Karkos was a local newspaper reporter.

David Lidstone was a logger, wildlife photographer, expert woodsman, and volunteer raven researcher.

Carol Nash, a nurse and sled racer from New Hampshire, bred Siberian Huskies (kennel name Canaan) and mentored Colleen.

Jim Parker, John's former scoutmaster from Kansas and an ornithologist specializing in raptors, just so happened to live outside Farmington, Maine, and he helped with trapping and tagging ravens.

Dr. Robert Patterson was veterinarian to John and Colleen's sled dogs.

Patty Parker Rabenold and *Richard Knight,* ornithologists specializing in social foraging, vultures, and ravens, advised us on laporotomies (Patty) and field work (Rick).

Larry Wattles, Anne Moody, and *Buster Nutting* lived near the New Vineyard roost.

Tom and Zetta Wojcik, landlords of John and Colleen, owned Hills Pond Associates and parented *Jennifer, Hilary,* and *Joshua.* All five participated in and supported the sledding and research addictions of John and Colleen.

Harry Wycoff, a local resident who supplied wood for a racing sled, raised a brood of baby ravens in 1989.

Animals

Boo, a sleek black Labrador mix owned by Henry and Lee.

Brodie, a rotund smooth-coated Border Collie of the Wojciks turned sled dog.

Granite and *Buster* were pure-bred Siberian Husky racing dogs adopted by John and Colleen.

Jocko, a noisy African Gray Parrot who lived with the Wojciks.

Kenai and *Sky,* the Siberian Husky pups owned by Colleen and John and the Wojciks, respectively.

Phoebe, Butch and Nancy Adams's boxer dog.

Sitka, John's dog, a smart mix of Siberian Husky and shepherd.

Topper, Colleen's dog, a mutt of various sheepdogs from the Navajo reservation who was prone to wander.

Woody and *Tilly* were pure-bred Siberian Husky racing dogs that John and Colleen often borrowed from Margaret Cook.

Following pages: Western Maine where we conducted our research. Important local landmarks, towns, villages, and research sites are indicated for orientation.

one

Can You Make a Living from
a Love of Natural Science?

Our future was visible, if blurry, as we crossed the Lemon Fair River in the verdant forests of Vermont. With meager savings, two good dogs, and new friends, we would apply our life's training to understand a new world. A safety net of friends and family who hosted us as we traveled east from Arizona faded to the southwest. Ahead were the Maine woods, a small cabin, and the secrets of hardy people and crafty birds. Our savings would get us through the winter, and with luck, pending grant proposals would provide support for the next three years. But presently there were no guarantees. We had only hope, hunches, and a deep longing to learn. How did New England's nature work? What were the people like? Can you make a living from a love of natural science?

It was late summer 1988. We were approaching the western mountains of Maine intent on studying the winter behavior of a wild bird. The Common Raven is an often reviled, jet-black scavenger. Its large size, dark eyes, and sable dress suit it well for tending nature's morgue. Provocative, funereal, wonderful, and mysterious, it lives around the globe from arctic to desert regions and temperate to tropical climates. The raven's influence on humanity's language, art, religion, and popular culture is unmatched in the animal world. Despite being familiar and influential, ravens were just yielding to scientific scrutiny, and we wanted to join the hunt to learn more. In the past months we had been consumed by preparation. We developed, proposed, and tested new ways to study wild ravens. We sorted our possessions, packed those deemed useful in remote field settings, and planned a route across the United States that would enable us to visit friends and sleep cheaply. Finally, our wish for an adventure in a new land with new people and wild nature was upon us. We were convinced that our savings and professional standing were worth gambling. As we drove, reality melted away and adventure began. We were fully in the raven's grip.

Years of study and serendipity had made this trip possible. Colleen and I had met six years earlier as graduate students at Northern Arizona University in Flagstaff. Only three years ago we had married. As a student, Colleen had followed radio-tagged Abert's squirrels around the pine forests to decipher their ranging and feeding habits, gaining experience with this relatively new technology. And she knew animal behavior. As a professional research technician with my graduate mentor Russ Balda, she had investigated the incredible spatial memories of jays and nutcrackers. These small birds consistently outperformed graduate students on standardized tests, remembering the locations of thousands of stashed pine seeds each year. I had just finished seven years of research for my Ph.D. on the behavior and ecology of the Pinyon Jay, a unique bird that lives in large flocks. It was this careful study of a close relative to the raven that brought us to a unique intersection. While arranging a meeting on advances in the study of animal social behavior at Northern Arizona University, we had read an intriguing story about raven societies by Bernd Heinrich. Bernd was known for his work on bumblebees, but his new raven interest fit well with the theme of the meeting. Con Slobodchikoff, who was organizing the meeting, agreed, and we invited Bernd to the meeting. He came and stayed with us. He arrived in summer 1987, looking much like a raven—lean, inquisitive, and carrying far too little for a weeklong stay. He was a professor at the University of Vermont, but he spent as much time as he could at his "camp" in the mountains of western Maine, where he had grown up and where he had become fixated on ravens. During his stay we hit it off immediately. On long runs in the Arizona pine forest and at home over drinks and meals, we talked with Bernd about ravens and science. We were captivated by his stories of Maine and its rural character. It took little time to convince us that we had to move to Maine to study ravens with Bernd.[1]

Postdoctoral study (or a postdoc) is not uncommon in our field. Few newly anointed Ph.D.'s get real jobs. Instead they flit from lab to lab working with seasoned pros in a sort of apprenticeship. During this time, productivity, especially in grantsmanship and publication, is key. A postdoc may do some teaching, but research is more common. Without the distractions of students and committees, postdocs are free to immerse themselves in a new research environment. This time is not all bliss; old research must be published, new papers must be written, and one's future is anything but settled. Freedom is wonderful, but job security is purposefully absent. Although stimulating, a postdoc is also stressful because one must always be looking for permanent employment while simultaneously proving research ability in a new venue. Postdocs are usually financed with grant money, for which I started applying a year or more before we crossed the Lemon Fair. I wrote grants to study jays in Arizona and Florida, which ultimately were not funded. Bernd and I wrote three proposals to the U.S. National Science Foundation for support that would fund the research and pay our salaries. As is usual for any new idea in science, we were roundly criticized but also encouraged to revise our ideas and try again. Bernd had enough money to gather preliminary observations, get me to Maine for reconnaissance, and provide basic support for the start of our work. From this small beginning and with little assurance of long-term support, I started my postdoc on raven winter behavior.

As little was known about the winter habits of wild ravens, we proposed a combination of field observations and aviary experiments that would build on Bernd's solid foundation. What Bernd saw, but could not fully explain, was quite simple. Usually large animal carcasses or other bonanzas of food left in the snowy Maine woods would be quickly discovered by just one or two ravens. Often these were mated pairs, and they vigorously defended their valuable finds from others intruding on their territory. But a group, often numbering more than fifty birds, eventually gathered to share the food with the territorial pair. Bernd's meticulous observations suggested that unpaired ravens formed loose aggregations, or "gangs," at foods, which allowed them to overpower the fierce defenses put up by the resident pair of adults. But how did these gangs of vagrants form? Did they actually recruit each other by giving *yells* at the food, as Bernd's playbacks of recorded raven noises suggested? Or were they more like bees, somehow dancing and calling at their communal night roosts to give directions to newly found foods? Why did they share information as apparently valuable as the location of a dead animal that might keep them well fed through the winter? We reasoned with Bernd that if we could catch vagrant ravens, house them in a huge cage, and control their access to food bonanzas, some of which were defended by adults, then we could answer these questions. As we brainstormed over proposals, we converged on the idea of building some sort of cage within which we could have a modicum of control over the actions of our study subjects. But ravens are big, weighing nearly three pounds apiece, and groups of ravens would need considerable space. If we hoped to learn anything remotely relevant to the actions of ravens in nature, we would need a super-sized cage. In it, with controlled experiments and supplemental observations of free-roaming wild birds, we could learn how and why young nomadic ravens share valuable winter meals. Our enthusiasm was endless and our hand-drawn plans fit easily into our proposal, but we were suggesting enclosing an area the size of a city block in wire. Just getting the materials to the site would be difficult. Actually raising the cage might not be possible. But we never considered this. Bernd did not know failure.[2]

Others, however, would require more than faith before they would fully invest. Proving that our concept was sound was essential. To the academic skeptics, Bernd was better known for his work on insect physiology than his work on bird behavior. But his detailed research on bumblebees in the field easily spilled over to experimental work on birds. He liked to manipulate nature to learn her secrets, punching holes in leaves, for example, to see if chickadees used the damage as a cue to the location of an insect meal. He had also manipulated what he could to learn about ravens. This involved moving dead animals here and there to determine which ravens discovered them, then cataloging the events that followed. I was also hooked on experiments and on using a combination of wild and captive animals to fully understand their behaviors. It was only natural that Bernd and I would build our research approach on a strong experimental foundation. Though an unproven young Ph.D., I had expertise in bird behavior. Colleen's experience with the new technology of radio telemetry and diverse training in animal behavior rounded out our skills. Our expertise and Bernd's experience made a good research team. But we had to show others that we could work together and accomplish what we proposed. We got that chance in 1987 after Bernd convinced the National Science Foundation to seed the project with just enough money to build part of the aviary and test it.[3]

On August 26, 1987, I began to turn our paper plans into reality. I flew to Vermont to meet Bernd and drive to his Camp Believe It in Maine. This trip was my first time with Bernd in the Maine woods, or to state it more accurately, cutting and clearing what seemed to be a significant portion of the Maine woods. We started to work in earnest the minute we pulled off Route 156 (also known as "the Weld Road") at the base of York Hill. We hauled gear and basic necessities, including a fresh-killed sheep for a party the following day, uphill a half mile to Bernd's cabin. The cabin had been unoccupied for several weeks and was musty and dank. We opened the doors to let in fresh air, and gathered wood and started a fire in the old cook stove to dry out the cabin. An old stone well, hand dug decades earlier, was nearby. I dropped a bucket into the well and retrieved it, hand over hand, to fill our water container. As camp life energized the cabin, we began to survey the aviary site.

We pushed our way through underbrush thick as a wolf's winter coat, over rough ground, and around a half-mile-wide grove of young maple and beech behind the cabin. Peering through the dense foliage of hundreds of trees, we could imagine a great cage rising up from the undergrowth. We fired up the chain saw and started felling, delimbing, hauling, piling, and clearing. With Bernd's friend Alice Calaprice and his young son, Stuart, we worked through steaming rain until dark. Coming from an elevation of 7,000 feet in the dry western United States, I wasn't used to the heat and humidity. Progress was slow but visible. The day's work made the bonfire in front of the cabin extra special, and the hard labor softened the scattered logs we sat upon. We were famished and eyed the sheep hanging in the birch tree just beyond the front door. The main carcass was off limits tonight. As a raven first goes for the entrails of a newly found carcass, tonight we would eat only the internal delicacies. Bernd and Alice cooked and shared the liver. Not having an appetite for organ meat, I cut out the tongue. A sheep tongue is not very big, but when skewered with a green maple twig and roasted over a crackling fire it sure is tasty. But it wasn't much, and with no other food in sight, I collapsed in my sleeping bag with a growling stomach and an important lesson learned. One should *never* go into the woods with Bernd without bringing food.

An enthusiastic army of volunteers woke us the next morning. In this part of Maine, friendships are strong and eager to be strengthened with manual labor. Bernd's relatives, former neighbors, and lifelong friends trekked up York Hill, and the work party grew to nearly fifteen. Now we had jeeps and an old military amphibious craft, known as the "coot," hidden for decades in a Maine barn, to do the heavy hauling of wire, nails, and tools up the hill. We had Lee DiSotto's homemade doughnuts, carefully packaged in wax bags habitually recycled from cereal boxes, to soak up the coffee. And we had muscle and skill, from a crew that ranged in age from six to nearly seventy, to clear the forest and construct a unique research facility. It rained all day, but as it grew darker we saw more clearly. Our work had shaved the ground clean, raised a four-foot-tall base wall of stout wire, or "hardware cloth," that we stapled to the perimeter trees, and perched a first-class observation hut at the height of the land. Supported by strong maples and stout granite, the hut would offer a commanding view of the cage.

Now it was time for a real Maine party. Wired to a sapling, the sheep had been roasting above a wood fire most of the day, carefully rotated above the smoke and fire by Charlie, Bernd's nephew. It smelled heavenly. The beer was cold and plentiful. Our knives were sharp. When the sheep was laid whole on the picnic table, we all rushed in to cut off a hunk. In this research, we may not have been able to eat our study species, but we sure did eat like them. Sitting on logs with the sun setting, we ate, drank, and told stories. Jack Daniels and Johnny Walker made an appearance, but it was the friendship that kept us warm. This was truly the social fabric of the Mainers I met: hard work, honesty, support, and celebration.

We spread our sleeping bags across the cabin floor and slept deeply. The cabin rocked with the gas and snoring fueled by the sheep and beer. The following morning we nearly finished the observation hut and secured flexible "chicken wire" above the hardware cloth base to create fifteen-foot-tall walls around most of the main aviary. By midday, the Mainers returned to their homes, and Bernd headed back to Vermont. I was able to stay a few more days and finish up a few tasks on the aviary and hut. Sunday was warm and sunny, and I enjoyed a dip in Alder Brook in between hanging tarpaper on the hut and unrolling wire for the cage roof. Just readying the roof for the next gathering—unrolling and arranging the springy chicken wire on the forest floor—took me more than a full day. The Ruffed Grouse were constant companions, and I began to explore the orchards and woods around the cabin. As I prepared to leave on Wednesday, September 2, the first corvids (the family of birds that includes crows and ravens) inspected the aviary. Not ravens, but Blue Jays. As they perched along the new forest edge they called in apparent disgust. I hoped they would understand. I went back to Arizona already longing to return to Camp Believe It in the Maine woods.

Bernd followed up on our first week of work by organizing two more cage-building parties during autumn 1987. By the time winter frosted the wire, a sealed aviary was ready to be tested. I flew to a snowy Portland, Maine, for three weeks in February of 1988. Colleen remained behind in Arizona, where she ran our dogs in their first dogsled race. Practicing my skills as an absent-minded professor, I left my driver's license in Arizona. As a result, the rental car I had reserved was unobtainable. Thankfully, Henry and Lee DiSotto answered my phone call and were more than happy to brave the winter and drive eighty miles to meet me at the airport. We figured Henry could rent the car and we would be off. But to rent a car one needs a driver's license and a credit card held by the same person. Henry, who lived within his means and not his credit, had the license, but he did not use credit cards. After hopeful negotiations with the rental car attendant failed, we figured I didn't really need a car after all. Henry and Lee would just take me to the cabin and three weeks later take me back to the airport. They would happily provide any other support during the research visit as well.

Although they had met me only briefly the previous summer, Henry and Leona (Lee) DiSotto treated me like a long lost son. Driving in the dark from the airport, we decided that I should stay the night at their house and go to the cabin early the next morning. Henry and Lee lived appropriately enough in Jay, Maine, seventeen miles from the cabin. Their house was a typical New England–style home, sprawling, with all parts connected together, even the barn (now a garage). Between the house and barn was the "summer kitchen," with many windows so air could flow through on warm summer days when Lee would do her canning. There was a black iron pump handle that drew water from a century-old, hand-dug well right inside the house. When they first moved in, the two-story, four-hole outhouse was still standing. It was now long gone, but the hand-hewn, wide pine flooring and ceiling planks of the house date to the original construction, finished nearly two centuries earlier in 1793. The upstairs was like a museum. Lee had collected antiques over the years and furnished the rooms as they would have been in 1859 when the town of Jay used it as the "poor farm," allowing four families to survive their struggles within its sturdy frame and fertile acres.

Lee was the matriarch of a very extended family, which grew by one that night. With white hair, a soft smile, and twinkling blue eyes, Lee was the ever-ready hostess, always eager to expand her family with newcomers. When Bernd Heinrich's family settled in Maine in the 1940s, Lee and her first husband, Floyd Adams, welcomed and nurtured them. A young Bernd was befriended by the Adams boys and quickly became a fourth son. Eventually, Bernd bought York (aka Adams) Hill from Floyd. Lee and Floyd had divorced decades earlier, leaving Lee to raise three young boys alone.[4]

Henry had married Lee and adopted her boys nearly thirty years before we came to know him. Times were challenging for a single mother of three, and Henry made sure the boys had presents under the Christmas tree even before the marriage. He worked for International Paper in the mill's warehouse in Jay. His demeanor was a product of hard work and service to his country during the Korean conflict. As a boy he had cut lake ice for refrigerators, and he spent his early years wrestling cordwood from railcars to the International Paper pulping vats. Working his way up to his current position as a crew boss in charge of loading finished paper onto trucks, Henry was union, and the union was now on strike. It had been for eight months (since June 1987). Between puffs on his cigarette, Henry was always joking. But his humor was only a thin cover for a deep concern over America's growing corporate greed. He knew the importance of the common, working American and would tell all listeners his views. As the strike raged, the union hall became his workplace. But whenever we called, he lent his wiry frame to the cause of science.

During that first winter visit, research went well. Bernd and I practiced catching and handling large groups of ravens in the trap just east of his cabin.

Henry (left), John, and Lee gather around the cook stove in Bernd's cabin for a hot dinner after a day of construction on the raven cage. Wet gloves dry above the stove.

We tested the aviary, which worked beautifully. Twenty ravens shared some of their secrets with us during that time. They fed as a tenuously cooperative group. Fights broke out, but only rarely because a strict pecking order guided their actions. Like barnyard chickens, ravens have dominance hierarchies that allow valuable resources to be shared without repeated, and potentially harmful, bickering. I observed and easily measured dominance status as one bird excluded another from choice food or a central feeding spot. Just as my larger dog, Sitka, would exercise her dominance over Colleen's smaller dog, Topper, with a growl, snarl, or stare, a dominant raven's sharp jab of the beak or direct gaze to a subordinate reinforced its claim and caused the weaker bird to cower, fluff its feathers, and back away.[5]

We were able to peer deeply into raven life. We began to decode basic signals, for example, the sharp loud calls that sounded like *yack*, which signaled that a subordinate was displaced. By observing the situation, or context, associated with the variety of calls given by our captives, we might come to understand the meaning of the hoots, yells, quorks, woops, kaws, knocks, gurgles, barks, clucks, rattles, and drips that filled the air wherever ravens roamed. Even behaviors rarely seen in nature were common in the aviary. After eating their fill, the ravens frequently rolled in the snow to bathe and played tug-of-war with sticks. These aspects of raven social life reminded me of our dogs and of young wolves that endlessly chase, tug, wrestle, and roll in the snow.

Two of the adults we had captured, apparently an established pair, were in constant contact, grooming each other like monkeys, calling in duet fashion, and defending food as an efficient team. Many of the younger nonbreeders in the cage, especially the most dominant ones, also seemed paired up. They often courted and preened one another. Rather than fight for dominance status at food, these paired birds appeared to have a joint status. Was the male's status conferred to the female or did females have their own hierarchy? Perhaps our observations could refine views of bird social relationships, much like detailed observations of individuals within wolf packs were refining our understanding of pack structure. No longer do wolf biologists describe wolf packs as simple organizations where an alpha male sits atop a chain of subordinates from the alpha female to the omega pup. Modern descriptions characterize packs as extended families co-led by a dominant, mated pair and several of their offspring, with flexible status relationships among themselves and with their parents. In the aviary, we would be able to determine the relative influence of individual character and the character of one's associates on a raven's status.[6]

When dusk came, the ravens were very cooperative. They roosted as a group in the shed we had built for them, snuggling shoulder to shoulder in the subzero temperatures. The birds in the aviary were very attractive to others outside. Wild birds were frequently trying to join our captive flock. At the end of the trial, when I opened the door to let the ravens loose, more came in (appendix 1 provides a summary of the aviary at this time). As with the reintroduced wolves of Yellowstone who were apprehensive about leaving their temporary pens after a couple of months of captivity, our ravens were in no hurry to leave the aviary. Apparently regular meals and protection from hawks and fishers were to their liking. Their approval led us to dub the aviary "Raven Haven."[7]

Our preliminary test of the aviary allowed Bernd and me to prepare a fourth proposal for the National Science Foundation. This was a realistic plan, rooted in our successful test of the aviary that proposed to combine aviary and field observations to study the food-sharing behavior of ravens. Colleen and I felt our chances of getting funding were sufficient to take the risk and move east. At worse we would stay the winter, write a paper, and apply for other jobs.

Quick, roll down the windows!

A dog farted as John and I neared Weld, Maine. We gulped at the pure air of the western Maine mountains. These mountains were older than the ones we knew out West—rounded, not sharply peaked like our familiar Rockies. Their bald granite heads poked above slopes richly cloaked in a wild diversity of trees. Steel gray beech, white birch, and luxuriant green pine, fragrant balsam fir, and spruce. Maples, both red and sugar, were everywhere. These forests were in direct contrast to the vast monoculture of parklike ponderosa pine we had left behind in Arizona. The rivers were wide, rocky, and seemingly alongside every roadway. They animated the scenery but worked hard fueling small power plants and, more commonly, paper mills that punctuated the rural setting.

The vagaries of traveling with dogs and their canine odors were nothing new to us. Both of us had always had dogs growing up. We had our share of Sams, Snoopys, and Bucks. Our dogs had, in many ways, made us who we were. As children, many of our adventures occurred in spite of or because of our four-legged pals. As a married couple, it was a nonissue whether we would have dogs. Our Maine adventure would not have been complete without our trusty sidekicks. In fact, it might not have been possible.

Not long after we had met Bernd and learned of his raven studies, we realized our muscle power might not be enough to carry out this study. As Edward L. Moody, a member of Admiral Byrd's expedition and designer of a first-rate, much-in-demand dogsled, said, "A smart man never carries on his back what he can put in a sled." With this in mind we signed up for a dogsledding class during our last year in Arizona. We started to train, believing that we would soon have wonder dogs possessing super powers for hauling heavy gear and sloppy raven food through the woods. And surely then they would be too tired to chase the many grouse, coyotes, porcupines, and moose we would meet on the trail. Noted scholars of animal behavior Raymond and Lorna Coppinger thought likewise, stating that with dogsledding, the reward for dogs is the social interaction with other dogs and people and "enhanced opportunities for feeding, reproducing, and staying out of trouble."[8]

Our first classes involved just trying to get the dogs to pull. Picture a dog in a harness with a rope attached. A tire that has an eyebolt drilled through the tread is attached to the rope. The "trainer" verbally coaxes the dog to pull this noisy contraption yelling, "HIKE!" In sled dog vernacular, "hike" means "go." Eventually the dog pulls independently enough to learn directional commands like "gee" for right and "haw" for left. For most northern breeds like Siberian Huskies or Alaskan Malamutes this task is easy. Centuries of breeding have instilled in these dogs an unquestioning desire to pull. We, however, were dealing with Sitka, a black-and-white three-quarter Siberian Husky with piercing blue eyes whose stubbornness rivaled a donkey's, and

Topper, an edgy, black and peanut butter brown mixed mutt with flop ears and gay tail of a guessed ancestry. Probably he was a combination of Australian Shepherd and Border Collie, but having found him as a stray adult from the Navajo reservation outside Flagstaff, we did not know his background. We suspected it involved herding. Training our canine duo was slow, but we knew our muscles would later thank us.[9]

After weeks of training, much frustration, and a few marital arguments, both dogs seemed fairly adept at pulling. We advanced to learning how to make our own ganglines (the lines from the dogs to the vehicle being pulled) and even managed to build our own three-wheeled cart for the dogs to pull. We knew that Maine would have snow most of the winter, so we decided to try our hand at building a sled. We purchased oak pieces, followed directions, and over a period of months bent steamed parts of it in our tiny shower. Finally, we had a sled of which we were extremely proud and "trained" dogs that would save us many hours of labor and muscle strain. Our four-by-eight-by-six-foot white utility trailer with "Raven Haven, ME" and "Raven Research Vehicle" stenciled in black on the side lumbered under the weight of sled, cart, and household belongings. But the four of us were ready to meet Maine's mountains as an efficient two-dog, two-person team.

Finding a home convenient for research in the hinterland of western Maine with a landlord who would tolerate ravens and dogs had not been simple. John went to Maine a couple of times before our actual move. Each time he would look for accommodations for us. It was apparent that Bernd's cabin (aka Camp Believe It) on York Hill, between Weld and Wilton, would be a great research cabin but not one for permanent living. Bernd and his friends built it by hand from native materials. It was a lovely, two-story log cabin chinked tight enough to keep the cluster flies inside. There were two stoves to keep out most of the ice during the winter. An old-fashioned wood cook stove sat downstairs, and a small but efficient modern woodstove heated one of the two upstairs bedrooms. The kerosene lamps added a romantic ambience. A

Bernd's hand-built log cabin atop York Hill.

kitchen sink actually drained in the warmer months, and the front windows offered a spectacular view to the south of Bald Mountain and beyond. The outhouse accommodated two at a time, and with only a roof and three sides it provided an uninterrupted view of the woods. The water was very tasty, particularly after it had been hauled 300 feet up the hill from the well. The area was utterly quiet—there were no noisy neighbors because the cabin was a half mile from the nearest road and neighbor (a mysterious man simply called "the hermit"). These amenities notwithstanding, we needed a shower.

With each place John found, something would turn out to be wrong. One had electricity but no running water. One had both but just an outhouse. As our departure drew closer and closer, I got more discouraged thinking that we would be living at Camp Believe It full time. I was starting to think we could forgo showers, but it would be tough to complete our research without a phone or electricity.

We leaned on Bernd's social connections to expand the home search. As a small boy in Poland, he fled the Nazis with his parents and sister. Landing in New York, the Heinrichs soon found western Maine. These mountains were Bernd's playground, and he knew every inch of the country and all the secrets of its flora and fauna. Fortunately for us, he also knew a lot of the local folks. Hilda, Bernd's mom, lived a few miles down the road near Jay. John had met a few of Bernd's friends on his previous trips and had put out the word that we were looking for a place to live near York Hill. Luckily this led us to Tom and Zetta Wojcik, who lived near the shores of Hills Pond, a mile from York Hill. They had a small cabin in need of tenants. We could rent it for $185.00 per month, including weekly laundry privileges at their house. I was relieved, and we decided to take the place sight unseen because it had all we needed—electricity, running water, a phone, and easy access to the research cabin.

Tom and Zetta had come to Maine from Michigan. We found many transplants to Maine were from Michigan. In their mid-forties when we arrived, Tom and Zetta were closely connected to nature and not far removed from the 1960s. They had their own ideals, including caring for their land so it could provide fruit, vegetables, and firewood; exposing their children to culture beyond the farm; and peering closely and openly into the nature and people that surrounded them. Tom was a Saab-racing, mechanical genius, able to repair sports cars and houses (his own was under constant improvement). His busy, active life energized his personality and kept him dark-haired and lean. He rarely paused from talking, even while flossing his teeth. His current day job was as a maintenance manager of several nursing homes in the region. Zetta ran the family business, Hills Pond Associates, which took on odd jobs and maintained summer "camps" (aka cabins). The Wojciks shoveled snow off roofs in winter and prepared cabins in summer for the "rusticators" ("summer complaints" or temporary seasonal visitors). No job was too small for them. Zetta's infectious laughter and nurturing demeanor assured that they

Hills Pond as seen across the highway from the Wojciks' house. Bald Mountain
dominates the skyline. Ice fits a loose lid on the distant water.

would always have clients. She embodied the temperament—cheerful and
giving—that others have used to characterize Maine residents. Tom and Zetta
had three active kids: Jenn, Hilary, and Josh. When we arrived they were
seventeen, fourteen, and eleven. The kids were all talented musicians as well
as efficient woodchoppers. They lived far from any other family, television
reception was dismal, and as a result the kids found most of their entertainment outside. Our arrival and subsequent activities boosted their entertainment significantly.

The Wojcik house on the Weld Road across from Hills Pond was once a
bar. Ideally situated in Perkins Township between two dry towns, it was a very
popular place at one time. The Wojcik clan made the house equally popular

because they attracted a plethora of human and animal life. They had one dog (Brodie), two cats, and an obnoxious African Gray Parrot (Jocko). Few weekends passed without houseguests.

Tom, Zetta, and their kids were part of Lee and Henry's extended family. Hitchhiking to work shortly after his arrival in Maine, with a scruffy black beard and wearing a peacoat, Tom looked in need. Lee, though unsure about the stranger, stopped to pick him up at the insistence of her son Butch, who made toothpicks and croquet sets with Tom at Forester Manufacturing in Wilton. They stuffed Tom in the very back of Lee's yellow Suzuki jeep. From that point on, he and Zetta were in the family. This connection would help us form an even stronger bond with Henry and Lee.

The day we arrived at our new home we were in for a surprise. We knew it was a one-room cabin, unless you count the bathroom as a second room. What we didn't know was just how small it was. By the time we set up the bed frame that had functioned as the sides of our moving trailer, we realized we would be very limited in how much we could put in our cabin, including visitors. The cabin was partially furnished with a small table and two kitchen chairs, an old armchair, a woodstove, a refrigerator, a small gas cook stove, a small desk, and a small chest of drawers. Four deer feet reached skyward from one diagonally tongue-in-groove wood-clad wall as a rustic coat hanger. The cabin was equipped with a wall-mounted, black rotary dial phone with a three-foot-long cord. Fortunately, there was a decently sized closet. End to end our new house was thirty feet and side to side fourteen feet. If we opened the oven door, it would hit the foot of the bed. Putting wood in the woodstove at night didn't involve getting out of bed. Rearranging furniture was out of the question. We were amazed to find three doors into the cabin. In a previous life, it had been the office for a lumber company, and it had been purchased and moved to its present site to serve as a home for an elderly man whom Tom and Zetta had befriended. A wraparound deck, covered front porch with a mounted deer head, and detached garage with a dirt floor had been added.

The cabin was snugged picturesquely under large maples between two un-named feeder streams of Alder Brook about 150 feet from the back door of Tom and Zetta's house. The front window of this cabin also had a spectacular view of Bald Mountain. We had found a home, complete with a family that stretched from Hills Pond to Jay.

two

Stocking the Aviary

Adrenaline choked me as I watched the ebony birds carefully enter the crude trap. I was alone just outside the trap, cramped and motionless, hiding in a dark pile of thick, snowy spruce boughs. My muscles were cocked springs, screaming from two hours of confinement. But the discomfort mattered little; my confidence was soaring. Surely I was near balancing the score with these ravens that had so far effectively eluded Colleen and me. The icy predawn of late December that bit at my face also pushed the ravens, now perched all around me. The lively, wild birds were everywhere—yelling, fighting, courting, digging at meat scraps buried in the snow inches from my face— and now they were slowly filling the trap, using their stout bills to pound the frozen deer and moose we had scattered as bait. The sight of others feeding is irresistible to ravens, and soon the entire trap was sooty with hungry birds. My heart was pounding, and it was difficult to breathe as I jerked the clothesline and sent the heavy door crashing earthward with a snow-muted *whumpf*. I crashed out of the spruce blind and yelled out to the cabin, "We got 'em!"

Twenty-six confused ravens tried to escape their wire enclosure as I crawled into the trap through a small door. The first one, now in my bare hand, gazed deeply at me. Its pupils were dilated. Its massive beak pinched my numb hand, twisted, and drew blood. I felt only euphoria as Colleen and our new friends joined me to bag ravens. All autumn, indeed, for much of the previous year, we had prepared for this moment. We had moved across country;

planned and revised our scientific approach; lured, chased, and been out-smarted by ravens; and built a huge cage. Now, with the ravens secured in burlap bags, we could stock our giant aviary and begin the experiments.

The crew that was now stumbling among the frozen meat, bloody snow, and snapping ravens had gotten an early start. The wind howled that morning, December 29, 1988, but Zetta and Jenn Wojcik along with local environmental educators Rick Ashton and Jim Parker trudged up York Hill for coffee, con-versation, and, we hoped, hands-on raven work. They arrived at 5:30 a.m. and joined Henry, Josh, and us, who had spent the night stoking the old wood-stove in Bernd's cabin. Hiking in the dark was a necessary precaution. Ravens begin feeding just after first light. We had been especially careful around the cabin during daylight for the past two weeks because ravens were feeding nearby at our trap. Late the previous day, Topper and Sitka had pulled load after load of meat on our dogsled up the now snowy path from the highway to the cabin. After we had baited the trap, they pulled us down the hill. These were crazy amusement rides. The dogs flew, and we rocketed through the dark, bouncing off embankments and trees, often ejecting passengers head first into the snow or ice.

The trap itself was only about 100 yards from the cabin, in the clearing to the east. It was a simple tent of poultry wire supported by a small grove of maple and fir trees. The wire enclosed an irregular, yurt-like rectangle about twenty by fifteen feet. It was six to eight feet tall with a wide, heavy door propped open by an eight-foot-tall sapling. Inside the door, throughout the trap, and around it we had placed hundreds of pounds of cow lungs, deer parts, and dead livestock. We had secured the door open while the ravens acclimated to the giant, gruesome bird feeder. The mouthlike door yawned open, hungry for ravens. Today we changed the arrangement ever so slightly. Ravens are patient and will wait for hours or days before feeding in a new situation. This morning while it was still dark we untied the door from its prop. Now only gravity held the door in place, balanced atop the sapling. No

Our assistants, Sitka and Topper, haul our first homemade oaken sled up York Hill. The frozen calf they are carrying will be used to lure ravens into the trap.

food was outside the trap, but the interior was littered with deer carcasses, piles of offal, and most of a moose. Its floor of raven-packed snow stained red, brown, and green-yellow belied the feast that had been raging for days. My direct connection to the trap was a stout clothesline running from the base of the door prop to a small clump of thick spruce branches that we piled together to form a simple, natural blind.

By 6:00 a.m. a concert of raven music was filling the cold morning air. With John in the blind, I worked on arrangements with the crew. We passed the time sipping coffee, eating homemade cake doughnuts, and chatting quietly about last-minute instructions. We waited anxiously for John's signal. At 7:00 a.m. we heard him yell excitedly. We threw on our parkas,

Working inside the trap, we quickly placed each raven in a burlap sack to calm
it down. The heavy trapdoor, now closed, frames the image.
Photo courtesy of David Karkos.

stuffed our feet into our felt-lined pac boots, grabbed the gunnysacks, and
dashed out the cabin door. The air was full of the birds not captured. Their
huge wings swooshed the air. We surrounded the trap and worked quickly to
catch and individually encase each bird. We loosely tied the heavy, jumping
sacks and carried them to the cabin for processing. As the birds thawed, the
smell of old burlap and bad bird breath blended into a sharp, smoky-sweet
pungency. We quickly associated this new smell with success. Two birds
escaped, but twenty-four made it safely to the cabin.

All hands busily examined the ravens. Everyone found a task and dug right
in. We fitted each bird with a numeric United States government leg band and
a set of hand-colored, vinyl wing tags bearing a unique color combination and
large painted number. This marking system would allow us to identify specific

David Lidstone (left) and Tom Wojcik weigh a raven in a sack.

individuals in the aviary or the field. The wing tags were also conspicuous enough to catch a layman's eye, which meant that we often heard from
Mainers who had seen strange "color-winged" ravens. We weighed each bird
and measured the length and depth of its beak. These measurements told us
something about a bird's condition (lean or fat) and gave a first clue to its
status and gender. In ravens, males and dominant birds are more massive than
females and subordinates. We opened each bird's beak and noted the color of
its mouth lining. Birds hatched the previous summer, "juveniles," have a
bright red lining that is distinct from the jet-black lining adorning mated,
territorial adults. Some birds had mottled, intermediate linings. We called

Y23, a wild fledgling raven. Wing tags were easily identified from a distance. The large bill and wedge-shaped tail that distinguish a raven from a crow are evident.

these "yearlings" and suspected them to be in their second or third year of life and without a mate or territory. Finally, we drew a small vial full of blood from a prominent vein under the wing. The vials were stored in our refrigerator to await later genetic analyses.[1]

Having seen the ravens pound and tear rock-hard, frozen meat, we were cautious around their beaks. We discovered that if you put something in front of a bird's beak, it would grab the item, and you could see the mouth color. Sometimes we would pick up whatever was near at hand. We happened to have a dog chew toy that was a sawed-off, hollow cow femur. After the birds bit it, we could easily slip the bone over the bill to prevent the bird from biting us while we finished all our data collection. This routine worked most of the time, but everyone who helped catch and tag ravens eventually suffered bites. Later we would use medical tape to safely secure the bill shut. The sharp, powerful bills really pinch. And when a raven gets hold of soft skin, it twists. The result for us was a badge of honor: a bloody finger and possible infection. For the ravens, their reward was pure satisfaction.

Work on the first ten birds was without incident. They were feisty, occa-

Topper (left) and Sitka watch from the cabin balcony as the crew below measures, bleeds, and tags ravens. Sitka has a "snow nose," so called because of the lightly pigmented stripe between her nostrils. Photo courtesy of David Karkos.

sionally ripping our cold hands with their strong beaks, and frequently showering our clothes with steamy, rank raven crap. But the eleventh bird was quiet in its sack. To our dismay and sadness, it was dead. The trapping was evidently too stressful for this mature adult. Fortunately this situation was unusual, and we marked and measured the remaining birds without further issue. Sitka and Topper had the best seats in the cabin, watching the excitement from the "bridge" between the upstairs bedrooms. They eagerly followed as we placed fourteen juveniles and seven yearlings in the aviary and released to the wild two others whose mouth linings suggested they were nearly adults.

Content that we had stocked the aviary with a gang of young ravens, we relaxed.

Later in the day we checked on the caged birds and found that six had escaped through a back door they had managed to bang open. After the door was fixed, we discovered that two more had escaped through a hole in the ceiling above a tree perch. These were strong, resourceful birds. Now more than ever we had to think like a raven to keep a smart step ahead of our caged flock.

8 October 1988; Colleen's Journal: "We're in our rented cabin staying warm until we have to go 'up the hill' for our work weekend and sheep roast. It's supposed to snow 6 inches tonight so we don't know how much luck we'll have getting people or work done. We have our fingers crossed."

Prior to our successful December trapping we were consumed by aviary construction. In late September we took a quick break from sewing wire and cutting firewood to visit the Common Ground Fair in nearby Windsor, Maine. The description of the fair intrigued us enough to make the drive. The three-day festival celebrating rural living was perfect for our first autumn. We saw sheepshearing, sheep herding, fiddling, and farming exhibits. Maine-grown produce was plentiful. We ate pickled fiddleheads and tasted maple syrup. Crafts and homemade goods filled the many colorful booths scattered over the multiacre site. We returned home to our cabin appreciative of the culture surrounding us and feeling ready to complete the aviary.

Our friends assembled for a last big construction party during the first weekend of October 1988. The maple leaves burned scarlet against the fresh Maine sky. Golden beech, orange sugar maple, and green pine framed a perfect autumn portrait. Tourists rolled by "leaf peeping," an economic force in this part of the world and one we had never before encountered. Our friends and new Maine family worked to expand the main cage by adding two long "arms"—literally 150-foot-long by 20-foot-tall tunnels of chicken wire

The main aviary crushed by an early, heavy snowfall, as viewed from the hut. Subsequent snows sent us into pole-shaking fits to free the wire from the deadly white coating. T-pole supports for the roof, listing badly under the weight of the wet snow, show how we customized the fit by placing rocks below a pole.

that ended in sizable 30-foot-diameter side chambers. One chamber was to eventually hold an adult pair of ravens, so it was outfitted with a small roosting and nesting shed. We placed large perches throughout the entire aviary complex and hung iron-framed wire doors in the tunnels where they joined the main aviary.

The snow began to fall around noon Saturday and more heavily after dark. The trail up the hill was slippery, but it didn't slow down our friends. The dogs gamboled ahead of everyone, anticipating a great weekend of free food and exploration. A dozen of us worked through the afternoon snow in preparation for the next day's final push. Sunday morning dawned bright white, but the usual calm was shattered by the sound of breaking limbs. Heavy snow and fall foliage do not mix well, and the maples were shattering under winter's early cloak. The aviary was a mess. Wet snow stuck and piled high on the wire roof. Its weight snapped our support poles and tore gaping holes in the roof of the main raven cage. Much of our previous work lay crushed before us. This, however, was nothing new to our hardy friends. They had always struggled with harsh winters and could shrug off defeat with more ease than we could. They had an "it is what it is" attitude and could dig in and tackle just about any job without complaining. After a quick breakfast of Lee's doughnuts and much-needed hot coffee, we all donned warm gloves and went back to work in the cold slush. By the end of the day, our work party had grown, and we had managed to repair and re-raise the main aviary roof and to complete one of the new arms and side aviaries. We added more support poles all around, like great masts of sailing ships, to carry the load of our wire tent. We had numb fingers but renewed confidence that this cage would weather future storms. We paused to eat sheep.

The following day we finished the sides of the other arm of the cage. We now had hung 133 rolls of chicken wire (roughly 50,000 square feet) on 225 maple tree supports. The side walls averaged 15 feet high, and the roof soared to 30 feet in places. We had enclosed one acre of Maine, about the size of half a football field or a small city block! Raven Haven needed only a few stitches here and there to be ready for its next feathered tenants. We were poised to toast the grand structure, when we discovered that our two four-legged assistants were nowhere to be found. After several hours, both dogs returned exhausted and humbled. They were getting comfortable with their new surroundings and probably had a story to tell if they could. Or perhaps they too needed a break from cage construction.

15 November 1988; Colleen's Journal: "We went into Farmer's Union and were asked how the cage was coming along. We told them, 'Great, it's almost done. We took time off yesterday to haul a 1,400 lb. cow up the hill.' An older guy overheard us and said, 'Bernd Heinrich must be involved in that.'"

Bernd, ever curious, has just returned to his truck from chasing ravens through the puckerbrush.

As we finished aviary construction in November 1988, our fingers, worn smooth by the galvanized, rough poultry fencing, stung in the cold mornings. The fourteen-gauge wire strand resisted our efforts to weave it in and out of the fencing. We were sure our friends and family wondered why our ten years of postgraduate education had us using our backs more than brains, but we were used to it. Manual labor like this is not uncommon for budding environmental biologists, who often spend much of their day-to-day energy in the construction business. Building a huge aviary was hard work, our largest construction project by far. But as we sewed the final stitches we thought about our new friends and the lessons they were teaching us.

Bernd was showing us how to get a job done, regardless of the obstacles. He made do with what he had. Curiosity drove him. Efficiency was rarely important. He would cut up dead cows with a pocketknife, haul them in the backseat of his small jeep, and drag them up frozen hills alone. His penchant for competitive ultramarathon races sealed his fate to most he met; this guy was crazy, in a good and interesting sort of way. To us, he was certainly interesting, and productive.

Our friends in Maine were guided by unquestioning generosity. Whenever we needed help, they were there. They enjoyed working together, being outside, and learning about the natural world. Through it all they kept a sense of humor. Dan Mann was eager to put his "coot," the amphibious vehicle, to work hauling wire and just as quick to point out that surely we could learn what science demanded by using black bantam chickens instead of ravens. Chickens, after all, wouldn't need a roof on their aviary. And just imagine the end-of-season barbeques.

The resourcefulness and deep roots of our extended family in Maine would prove crucial to our survival. Lee was a strong, opinionated woman. You knew how she felt. She once asked Henry to turn around while driving home so that she could point out a large pothole in the road, only to tell him, "Go ahead and drive through it! You might as well," she quipped, "You hit all the other ones." Henry did as directed. Lee's resources were simple but seemed endless. Drawers and cupboards held recycled string, neatly sorted fabric, grommets, leather, boxes, and bags. Little was wasted, and most was used repeatedly. Lee would listen to us, help us, and most of all feed us well. Her three sons, Floyd, Vernon, and Clifford, had practical skills. They rarely used their given names. It was at least a year until we knew "Butch" was Vernon, "Billy" was Clifford, and "Jim" was Floyd. Jim and his wife Janice were dairy farmers with five kids. Their connections would put us in touch with farmers anxious to donate dead stock to hungry ravens. Butch (an electrician), his wife Nancy, and their two daughters lived next door to Lee in a lovely cabin they had built themselves. Their construction skills, snow machines, and ingenuity solved problems. Billy, a pattern maker for a shoe company, and his wife Lili ran a daycare from their home with their daughter and son. When I met Billy we had an immediate bond, and I came to know him well over the years. He worked in all phases of our research, always ready to catch, watch, and track ravens. But it took a lot of careful listening before I realized that he was a cobbler, not a "patent" maker. I was beginning to learn the Maine lingo with its dropped *r*'s, where "ern" is most often pronounced as "ent."

19 November 1988; Colleen's Journal: "We are having Thanksgiving dinner (early one) at Lee and Henry's tomorrow with a bunch of people. We're making sweet potatoes and bringing white wine. Ed is making mashed turnips."

Joining a new family allowed us to experience the joy of the holidays from a fresh perspective. Thanksgiving in rural Maine had changed little since the first colonial festivities. Extended families welcomed new friends from distant shores to share customs and celebrate the earth's bounty. We joined Lee and Henry at their house for an early celebration. This allowed the whole clan to gather without disrupting later, more intimate celebrations on the actual day of thanks. We made favorite side dishes and brought along Ed Hathaway, a friend from Arizona who was helping us build the aviary and enjoying a wilderness reprieve from his native Boston. Ed was a big, strong, analytical, bunny-hearted environmental scientist intent on reducing our abuse of the earth, but until a job was available he was content to simply enjoy nature. His Irish blood rarely boiled, and he tended a large Alaskan Malamute and a German Shepherd. On this occasion, his two big dogs stayed home at our cabin to guard the carcasses.

It snowed throughout the day as thirty-two friends and relatives sat down to a memorable feast. The extra-long table, formed from many cobbled together, groaned under the weight of two turkeys, each in the thirty-pound range, and more trimmings than ought to be allowed. If that weren't enough, there were nine pies, three cakes, and plates of cookies for dessert. Everyone was anxious to get a bit of exercise after dinner, so we decided to take advantage of the new snow and try some backyard dogsledding. Sitka and Topper had come with us and waited anxiously in the car. We had put the sled on top of the car, hoping we would get enough snow to try a "fun run." We hooked them to the sled and added Boo, Henry and Lee's little black lab mix. Butch brought Phoebe, his typically high-strung Boxer, so we had a team of four. With no well-marked trail to follow and two untrained dogs, sledding was a disaster, but we managed to burn a few calories in the attempt, mostly from laughing. We also managed to further our new friends' case for just how crazy we were. We could imagine their thoughts: "These foolish youngstahs from away don't know what theyah doin', chasin' ravens and runnin' behind dogs."

After such great trapping success on our first attempt, we decided to try again on New Year's Eve. This time we had Steve Freshette, from the local Audubon club, Harry Turchan, who had a small farm nearby, and Harper, a friend of the Wojciks who had his arm in a sling, to help us. The birds were apprehensive about the trap. We caught only five. One escaped, and one was a recapture of one of the original escapees from the aviary. We returned the escapee to the aviary gang. Disappointed in our attempt, we knew another big group was needed and decided to schedule another "raven round up" for January 2. Birds continued to visit our trap and we remained optimistic. We took a few days off for some rest and, we hoped, to give the trap time to fill with naïve birds.

Meanwhile, we went to a New Year's Eve dance in Jay. We had purchased tickets from Lili a month before, longing for social getaway. Billy's rock band played long sets of old favorites through the heavy cigarette smoke that blued the air in the community dance hall. Everyone danced, drank, and talked until well after midnight. We all brought our own snacks and beverages, in coolers

John (left) and Bernd with ravens inside the trap in a fresh morning snow.
Photo courtesy of David Karkos.

or simple brown paper bags. This was a time to catch up on others' lives and simply share a good time. We enjoyed ourselves and made new friends. We were made to feel welcome, but still we were not fully vested in this new society. In our lives as perpetual students, we had been insulated from much of the real world. Now, as we drove home, we felt like we had watched a documentary about the social life of a rural paper mill town. But we were living it.

Bernd joined us for the next trapping party. After a cold hike up the hill in the predawn hours of January 2, we watched as he closed the trap on a crowd of fifteen juveniles, four yearlings, and three adults. It had taken awhile. Sitting in the cabin we wondered why Bernd hadn't fired the trap sooner. It seemed full of birds. Was he asleep inside the spruce blind? No, on his first heave, the clothesline scared the birds as it ripped through the frozen ground, snagging short of the door prop. A second jerk after the birds resettled in the trap did the trick. The tagging crew of Billy, Zetta, Hilary and Josh Wojcik, and Dave Karkos (a local reporter whose name is aptly pronounced "carcass") helped us band, tag, and draw blood. We put a recaptured juvenile in with the aviary gang, put the three adults in the left arm of the aviary, and released the rest. It took only a day to see that two of our adults were a mated pair. They preened each other, called together in soft and loud duets, and excluded the third bird from the roosting shed at night. We released the loner and knew we now had all the ingredients necessary for a productive winter of aviary experiments. We looked forward to knowing the ways of young ravens and investigating their interactions with adults in a controlled setting. Dave's article was helpful as he broadcast our eagerness to "welcome any gifts of dead animals." Now we could really use them.

14 December 1988; Colleen's Journal: "John went to a dairy farm and picked up a 1,400 lb. Holstein (black-and-white) that had died of mastitis. He had to gut it via the anus and then remove the stomachs which were left behind. Then he cut it in half with a chainsaw. What a bloody mess."

Word of our carcass needs spread quickly through the local community. Farmers were eager to engage our services. Rather than pay someone to take their downer cows, horses, pigs, and sheep, they learned we would do it for free. When they called, we hitched the trailer and drove to their farms. With tractors and saws we put bloated beasts in the trailer and drove back to Hills Pond. Our white trailer with the black raven logo, often containing stiff legs pointing skyward, became known to many. Nearby residents would deposit small carcasses in it. It was rarely empty. Sitka and Topper kept a close eye on the trailer, ever ready to test if the contents tasted as good as they smelled.

Castonguay's slaughterhouse in Livermore was a perennial source of raven chow. We would go there for the tasty cretón-spiced meat spread meant for human consumption. But Frank and his son Don would save lungs and other scraps for us. Weekly we would pick up two, three, or four fifty-gallon drums of the offal. They would jiggle all the way home.

Getting road-killed deer and moose, the favorite raven food, was not easy. It was not that few were available. It was that they were so valuable we had to race others to them. If we were lucky, the game warden or sheriff would tip us off to a recent kill. More frequently we wouldn't learn about the animal until its location was announced on the police radio band. Apparently, some hungry Mainers regularly monitored that frequency, and they often beat us to the site. When we arrived, all that remained was a bloody spot on a snowy road.

On January 16 the game warden from Rangeley called to let us know he had a moose. Anxious locals would not beat us to this prize. The warden said to just drive on up and he'd shoot it and load it into the trailer for us. Huh? Our moose were usually dead, but this one was not quite dead. She had "brain worm," or meningial worm (*Parelaphostrongylus tenuis*), a debilitating nematode some moose got from deer. A moose with meningial worms often contracts severe cerebrospinal nematodiasis, a disease of the nervous system, which causes moose to stumble, act abnormal, and often die. Mainers go to all lengths to spare a moose from unnecessary suffering, so this one was going to be put out of her misery. We met at a logging camp a few hours later and easily received the large, and now lifeless, cow moose as she was dragged behind a speeding logging skidder. We drove happily home with a blue tarp over the just-dead moose, whose nose and tongue hung over the side, not quite covered. Lifting her into the trailer had been mechanical. Getting her out was another matter.

Getting big dead animals out of a trailer is a fairly common problem in western Maine. We were advised to tie a rope from the animal's legs to a tree and drive away. It worked. Now we had a dead moose just off the Weld Road across from the trail to the aviary. We covered the 700-pound carcass with a blue tarp and hoped the falling temperatures and new snow would quickly freeze her and obscure her from passing motorists. Billy and Butch were eager to help us haul the moose up to the aviary in a couple of days. They had a snow machine that would allow the dogs to sit out this carcass haul. Topper and Sitka had been working overtime all week hauling chunks of a huge draft horse up to the aviary. At 4:45 a.m. on the morning we were going to haul the moose, loud footsteps preceded a strong knock on our cabin door. A sheriff's deputy asked, "Ah you responsible foah that moose up the road?" "Yes, we are, but how did you see her under the snowy tarp?" we wondered. "Tahp? Theahs no tahp, justah moose," came the reply from a deputy well fueled on coffee. Blue tarps were valuable out here, and ours was apparently enjoying a new life elsewhere. Butch and Billy complimented me on my sense of rural Maine life when I suggested we would probably be able to buy the tarp back down the road at a yard sale. Thankfully the moose was still present, but the tarp thieves sure must have been surprised when they lifted the blue plastic out of the snow. We asked the deputy, out of curiosity, "How did you track the moose to us?" His answer: "Communication." Our reputation was spreading.

Later that morning, when the snowmobile could not budge the frozen moose, we decided to cut her up. We were getting used to chainsaw massacres and retrieved our Stihl Woodboss, which we had purchased three years earlier with our wedding money. The romanticism of the saw quickly faded as I sliced through the moose's midsection. Fermentation in the stomach of this large vegetarian prevented complete freezing. A reddish brown, distinctly green streak of warm, blended moose blood, guts, and last meal shot across the snowy road, like spilled wine on starched linen. Billy lost his breakfast, but we soon had six pieces of moose efficiently hauled by snowmobile up at the aviary. I can still smell that morning's peculiar mix of exhaust and scorched moose meat.

Before the snow was suitable for dogsled or snow machine power, we mostly used an old wheelbarrow we scavenged from the Jay municipal dump to haul food to the ravens. The rusty hulk squeaked as it rolled, but it was porous enough to self-drain. Pushing the wheelbarrow up the path to our trap atop York Hill during our first autumn was never boring. On our maiden trip, barely able to hear each other over the squeaky wheel, we suddenly were shocked by a growl from along the trail. Certain it was a bear, we yelled. To our surprise a gray, fuzzy "bear" leaped from the brush. Unzipping his new bear suit, Bernd was barely able to control his laughter. Bernd loved practical jokes. Later Billy would tell us of the many summer evenings when growls from the near shore kept him and his brothers in their canoe and away from dinner. A young Bernd never let on to his game. We had now gained enough trust to be teased, and Bernd was comfortable leaving the day-to-day responsibilities of the research in our hands.

Later in the autumn, a female moose paralleled me step by squeaky step up the hill. As the clearing by the cabin came into view, the moose suddenly turned to me and grunted loudly. Her hair stood erect on her back, and she locked eyes with the squeaky stranger. My neck hairs were also standing on end but to little effect. She stomped the ground. Clearly she was perturbed, but why? Then her calf stood up a few yards away. Rather than cross between mother and daughter, I dumped the load of cow lungs on the trail and headed back down to the highway for a second batch. The moose were gone an hour later when I returned. Surely eviscerating the rusty wheelbarrow had bolstered their confidence!

Living in nature, especially collecting and distributing food for our ravens, and cutting, splitting, hauling, and stacking firewood, kept us fit. The dogs, too, were in top shape, using their sledding know-how to haul cut logs from the aviary to the growing woodpile behind Bernd's cabin and bloody raven food from the highway uphill a half mile to the aviary. We carried the meat in the bed of the sled, but a simple line from the dogs' harnesses to a downed section of tree allowed the duo to skid logs much larger than we could carry. Dogs can be thought of as "just smart enough to do a job and just dumb enough to do it." That fit our team well; we were smart and dumb but eager to watch ravens and learn. Even if our proposal went unfunded, we were now confident about learning some of Maine's secrets this winter.[2]

Fortunately, disappointment was not the case. Two days before our first Thanksgiving in our one-room cabin we received a phone call from Fred Stollnitz, the program officer for animal behavior studies at the National Science Foundation. He was happy to tell us that the reviews of our fourth proposal were positive, and if we could cut $16,000 to $18,000 from our annual budget, he could fund us at a rate of $50,000 a year for three full years. We called Bernd, who was in Germany at the time, to give him the great Thanksgiving news. We were ecstatic. Our gamble to leave our familiar West and work together as a human and dog team had paid off.

Cutting research budgets was standard practice at the time, but it was painful. Directors such as Dr. Stollnitz often asked researchers to make deep cuts so that scarce federal investments in basic science could be stretched a bit further. Our euphoria sobered as we tried to trim nearly a third of our requested budget from the project. Most of the budget was salary for John and me. This project was John's postdoc, which technically is a faculty position that required a minimum annual salary of $20,000 at the University of Vermont. Bernd received no salary from the grant and only minimal travel support to trek between Burlington and Maine. After many difficult discussions we saw cutting my salary as the only logical solution. But how could we maintain medical insurance and a joint salary sufficient for even our simple life? I had been working as a tech II for Russ Balda at Northern Arizona University, and I felt it was important to maintain a similar level of pay, if not recognition, given my experience. But cutting a tech II salary in half was still not enough. We got closer to our budget target by removing my medical coverage, which could be provided to me as a spouse under John's coverage. Despite these adjustments, we still had to reduce John's salary by nearly $5,000 over the second and third proposed years. I would work full time most of the year for my "part-time" salary. I felt as if my professional experience was formally undervalued. But John and I were entering this as a team, and I was willing to make a sacrifice. Our financial resources were pooled anyway, and in making these changes everyone came out ahead.

When the numbers were finally crunched, we would make $26,000 per year. The University of Vermont would receive just over $11,000 annually to administer our grant and provide "overhead," resources needed to keep the lights and heat on at Bernd's academic office. We also had a few hundred dollars each year for travel to scientific meetings and basic field supplies. We would gladly use our car and fuel for daily research travel. When our land-lords, Tom and Zetta, weren't using their office, we even had the necessary facilities for data analysis. Finally, we could stop looking for odd jobs and fully immerse ourselves in the lives of ravens and Mainers. In a depressed rural economy, the job hunt had been difficult anyway. From conservation educator to kennel help, we weren't a good fit. Raven ecology in winter, according to National Science Foundation, fit us just fine.

Not everyone was so sure America needed to invest in basic science, espe-cially our brand of science. Dick Milne crowed in the *National Enquirer* that the federal government was spending the huge sum of $50,000 per year to find out how ravens got dinner dates. Representative Carroll Hubbard of Kentucky was quoted as saying, "With the nation's many homeless people roaming the streets in search of a decent meal, I find it appalling that the NSF would approve funding such a grant." The tensions between funding basic academic research and solving society's urgent problems were apparent to us. We understood our privilege and were grateful. But we were surprised. Hav-ing grown up around universities, we had always lived in a culture that valued science. Many of the things that meet our needs and improve daily life came from basic scientific investigation: superglue, tin foil, Velcro, microwaves, and televisions, and an appreciation for the ways of other peoples and other species. Thankfully, our friends in Maine, while often out of work and living on fixed incomes, never questioned why their government should support research. To them, knowing more about nature was reason enough.[3]

25 November 1988; Colleen's Journal: "John and I journeyed down to Freeport to the big L. L. Bean $2 million warehouse sale."

Since funding had thankfully materialized, we decided we could afford to visit L. L. Bean in Freeport to stock up on warmer clothes. The huge warehouse sale that was going on made the trip even more appealing. Penny-pinching is a habit that is hard to change, but temperatures were dropping and we needed insulation. We bought $355 worth of winter field clothes for around $172. A week later we returned to buy more warm socks and almost all our Christmas gifts.

Many have asked why we didn't venture farther afield to study nature in the jungle or savannah. Surely this is where the real secrets of the earth reside. But for us, nearby nature was more relevant. Here in the wild spaces near people we could practice biology and learn about a new culture. We were also practical. We concluded that foreign travel would preclude many of our desires, including owning dogs. John desired a novel research setting where experimentation was possible, not logistically preempted. Rather than observing a few rare animals, he wanted to test scientific hypotheses using an experimental approach. Experiments depend on abundant, accessible animals and unique field facilities. He was ready to answer new questions but wanted to query the animals he knew best—the crows, ravens, and jays. I wanted a rural lifestyle and a chance for real adventure with my budding sled dog team. My choice to join in this adventure had more to do with academic burnout and my introduction to bird behavior studies than with making a sacrifice for John. I never thought of it as a tradeoff or that one day I would have "my turn." It was a chance to share the adventure and learn as much as I could about an exciting topic along the way. I also had a long fascination with Maine. Sanford, Maine, was named after my ancestors, who settled throughout the state. I wanted to research these relatives and share my findings with John. Many of our colleagues and mentors had struggled and failed with their marriages. We did not want to be one of those statistics. If you had asked me years ago if this is where I saw myself, I could not have said "yes," but neither could I have predicted where my life would lead. We had all we could hope for here in the wilds of Maine: new friends, faithful dogs, scientific rigor, and most important, each other.

three

Torture in the Hut

It was still dark as we slipped from Bernd's cabin, locked the dogs in their makeshift kennel, and snuck around the aviary to the small tarpaper observation hut. We shuffled through the snow-quiet woods. Stooping beside the elevated, frosty floor, we creaked the hatch inward and upward. Our entrance was becoming automatic: reach into the porthole and palm the inside floor of the hut, jump, flex, and wriggle to avoid the stove and piss pot, pull knees toward chest and touch down quietly inside the cramped but dry shelter. We built a fire in the woodstove and got ready for a day of raven watching. Our captive flock was also dry, nestled in the roosting shed a half a football field away at the distant end of the aviary. In only a few minutes the seasoned maple and birch kindling burning within the old stove began to thaw the sixty square feet of hut. We peeled off layers of clothes and breathed deeply of the piney air; the resin in the rough lumber walls was softening and vaporizing. We unfolded our metal chairs, pushed a long, foam-insulated shotgun microphone out a small hole, connected it to the tape recorder so we could capture any utterances from the ravens, and leaned onto a small wooden shelf turned crude desk to begin writing:

12 January 1989
Cloudy, flurries, 0° (−2°F last night)
6:30 Soft woo-woos as birds wake up
7:10 Birds relatively quiet, adults feeding, juveniles spread out on perches

The hut as viewed from inside the aviary. The aviary is not yet roofed,
but the hut is complete with its tarpaper skin.

Our hut had a full view. Out the right window we looked over the captive
adult pair defending their 120-square-yard caged territory. A natural ledge
supported a 25-yard-long chicken wire tunnel that connected their abode to
the 1,600-square-yard main aviary sprawling in front of us, completely visible
from our large front window. A second, 46-yard-long tunnel of wire arced to
our left, invisible in places despite a small third window in the hut, toward a
second, 120-square-yard unoccupied aviary. The juveniles in the main aviary
could see the adult or the empty aviary. No ravens could see us. We watched
from behind one-way glass, darkening our view but fully reflecting suspicious
raven gazes.

Absorbed in watching and noting, we forgot about the fire. The chilly
winter quickly cooled the hut, and smoke choked in from a gust of wind. A
newly kindled fire solved both issues, and we enjoyed a hot mug of coffee from

just-boiled water. We welcomed the coffee's heat but fought its inevitable diuretic side effects. Alas, we had to succumb and retrieved the two-pound coffee can from next to the stove. We developed a technique for the elimination process that involved avoiding the hot stove and, for Colleen, precise squatting. True love at its finest!

Relieved, we continue the vigil:
YW displaces BRG
BrW displaces GY
10:30 Yells coming from free birds at food to the west; caged birds calm (no wind)
RYR preens WY and RB bites her softly
RYR knocks three times with puffy head and wings spread, V-like, as she switches to preen RB

We recycled a thick layer of old manuscript paper into a sheaf of daily notes until darkness again ushered the ravens back to their roost shed. We identified individual birds using shorthand reference to the color wing tags they wore: BrW for a male whose tag was half brown and half white; RYR for the female whose tag was striped red, yellow, and red. As tempted as we were to name them based on personality quirks, habits, or physical appearance, we stuck to tag abbreviations only. We used objective names for our ravens to prevent our personal interpretations from biasing the basic data we were collecting.

Our knowledge of the intricate details of raven life had expanded. We rose stiffly from the increasingly hard chairs and slithered through the trapdoor into the snowy wild. Following our deepening trails through the snow back to Bernd's cabin, we gathered up Topper and Sitka and enjoyed the cool clarity of the hike downhill to Weld Road and the short drive home. We chattered constantly, finally able to speak without fear of disrupting the ravens. Tomorrow we would gather meat for the ravens, check on field experiments, and return to the hut for more observation. We were multitasking a blend of ranching and science—feeding, tending, and watching our black flock.

A hungry group of ravens inside the aviary begin to eat a frozen raccoon. Unique, alpha-numeric tags are affixed to each wing. C18 (left) has a fuzzy head signaling subordinate status. Dominant birds with sleek heads are the first to eat. RYR (C8) moves in close to her preening partner, the alpha male C22 (back toward camera).

First week in January 1989; Colleen's Journal: "We watched the birds from the hut one day (the stove from Camp Kaflunk barely keeps us warm). The day before, we went up with some meat and to do some repairs and some construction (rearrangement). By the time we left it was −10 degrees with a 30 mph wind! John came in with a white nose. The ride in the sled down the hill was painful! The dogs ran like hell (their feet hurt)."

The dogs were invaluable assistants. They hauled horse each day for more than a week to bait the trap and feed the aviary birds. The farmer who called just after Christmas to say his horse of thirty years just died encouraged us to take her. He would even deliver her to our cabin. So we weren't surprised to come home to a horse carcass in the driveway. But a 1,200-pound draft animal?

It was cold, but a big horse took time to freeze. After a few days, the animal was expanding from the trapped gaseous by-products of fermentation. I opened her up, released the pressure, and while choking on the thick air, shoveled snow into the body cavity to speed the freezing and stop the stench. The hay and grain in the horse's stomach had a life of their own! As with the moose, fermentation prevented freezing; I shoveled and hauled by wheelbarrow load after load of brownish-green stomach contents from the horse to Zetta's garden. When spring came the manure-in-waiting would fertilize the crops. That is, if any was left after Brodie, the Wojciks' rotund Border Collie, was done rolling in it, eating it, and puking it on Tom and Zetta's bedroom carpet. The horse did not make us popular tenants, but it taught us to be careful where we scattered what the ravens would not eat. Brodie was not the only issue: the stout legs and huge horse head I cached by Hills Pond were found later in the summer by hikers. The game warden and sheriff figured out quickly who was responsible for the mysterious horse massacre.

19 January 1989; Colleen's Journal: "The dogs' hair grows thicker, especially between their toes. We hear the deck and even the trees popping, like shots from a rifle, especially when the temperature drops below 0°F. We learn that the tree shots are in reality dead xylem cells shattering in the cold."

Every day in the hut was a new experience. We learned the idiosyncrasies of the cranky woodstove, and we finally replaced our reliable coffee can with an antique white enamel chamber pot with a much larger diameter. Because we could identify each bird by its wing tags, and because we provided all the food and watched many of the birds' interactions with one another and with visiting free-flying ravens, we could interpret much of what we saw with unusual clarity. The ravens' pecking order, or dominance hierarchy, for example, was clear within a few weeks. As ravens settled into their caged life, we recorded every aggressive interaction—a forceful jab, slow push, or loud scuffle—as one juvenile raven displaced another from a favorite perch or feeding spot. We

RB (C22), the alpha male of our first aviary group, yells from a dominant posture toward a subordinate cage mate, who looks away and cautiously approaches a new food item out of view in the ferns.

noted many each day—118 on January 11 alone! Compiling nearly 2,000 displacements over the first winter confirmed what we had learned during my brief stay last winter: large, presumably male, ravens are dominant to smaller females. With more observation time it became clear that the hierarchy in the aviary was stable with each bird having a fixed place. Male RB was the alpha raven, male GB the beta, male GY the gamma, and so on down to BrB, who was the low female raven on the totem pole. Scientists studying social order often refer to animals using an ordered sequence from the Greek alphabet. "Alpha," signifying to Grecians the first or most significant occurrence, is used to denote the highest-ranking member of an animal group.

The chain of command was fairly consistent and rarely reversed. It was much simpler than the multigenerational, family arrangement of wolves. In wolf packs, a dominant pair reigns supreme, but in some cases the alpha female calls the shots and in others it is the alpha male who is in charge. Subordinate wolves have even been known to rise up and kill a dominant tyrant, but in ravens role reversals were rare, subordinates rarely challenged, and dominant males always seemed to run the show. Over the entire first winter, we saw a subordinate displace a dominant only 58 times. The birds' interactions were not random; fights were rare between birds of extremely different status, and stable partnerships formed among some males and females. Partnerships were reinforced with social grooming, or allopreening, where one bird uses its bill to probe the other's head and neck feathers for unreachable parasitic flies and lice, which can easily become problematic to animals that live together in groups.[1]

Grooming ravens reminded us of intent apes, but this interesting activity is fairly common among social animals, including gulls, albatrosses, and penguins. It likely fills multiple needs beyond the practical removal of pests. Grooming can cement social bonds and reinforce dominance. Dominant ravens typically initiated grooming sessions, and often grooming turned to aggression. Dominants may even be repaying subordinates' diffidence by helpful preening. After all, a dominant needs the company of subordinates to survive.

A well-respected social hierarchy built on aggressive and supportive relationships has clear advantages in reducing overall aggression within a flock. It is absolutely typical of caged animals that fight regularly when first brought together but gradually come to know each other as individuals and then defer without battle to higher-ranking group members. A hierarchy of social status ensures dominant individuals priority, but not always exclusive, access to important resources. This hierarchy also provides a structure to group life that may reduce overall stress and therefore benefit subordinate animals as well. A stable hierarchy also implies that ravens know each other as individuals.[2]

But we did not simply observe the caged ravens. By late January we were literally pulling strings to conduct our first experiment. Six nylon-coated clotheslines led from iron-framed, wire doors in the aviary arms through pulleys to the hut. Each arm had three doors: one at the junction where it tied into the main aviary; a second five yards down the arm; and a third where the arm joined the satellite (either the adult or the empty) aviary. We pulled the line to the first door to open it and allow the ravens from the main aviary into the vestibule of the arm. Pulling the second gave the birds full access to the arm. Pulling the third allowed the nonbreeding flock to explore the entire length of the right arm and encounter the adults in their territory, or to explore the full left arm and discover the isolated, undefended satellite aviary. Appendix 1 illustrates the aviary complex, including the arms, doors, and various aviaries.

19 January 1989; Colleen's Journal: "We are conducting our first experiment this week on recruitment to food in front of the adult pair. It means getting up early both tomorrow and Saturday and spending the day in the hut."

Our first set of experiments was designed to test Bernd's hypothesis that young ravens yell with loud and powerful calls at defended foods to recruit others. Recruiting others would benefit the caller because a gang of young birds could negate the adults' defense and allow access to the rich, but guarded, food. But was the cacophony around a carcass really a purposeful cry for help, or was it a simple side effect of sharing a meal? Bernd's observations and ideas had great public appeal because they were interpreted as evidence that young oppressed ravens purposefully recruited help to overthrow defensive adults. In the aviary we could test this hypothesis directly. We would compare the calls of young ravens when they were allowed to find defended foods (those in the adult aviary) versus undefended foods (those in the peripheral, left aviary). If ravens yelled to attract recruits, then they should do so only in the adult aviary. More interestingly, if ravens yelled to purposefully recruit help, then yelling should be directed at possible recruits and not at the food, the adults, or those already recruited.

It was possible for us to study both the mechanics of recruitment and the function of sharing a meal. Confusing the function, or evolutionary explanation, for a behavior with the mechanics that produce, or immediately cause, a behavior had befuddled psychologists and the public's perception of the abilities of animals for centuries. Clarifying the various meanings behind the simple question "Why?" was perhaps the greatest contribution to the field of animal behavior made by one of the founders, Niko Tinbergen. Consider why a wolf pup plays. A young wolf may be stimulated to play by a simple cue—a sibling bowing down with rump high and tail wagging. The pup's lunge toward his sister may be an automatic behavioral response to a "proximate" cue, the play bow. The mechanics of play are the lunge in response to the bow. Bowing causes play. Playing may also have "ultimate" survival value, shaping the pup into an effective hunter. Play functions to improve hunting. This ultimate interpretation provides a different answer to the question about why a wolf pup plays. But the proximate and ultimate answers are easily confused. Improving one's hunting skill need not be understood by, or directly motivational to, the young, playful wolf. As observers we might say that the young wolf plays to increase its survival skills. But this shorthand statement, while true at the evolutionary level as an explanation of why natural selection has favored playing wolves over standoffish wolves, is also presumptive at the mechanistic level. It presumes, often incorrectly, that the wolf knows why play is important. Without detailed observation and experimentation, we cannot know what the wolf knows. The same is true for the recruitment to food by ravens. So we set out to untangle the mechanics of recruitment—how it was done and what cues were used—from the function of recruitment—why natural selection would favor its evolution. Our critical thinking about the mechanics and functions implied in Bernd's initial experiments led to tense, but insightful, discussions among Bernd and us.[3]

Bernd would argue that ravens yelled, that yelling attracted others, and that attracting others could be advantageous to the yeller. Thus a function of yelling was clearly to attract recruits. But we would counter that yelling might simply be a response to hunger. Hungry ravens yell. Natural selection could shape yelling into an effective recruitment call, but an individual raven still just yells because it is hungry. Demonstrating a complex function of yelling, like group assembly, does not mean that those actually yelling also understand this function. Ravens need not consciously or purposefully yell to attract others. They might. It was certainly more interesting if they did. But we needed to decode the proximate stimuli for yelling and unravel them from the ultimate advantages to be certain. To date, Bernd had focused only on the ultimate. When Bernd would say, "Ravens yell to recruit others," he meant this in an ultimate way: ravens yell *because* natural selection favors yellers who recruit, eat, and survive. This was missed in the public press where readers were led to believe that ravens consciously and actively yelled *to* recruit. This was certainly possible, but it was untested. We started pulling strings, raising doors, and moving meat to clarify the proximate reasons ravens yelled.

On January 18 we put a cow lung in each vestibule and opened the first door. The birds were hesitant to move under the open, suspended door. Perhaps it reminded them of the trap. After several hours, BrYBr, a subordinate, ventured from the aviary into the vestibule of the arm and began to peck at the frozen, carnation pink, Styrofoam-like lung. Finally, after nearly three weeks, the birds were willing to explore beyond their main aviary for foods. The alpha male, RB, hung back and yelled frequently as his subordinate began to eat. RB was risk averse, royally chasing others and stealing mouthfuls from them rather than going directly to the lung. He was the only bird yelling. As the ravens swarmed the lung, RB eventually joined the feast. Subordinates moved away as he strode in to claim the central spot atop the lungsicle. Had we not known our birds, we would have concluded that RB was the local territorial adult. His behavior was fully adult. He even appeared to have a mate, RYR, whom he often preened and defended from the other high-ranking males in the flock.

We hid food in new places throughout the aviary to acquaint our wary birds with their entire terrain. The same outcome was repeated at each new discovery. The dominant male yelled as he watched others test new foods they had discovered. His yells were strong, given as he bent forward with slightly erect feathers, sounded like *Who! Who!*, and were clearly directed at the subordinates. We had noticed other yellers. But they were not in our cage. They were wild birds visiting the aviary, perched alongside our feeding flock. They too were clearly yelling at feeding birds. Their yells were often more plaintive, ethereal: *Youoo! Youoo!* These were the yells Bernd had described. Occasionally these visitors walked beside our flock, separated from the feast by a thin wire wall. Some gave strong yells like RB. This vocalization immediately attracted the attention of the dominant insiders, mostly RB and GB, who strutted stiffly, like mechanical wind-up toys, to the fence with their belly and head feathers erected (a posture Bernd referred to as "ears up and pants down"), bowed, flared their wings, and uttered choking vocalizations. Full out vocal wars would ensue if the displays escalated further. Dueling ravens on either side of the aviary would stretch their necks and utter loud, reedy, descending, harmonic trills, emphasizing each call with an upward or downward thrust of the neck. Strutting, trilling dominants faced off, unable to physically contact each other. To us these trill wars sounded like courting Sandhill Cranes. We felt the aggression in the calls. Nothing in these first glimpses suggested ravens yelled to attract recruits. If anything, they yelled to intimidate others or out of frustration at not being able to join a foraging group.

A young Northern Goshawk landed atop the aviary and startled the juveniles on January 31. The heavily streaked predator did not yet have its sizzling red eyes, but it mattered not to our ravens. They were potential prey, and they scattered for the shelter of the roost. Later in the afternoon, after the hawk had moved on, the ravens started prospecting for food. The only food available today was in the adult aviary and was strongly defended by the pair, with whom the juveniles had not had contact since their capture in late December. GY was the first juvenile to pass beyond the vestibule heading toward the adults. We closed the door behind him and opened the door at the adult aviary for the first time. We were barely able to breathe. What would the third-ranking gamma juvenile do when he encountered the adults? Surely he would yell and bring an army of recruits into the vestibule, eager to get fully down the arm.

GY entered the adult aviary at 12:10. We were stunned when he walked right up and took a bite from the adults' food. But he got only one bite before the territorial male dropped on him like a black hammer. The male bit him, kicked him, and chased him deeper into his lair. The adult female looked down from her perch. This was a male thing, but it was not a fair contest. GY puffed his head feathers out in a show of submission, crouched, and begged like a whining child. The demeanor of a confident juvenile changed instantly as GY now groveled at his superior's feet. The adult's attack shifted from physical to mental; simply looking toward GY caused the juvenile to cower. GY did not yell once. In two hours he fed for only three minutes, but GY begged incessantly. When a few wild birds gathered outside the fence, he suddenly snapped back into the juvenile social scene. Being the only juvenile near the food, he was by default the alpha bird. And he knew it! He strutted toward the outside juveniles and trilled. The territorial male dropped again, and the trills of a dominant became the begs of a subordinate. There was room for only one king here. The mechanics of begging were clear. Adult aggression is the proximate cause of begging. We watched the juvenile's begging turn on and off in response to the adult male—as abruptly as if the male had a switch wired to the submissive youngster.

Shortly after 3:00 p.m. GY left the adult cage on his own, and we again lowered the door, sealing the adults in their domain. We opened the vestibule door and GY returned to the main aviary to join the flock preparing to roost. With flock tucked in the roost, we bolted from the hut confident that we had set the perfect experiment. GY was the only juvenile who knew where to find tomorrow's food. When we opened the doors in the morning, surely he would lead the others to the adults.

It was still dark when we struck a fire in the hut on a cold February 1. By 6:20 we had all the aviary doors open. The ravens, hungry from two days with only scraps to eat, could explore anywhere. We eagerly watched every step taken by GY. Finally, at 7:03 he was moving. But he went left down the arm away from the adults and the moose he had discovered yesterday. Finding only a few caches, he returned to the main aviary and at 7:43 headed down the right arm toward the adults. He wasted little time returning to his prize. The juvenile alpha male, RB, was right behind him. RB yelled strongly, *Who! Who!* The adult male dropped swiftly, surely, and attacked both intruding juveniles. GY and RB instantly begged, cowered, and puffed their feathers. The signal of submission in ravens is the opposite of the signal of dominance—a weak versus strong voice, cowering versus upright posture, and fluffed versus sleek head. Charles Darwin long ago noted this "principle of antithesis" as he observed posturing dogs. It is common among social animals, where graded signals code one's motivation and the cost of mixed messaging is high.[4]

At the sound of begging, every other juvenile in the main aviary headed en masse down the right arm toward the commotion. Now the territorial female joined the fray, attacking RYR, the juvenile partner of RB. After only a few minutes the fighting was over and the feasting began. Like a stylized dance, the fighting was mainly ritualistic—a peck or two from the adults elicited begging and submission from the juveniles, which stopped the physical attack. No injuries ever occurred, even in the confines of the aviary.

As the adults and juveniles feasted, social manners governed the eating. The dominance hierarchy still determined who fed freely and who had to cower or push their way to the choicest feeding spot. The adults spent most of their time preening each other from the perch above the feeding juveniles. When the adults approached the food to eat, the juveniles backed away. Adults dominated all juveniles; the adult female ranked well above the alpha male of the juvenile flock. Among the juveniles, the dominant ones ate at the prime spots, where the skin had been peeled back to expose the burgundy muscle, when the adults were absent. Now, with plenty of moose every bird got its fill. As afternoon changed to evening, the juveniles returned to their roost shed and the territorial pair stayed in their aviary. We closed the doors on a fast, full, and somewhat surprising day in the hut, confident our contrived setting was mimicking nature.

The scene from February 1 was replayed many times our first winter. The basic pattern was always the same. Juveniles who discovered defended food might yell once or twice, but this behavior immediately changed to begging as the adults attacked. The adult male selectively attacked juvenile males, whereas the adult female took on the juvenile females. In response to begging, two behaviors occurred. The adult attack rate declined, and other juveniles flocked to the scene. In contrast, when foods in the undefended aviary were discovered no begging took place. The top male juveniles might yell as subordinates closed in on an undefended food, but without adults there was no begging. Begging was clearly given to the adults as a signal of surrender, just as a young pup crouches or rolls over to expose a vulnerable underbelly, whimpers, or licks lips to appease its owner or a dominant pack member. But this proximate explanation does not mean that begging could not also have evolved because it attracts recruits. Certainly nearby ravens who hear begging should wing toward this dinner bell because their presence might give them access to food. Their presence might also give the beggar access to food: the beggar not only appeases the adult, it also increases its chances of stopping adult aggression altogether as a crowd forms. All could feast where previously only a few groveled. The begging itself is not only a response to an adult presence but also a proximate cue to possible food. We were seeing a benefit of listening as well as begging, much as Bernd hypothesized for yelling. But in the aviary, yells seemed to have little to do with recruitment. Yells signaled status; dominants yelled *Who! Who!* Yells also signaled hunger and frustration; hungry juveniles and those unable to join a foraging group (and therefore not attacked to the point of begging) yelled airily, *Youoo! Hoooaa!*

Our emerging view of begging and yelling was that recruiting others was not the proximate reason for these vocalizations. Instead, ravens yelled and begged for more immediate needs, expressing their physical states and emotions. These signals might be pirated by others in search of food, which by benefiting caller and thief could reinforce the evolution of yelling and begging. But calling ravens did not appear to be anticipating a future need, such as the need for recruits to overpower a dominant defender. We confirmed the imme-

diate drivers of raven calls over the next five months by observing our juveniles' behaviors as they discovered defended and undefended foods. We also
systematically varied their level of hunger and the placement of food, and we
observed their responses to our tape-recorded calls. Our observations were
clear-cut. Plaintive yelling increased in direct proportion to hunger and was
especially frequent when food was visible but unobtainable. Juveniles begged
only when attacked by adults, and these calls were highly attractive. We could
draw our flock anywhere in the aviary complex simply by broadcasting begging from a speaker.[5]

If only controlling Topper and Sitka were so easy. While we were sequestered in the hut, our dogs would spend the days trying to escape from the
small haphazard kennel we had built alongside Bernd's cabin. The snow
fence, wire, and bales of straw were neither adequate nor interesting enough
for a young Border Collie mutt and a husky. Just as we learned from the first
raven escapes, we knew we had to think like a bored dog to contain our canine
duo. Sitka interrupted one of our early experiments by joining us at the hut
after she chewed a hole in the snow fence. The ravens flushed from feeding at
the sight of the streaking canine.

With ravens initially apprehensive about exploring the full aviary, hut time
could be dull. But because the trees had dropped their thick summer wares,
we could survey a broad reach from our small hut. Dog watching was a
welcome break. Some of our slow raven days had more notes on the dogs than
the birds, especially regarding their problem-solving ability. After her first
escape, we reinforced the kennel and grounded Sitka with a nylon cord. She
chewed through the cord with a few chomps of her shearing, carnassial teeth
and squeezed through the fence again. A cable tie managed to keep her in after
that, but now Topper squeezed through the fence. We sat helplessly peering
through our binoculars as he ate moose from a carcass in front of the cabin. He
soon tired of "wild" meat and moved to the other side of the cabin, where he
dug up our "refrigerator," a hole in the snow where we cached perishable
foods, and ate part of our dinner casserole and prized ham. Funnily enough,

he jumped back into the kennel after an hour and stayed there the rest of the day. Did he think we wouldn't see him? Did he think we would never know? (This routine was typical for Topper. He had perfected the art of conning us into thinking he never left the yard in Flagstaff. Tattletale neighbors filled us in.) Thinking we could outsmart him, the next day we tied him with the nylon cord in the kennel. He chewed it, ate more moose snacks, and then headed up to the hut for a visit. Colleen snuck out and intercepted him before he ruined an experiment. After that, we often left the two troublemakers at home, contained in the Wojciks' yard, when we had a long day in the hut. Maybe our dogs were just like the wolves and coyotes with whom the ravens often dined, but we didn't need the added variable. As much as problem solving in the domestic dog would have been an interesting side study, we had our hands full with the ravens.

Our time in the hut, while trying on the dogs and sometimes our patience, provided an understanding of the basic mechanics of raven communication. We had not discovered a secret dance or call used by the birds to purposefully recruit, but we knew how begs and yells given by intimidated, hungry, or bossy birds worked to incidentally attract others. It seemed that much of the magic of recruitment was actually a by-product of simple, direct status signaling. Natural selection often works this way, molding the simple into the wonder of the complex. While pragmatic, we were still awed from time to time.

On February 14, RYR, the dominant juvenile female, had just entered the adult aviary with two other juveniles. The territorial male predictably attacked GY, the beta male, who immediately switched from yelling to begging. But then RYR left the adult aviary, flew back to the main aviary, and perched next to RB, GB, and RWB. She leaned forward, spread her wings, and gave a series of knocking calls. One minute later she returned quietly to the adult aviary followed over the next twenty-three minutes by each of the three birds with whom she had just perched. No others came into the adult arena for another fifteen minutes. Surely RYR had actively recruited help. She had knocked, a general signal of excitement, apparently to convince her preening partner and a few others to follow. And it paid off, because adult defense declined with a growing army of recruits, and RYR was able to eat by sidling next to RB, the alpha juvenile. Such glimpses into the actual intelligence of ravens would remain just that, glimpses that impressed us but that we could not replicate.

The benefits of recruitment, on the other hand, were consistently and easily duplicated in the controlled environs of the aviary. From July to November 1989 we entered the main aviary with large nets, designed to ease lake trout, or as Billy called them, togue, into an angler's boat. We systematically scooped up juveniles in groups of one, three, five, seven, ten, or eighteen each day. We placed these randomly constituted groups into either the adult or the unde-fended satellite aviary. Then, we carefully recorded the juveniles' abilities to eat and the adults' abilities to defend. Our results were straightforward: groups of ten or more juveniles consistently overcame adult territory defense and fed at higher rates than did smaller groups or lone ravens. Feeding rates increased because the number of attacks by adults dropped and the adults relaxed their monopolization of the food. But increasing group size also reduced the fear juveniles typically had for new foods: a single juvenile would rarely dare to touch a new food, even without adult defense. Dominant juve-niles benefited most from recruitment. They fed over three minutes of a five-minute period when a group of eighteen assembled, compared to no feeding when alone and less than two minutes within groups of ten or fewer. But subordinates also benefited, feeding just over one out of every five minutes in groups of ten or more. Dominants even benefited by feeding with large groups of other juveniles when no adults were present because they were less skittish, more secure, than when alone. Subordinates, however, benefited only when groups were of about ten birds; their rate of feeding was low with smaller, skittish groups, and also low with larger groups because dominants monopo-lized the food much of the time.[6]

The benefits of social foraging were not equal among individuals in groups of juvenile ravens. All juveniles benefited in small groups, but social status de-fined the benefits in larger groups. Therefore, we expected dominant juveniles always to recruit others and remain at foods even when large groups formed. Subordinates should never recruit others to undefended foods and might even benefit by leaving a feast to search for less crowded fare when groups exceed twenty ravens. Our picture of juvenile group dynamics was clearing. The ultimate benefit of recruitment was a full stomach and survival, and through these rewards natural selection favored noisy begging and did not silence dominants yelling *Who!* or subordinates plaintively yelling *Youoo!* at large, defended foods.

Tantalized by our initial discoveries, we put in a long first season at the hut. From January to September, we spent 375 hours during 110 days gazing through the one-way glass of the hut. Temperatures ranged from −10 to +75°F. We enjoyed watching our ravens track the changing seasons. They took baths in fresh snow, plowing headfirst into powder, twisting, reveling, and then puffing their feathers and shaking off the crystals of ice like a dog shakes after a refreshing swim. When temperatures soared, the ravens snored. In bright sun they would collapse over perches or on the ground, alarmingly moribund but simply sunbathing. These ravens were fastidious, cleaning the gore of their scavenging lifestyle off their feathers by snowbathing and turning on the production of vitamin D by sunbathing. Sunbathing may also warm and enhance the action of the oil ravens apply from their preen gland to their feathers, and it might even cause parasitic flies and lice to more easily be detected and removed.[7]

Most of what we learned in the aviary helped explain what we were seeing in nature. We were often surprised when a lone juvenile, on finding a new carcass, looked and acted dominant, just like an adult. From our observations in the aviary we began to understand that this was a response to a unique social setting. When we kept social change to a minimum in the aviary, a fixed and stable dominance hierarchy developed. This hierarchy was rarely contested when all birds could access one another, but all it took was removal or isolation of one of the top ravens to see a massive shift. When we removed RB from the juvenile group late in the first summer, GB, the formerly quiet beta male, instantly assumed the posture, demeanor, and vocal repertoire of the alpha male. He immediately acted as the new top raven, and he was not challenged. He increasingly preened with RYR, who was previously RB's partner. When both RB and GB were removed, GY immediately displayed dominance and accrued all the benefits of being alpha. The stability we had assumed to be characteristic was temporary, quickly mutable into a new social structure defined by whoever was physically present in the group. It really seemed that each male was an alpha bird in waiting. Simply excluding the current alpha on one side of a wire gate, within a meter of its former group and in plain sight, caused the beta to immediately transition into the alpha role, yelling *Who! Who!* as he approached food, defending against the former alpha across the wire, commanding the top feeding spot, and preening the top female.

Flexible social roles seemed to fit the vagaries of raven social life. At consistent foods, like garbage dumps, we expected to see stable hierarchies just as in the aviary. Fights should be rare and the same ravens should often be present. This is indeed the case. But at ephemeral foods, like moose carcasses, we would expect hierarchies to be in flux because in such instances turnover in group membership is frequent and initial group composition somewhat random. Dominant juveniles should remain and fight all newcomers, but subordinates might do well to wander off and discover a new carcass where their status might be elevated, as was the case when we removed or isolated the top ravens from the aviary. Discovering ravens, whom we saw act dominant in the wild, might behave like those inside the aviary who could display their status to those outside it with postures and calls, thus gaining at least a momentary advantage. Our observations and experiments taught us that ravens have a very keen sense of their social milieu. And the dynamic nature of their flocking in the wild continually stirs their social arrangement, thereby placing a premium on knowing one's social setting and adapting one's status to fit within it.

Sometimes I would escape for my own socialization and sanity. Sitting in Lee's cozy kitchen one day, I felt a sense of contentment. We had been puttering around the house finding materials to make a harness for Lee's dog, Boo. Resourceful as ever, Lee put together some old fire hose and fake fur scraps, copying Topper's harness. Her old super-duper sewing machine that could go clean through a finger easily punched the hose, and we quickly had a usable harness. Anytime I had an opportunity to spend time with Lee we would chatter about all kinds of things, especially marriage. I could discuss my frustrations with John or his decisions as they related to our relationship with Bernd. Lee had listened to me do most of the talking that morning. A few "ayups" and chuckles showed her empathy for my marital woes. We sat down with a cup of coffee and I vented; then Lee talked. She told me about her first marriage to Floyd Adams. She told me stories about Bernd, because she had known him since he was a child. I left relaxed, feeling better about my relationship with John and with a new perspective on Bernd.

We continued to learn more about our social setting as well. When Zetta found out we were interested in antiques, she suggested that we try the auction in New Sharon on Saturday nights. Who could pass up fun and free entertainment? Clyde Allen, the auctioneer, had a great sense of humor. Different items brought different commentary, but they were all "cleaner than a smelt." We met some real characters who enjoyed telling us what was what. One called us "foreigners" and not just "from away." The room was smoke-filled and noisy, but we walked away from our first auction entertained and determined to save our money for the next one, if we could rustle up the courage to bid. We went back and bid. And bought. We got crazy items, including a garden decoration that depicted the back end of a lady bending over. That one was for a gift. We bought a worthless old oil-burning stove for $2, and a leather stitcher for $6. The auctioneer threw in a homemade deer spreader (de-ah spre-dah). For all we could tell, it was a stick. Having served time between a deer's hind legs, though, it was auction worthy. We had caught auction fever.

We searched the Maine roads not only for raven food but also for unique human food. In much of New England, but especially in Maine, community suppers are common. The public supper is a 200-year-old tradition and often a fundraiser. Commonly they are held at churches or granges, and the fare is baked beans, steamed brown bread, various casseroles, and more desserts, especially pies, than you can count. Henry and Lee had suggested we join them for a baked bean supper at their church. These "suppahs" usually attracted locals, and for us it was an opportunity to meet them as well as an excuse to eat out cheaply. One man in particular became a good friend. Roger Lane looked like a fishing boat captain, and he was more than happy to share stories over multiple cups of coffee through many church suppers. He always called John the "mountain man."

Roger introduced us to Maine Maple Sunday, a long-standing tradition that fell every year on the fourth Sunday in March. By late March the sap would be running: nights below freezing followed by sunny days with temperatures in the forties cause the sap to flow. Most maple farms are well-established enterprises because it takes forty years to grow a sugar maple large enough to tap. On Maple Sunday sugarhouses throughout the state opened their doors to celebrate this very busy time for those whose livelihood depends on maples. We joined in the festivities and learned how the sap is collected and then boiled down into syrup. A special treat was the free samples of maple syrup on ice cream shaved ice, or, when available, on snow.

30 July 1989; John's Field Notes: "A coyote's howl welcomes another warm day to the hut. I enjoy the trickster whenever he speaks."

Some days in the hut were anything but routine. One steamy July day the ravens were hunting insects in the thickening grass, ferns, and shrubs of the aviary when suddenly they flushed up in alarm. All but one. It ran crazily around the aviary, darting in and out of our view. I feared it had somehow been injured, but when it clucked I knew I had been tricked. Bernd had slipped a live chicken into the aviary just before heading back to Vermont. He must have had easier things to eat during his visit or else that bird would surely have been dinner. I am sure he was laughing all the way home, imagining the strange notes I'd be gathering to document his fowl play. It took me several hours to catch the chicken with a long-handled fishing net, but it gave me a good laugh and helped break up the summer doldrums.

With Bernd, you never knew what would show up at the cabin or aviary. Or who. A few weeks before the mysterious chicken episode, just after 6:00 a.m. I was shocked to see a large, bearded man in shorts amble around the aviary. I opened the hut hatch and squeezed in Professor Ebo Gwinner from the Max Planck Institute in Germany. Ebo pioneered captive raven behavioral research, following closely the lead set by his graduate mentor and Nobel laureate Konrad Lorenz. I knew and deeply respected his work, but I had no idea he was coming for a visit. The hours flew as we talked ravens, comparing the behavior of European and North American birds. Ebo, who died in 2004, was eulogized as an eminent naturalist and experimentalist, as well "as a modest man . . . who communicated with ravens." Colleen and I were fortunate to spend a few days in the hut and field with him surrounded by the animals that intrigued, fascinated, and perplexed us all.[8]

On warm summer days our stints in the hut were usually short, one or two hours. But during the deep of the winter, we typically spent six to eleven hours, often sunup to sundown, in the hut, while Topper and Sitka were imprisoned in their kennel or at the other cabin on their cable tie outs. We enjoyed the silence of the hut and the concentration it afforded, but for active people and dogs these long days were mostly torture. We craved fresh air and unconfined space. So in addition to aviary work, our first year we spent considerable effort chasing free ravens through the forested mountains. Hauling meat, climbing promontory trees, and fighting the cold in outdoor observation blinds provided the release we craved. A mixture of aviary and field research was not only a satisfying blend of physical and mental exercise but also essential if we were to fully understand why ravens slept together each evening. Wild ravens lured us away from the aviary even while we were busily finishing the giant cage. They continue to do so to this day. But now we take a step back to September 1988, our first autumn, as we follow these mysterious birds beyond the aviary to glimpse their nighttime secrets and better acquaint ourselves with western Maine.

four

Raven Nights

28 September 1988; Colleen's Journal: "We went to New Vineyard to check out the raven roost there. A beautiful view back to Bernd's cabin. No ravens, but met all the people who watched ravens."

We walked into the sun-starved, conifer forest where ravens roosted. There was little shrub growth ("puckerbrush") under the thick canopy so the walking was easy. There was also little whitewash to suggest recent roosting. It was late September 1988, barely two weeks after Colleen and I had arrived in Maine. We had come to this pine grove just below the crest of Taylor Hill near the town of New Vineyard on the advice of Larry Wattles, who had shown Bernd a nearby roost the previous winter and now pointed us up Taylor Hill. York Hill and Taylor Hill were only twenty-five kilometers apart, as a raven flies. There were only a couple of farms along the gravel road that bisected the hill, and their tenants, Anne Moody, a careful and longtime observer of nature, and Buster Nutting, a local trapper, confirmed that this location was a historic raven roost but agreed that the winter roosting season was not yet upon us.

Our exploration of Taylor Hill and its raven roost was one of many activities that autumn. We were also building the aviary, catching birds, and watching them under controlled situations. To provide a realistic context for our investigation of the mechanics and functions of food sharing in the aviary we needed to observe these behaviors in the wild. In addition to baiting traps and feeding our captive flock, we spread animal carcasses and offal liberally from York to Taylor Hill to see how ravens discovered and exploited valuable foods. Our observations at carcasses were somewhat redundant with Bernd's early, formative work, but our simultaneous observations at food bonanzas and roosts were unique.

15 November 1988; Colleen's Journal: "Today we watched the ravens come in to a roost. Mostly they came in singly or in pairs."

We returned to the roost on Taylor Hill on the afternoon of November 15 for another look. John climbed a tall spruce that overlooked the area where ravens were known to sleep. I stayed on the ground to write and time his observations, and periodically noted how rapidly the temperature was falling. It was getting dark, and ravens were flying toward the patch of white pine a hundred meters to the west. They came in small ragged groups, as pairs, and as singletons. I recorded what John yelled down to me:

1 from the west at 3:50,
2 from the northwest at 3:55,
17 from the northwest at 4:30.

The ravens settled but not for long. Uneasily, they flew, settled on branches, only to jump up and fly wildly. Some left while others returned. It was confusing to tally the total, but slowly the numbers in the pines grew. Soon thirty-nine of the rocketing, ebony birds had blended into the thick conifers. The noise was Amazonian. Growls, hoots, rattles, long quorks, gurgles, bells, and metallic qwaanks came from the forest. If someone had told me there was a restless group of monkeys in the woods, I would have believed them. These ravens were discussing, fussing, and fighting for space. As it darkened more, the noises faded. Stars brightened. I reported that it was 10°F. John's hands already knew that. As we thawed out in the truck before driving home we talked excitedly about returning in the morning to watch the birds leave the roost.

Much to the dogs' disgust, we rolled out of a warm bed well before sunrise and arrived back on Taylor Hill in the darkness. Climbing the spruce tree warmed me up. It was decidedly calm as light crept from the eastern horizon. Where were the ravens? Would we be able to observe them leave the roost? Were we too late? I heard a slight honking. Geese? No, ravens. The roost was stirring. Growls, trills, and knocking sounds came out of the distance. More honking and swooshing wings. A few rapid-fire knocks and kaws as they flew over us. Black shadows against a gunpowder sky. Counting was an estimate. But the departure was in direct contrast to the previous evening's arrival.

13 to the south and 14 to the west at 6:25,
2 more to the west at 6:26.

That was it. A quick, unceremonious, nearly unanimous departure. Despite having arrived from all directions the previous night, the birds were unified in heading south and west toward York Hill this morning. Was this typical?

Another twenty-eight nights and mornings convinced us that scattered arrivals and unified departures were the rule at this roost. Atop the spruce the work was exciting, ever changing. Repeating observations can be tedious, but it is a key part of science. Replication allows us to explore the variation in nature, variation that left alone confounds our insights into the motivations and meanings of an animal's behavior.

The pattern of coming and going from roosts—arriving from random directions over a period of an hour in the evening, but leaving in synchrony each morning—was completely consistent with a controversial theory that some animal gatherings functioned as "information centers." This novel idea suggested that animals who routinely returned to consistent locations—nesting colonies, day or night roosts, for example—might pay attention to their neighbors and use them to track unpredictable and distant resources. Honeybee hives are a classic example. Bees that find food return loaded with nectar, pollen, *and information* to the hive. They offload their tangible goods to nourish the queen and larvae, and they dance to transfer information to other foragers about the distance and direction to the flower patch. Less intricate means of communication might also be equally effective in transferring knowledge from successful to needy foragers. Naïve individuals could wait at the nest or roost for knowledgeable ones to return and then simply follow them back to food. And, as a result, an observer might expect departures to be more clumped in time than arrivals.[1]

Researchers were beginning to watch the traffic in and out of animal aggregations to test the information center hypothesis. The results were mixed and confusing. Arrivals and departures were highly synchronized in some heron colonies, whereas only departures were synchronized in others. Skeptics argued that synchronized heron departures—seaward from bulky nests—might simply be due to the birds' tendencies to arrive together or time their exit with the prevailing wind, not each other. This behavior seemed less likely in Osprey, the cosmopolitan fishing hawk that often nests in loose coastal aggregations. Ospreys really seem to be using information at the colony. They are picky about whom they follow, winging after others who have returned with a fish and especially those who hold fish known to live in schools. Following fishers of schooling species pays off because naïve birds can accurately track locally abundant but mobile foods, such as alewife, pollock, or smelt.[2]

Evidence was also accumulating that roosts were assembly points where knowledgeable and unknowing animals gathered to share information about the location of ephemeral and widely scattered, but rich, foods. But roosts had many functions, such as protection from the cold; massing to confront, confuse, or avoid predators; finding mates; or reducing commuting costs to feeding locations. Proving the importance of roosts as information centers was also difficult because all the individuals within a roost need not be together for the same reason. Maybe some roosting individuals were there to share and receive information and maybe or maybe not gain the more traditional benefits of communal roosting. It would take multiple sources of information, from the aviary and the field, to understand the relative use of information by roosting ravens. But we were encouraged to try. Breaking research suggested that naïve Black Vultures and Hooded Crows, two species that forage on dead animals just as do ravens, selectively followed knowledgeable roost mates.[3]

The problem that made information sharing controversial, and difficult to prove, was that it seemed at face value to be costly for knowledgeable animals. Could the other benefits of roosting or nesting colonially really outweigh the costs of having to give up information that might be critical to keeping you or your offspring alive the next day? Bees within a hive are extremely close relatives, almost clones because of their unique breeding system, so it made sense for them to share precise information. But sharing among unrelated individuals flew in the face of Darwin's theory—until you consider vampire bats.

Vampire bats roost during the day. Nursing females roost together in clumps of relatives and unrelated bats. At night they leave their roosts—cavities in dead trees—and fly to find cows, tapirs, or other large mammals and secure from them a meal of blood. Engorged bats return to the roost to digest, nurse, and, as it turns out, share. Bats who have not found a suitable mammal to suck are fed by others in the roost who found blood. Sharing blood meals occurs between related and unrelated bats. And here is the key: sharing is reciprocated. It pays to share today because tomorrow you may need to receive. *Hoy por tí, mañana por mí*—the golden rule of reciprocity—I'll do it for you today; you'll do it for me tomorrow. Vampire bat roosts were pretty small, eight to twelve adults and their offspring, so reciprocity was feasible. If reciprocity worked in larger roosts of birds, then information sharing could evolve and roosts could function as information centers. Roosting ravens could be sharing and reciprocating good deeds. We could not study this long-distance sharing in the aviary, but we might just be able to in nature.[4]

For ravens, long-distance sharing meant that vagrant, nonbreeding individuals would search widely in many directions for food each day and assemble at a roost to compare notes each night. This habit might explain why each evening birds came from many directions and in parties of various sizes. Larger parties included lucky, successful hunters returning from bonanzas. Small groups and singletons either had been unsuccessful at finding food or had perhaps discovered new foods where defensive adults prevented them from eating. Then, either through mutual understanding of shared knowledge, or perhaps simply by naïve birds following knowledgeable ones, all roost mates would leave together for known feeding locations each morning. It was clear that roosting ravens shared information on the whereabouts of food. But how did they do this? And why?

18 November 1988; Colleen's Journal: "We got up the next morning to watch the birds leave. The fog was as thick as pea soup so we couldn't see much. We figured they left to the east where we couldn't see them. This morning John went to watch again and they disappeared again. He went to see Larry Wattles, and he told John how to get to the New Vineyard dump. Sure enough, there were maybe 100 ravens there! How frustrating, the ravens prefer garbage over a nice black-and-white cow!"

Maybe it was the morning honking of the birds that cued those seeking knowledge. Honking might coordinate departure, as do the cries of gulls leaving their rocky abodes, but we would never be able to see who honked, if honkers led, or if other signals in the roost might explain how ravens shared their local knowledge. On November 21, that did not seem to matter. It was a bright afternoon, and the roost sparkled with light snow. As the ravens gathered they shared a deep secret. At 4:22, 103 ravens gathered on the wing above the roost. They rode the wind as a large, swirling, soaring flock. This kettle of birds drifted and flew a wide circuit around the roost. Others joined the group. Then at 4:27 they vanished. As a group they flew southwest. What information had caused this sudden shift? We never learned where these ravens went, but numbers at the roost were low for the next several days. Less than a week later, hunters told us they had heard lots of ravens up the Avon Valley Road, which was generally southwest of the roost. Maybe the New Vineyard birds were enjoying some early season deer.[5]

The next weeks were confusing. The soaring display seemed an obvious signal, but we could not link it to the discovery of new food and sharing among roost mates. The number of ravens roosting varied from day to day. Some evenings the group split into several satellite roosts. On others they would quickly and quietly enter the traditional pine grove. Soaring always preceded large roost departures, but where were these soaring ravens going? Those we could follow fed at the nearby dump or on deer frozen into Taylor Pond. An obvious, long-distance signal like soaring wasn't needed to cue ravens to these nearby or reliable foods.

We were getting hooked watching the ravens come and go from roosts, but we would need marked birds to test the information center hypothesis. With marked birds we could prove who shared information with whom and who benefited from the apparent reciprocity. We had not yet captured birds for the aviary, so as we watched the roost and finished the aviary, we also visited rich, but less aesthetic settings in the hope of catching or at least observing ravens. With Larry Wattles's help, we had followed ravens from Taylor Hill to the small New Vineyard landfill, and we also checked on landfills outside Wilton and Weld. The pile of rubbish outside Weld often held ravens and bears. Black clouds of crows and ravens, salted with white gulls, covered the larger dump maintained by the town of Wilton. Surely with so many ravens predictably visiting these rich sources of food we could catch our quota.

We directed our energies to the New Vineyard dump. It was an ideal field site. After parking behind a drooping chain that set the entrance road off from the main highway, we could sneak in to the dump through the forest or along the rocky, cratered approach road. The landfill itself was a steep-sided, ten- to twenty-foot-deep pit filled with rotting garbage and other discarded items.

Perched atop the level ground surrounding the pit was a four-by-four-by-six-foot shack, the weekend dumpmaster's refuge from the weather. The shack was a tribute to the riches of the dump. It was made of wood, windows, and doors scavenged from the pit. When we were inside, old magazines insulated us from the cold, and a small wood stove rescued from the detritus provided excessive heat and smoke. To fuel the stove, we used wood that had served many purposes—a chair leg, false wall, or picture frame. I spent hundreds of hours in that shack and watched up to seventy-five ravens recycle the pieces of Maine that others left.

Each day at the dump was an adventure. Early morning concerts were common. Coyotes and ravens—brothers of the dump—were the musicians. After watching ravens we'd see what the Mainers had left. Dump-diving was a window into Maine's past. Newspapers and magazines from decades earlier were common. A neat, bent wood "lobstah" trap fished from the sea of garbage took only a little refurbishing to become a proud end table. It still sits beside our front door.

Trapping ravens at the dump called on our construction skills. We were low tech. At the time, we had no experience or access to safe leg-hold traps (like those used to catch all manner of fur-bearing animal but with weaker springs and padded jaws), cannon nets, or net guns (ballistic-powered nets one can remotely shoot over feeding birds). These mechanical devices are effective, but they were far from our thoughts and beyond our budget. We had seen a design for a "Swedish crow trap" that seemed promising. Ed Hathaway was back from Boston, looking for a break from the city. He and I quickly built a Swedish crow trap at the far end of the dump. Everything we needed was on site: wood for the frame, wire mesh, and an old ladder. The trap was simple. It consisted of a rectangular three-by-eight-by-three-foot main compartment made from old lumber and poultry wire. There was a small trap door on one end so we could climb in and grab the ravens that entered the cage. The top of the cage was the sneaky part. Instead of constructing a lid that could be closed on birds in the cage, some Swede figured out that a ladder crossing the central section of the cage roof would act like a one-way valve—ravens would drop into the cage between the rungs, but when they tried to fly up out of the cage their open wings would not allow them to pass through the ladder's rungs. All we needed to do was to get ravens moving into the trap, and it would fill up. Even if we set it in the evening, it would trap during the morning without our active participation. We could sip coffee and come in mid-morning to load up the trapped birds. In theory.[6]

We baited the trap on November 24. A nice calf would surely be irresistible to these ravens who strained through plastic for a bit of chicken or bread. We started with the calf outside the cage. The calf was untouched for nearly a week. Calves were not common at the New Vineyard dump, and ours must have aroused too much suspicion by the garbage-tuned ravens. Ed was unable to be as patient as the ravens and returned to his job in Boston. I was also growing impatient, so turned to local fare, "matching the hatch" with meat scraps and trash. When the ravens started flocking to the hunks of chicken and pork outside the cage, I moved the meat into the cage. The entire top was open—no ladder to impede the movement of ravens or trap them until they were comfortable with the cage. They perched on the cage and went in and out with comfort, eating my offerings. Before dawn on December 7, I put the ladder in place, setting the trap, and put meat on the ladder and in the cage. Coyote music seemed to lighten the sky. Ravens started to appear. As I eagerly watched from the shack, the trap started to fill. It was working. There were at least ten birds in the cage, so I decided to dash the fifty yards from shack to trap and collect my bounty. My heart pounded then sank as each of the birds deftly flew straight out of the cage, between the rungs of the ladder. These were not Swedish crows. Or maybe I didn't have a Swedish ladder.

On December 13, our luck began to change. Twenty-eight ravens, most from the west and east roosted on Taylor Hill. In the 20°F morning of December 14, nearly every bird headed far to the southwest, the direction of Bernd's cabin and our trap on York Hill. I drove anxiously along the winding back roads to meet Colleen and see if the birds I saw leave the roost were now visiting our trap. At 8:20 I heard ravens as I walked up York Hill to the cabin. They were all over the meat scraps we had been scattering about since mid-October. Colleen and the dogs had stayed overnight at Bernd's cabin and had been serenaded by the ravens' raucous calls starting shortly after daybreak, at 6:30. Surely some of these ravens enjoying the meat had come from Taylor Hill this morning. If so, we expected they would soar and advertise their new find tonight.

Most of the fresh snow had melted by the time we arrived at Taylor Hill on the afternoon of December 14. Our hopes were dashed—only thirteen ravens roosted. They had come from the direction of York Hill, but there was no soaring. Ravens continued to eat our offerings on York Hill, and as the westerly wind blew on December 15, they gathered on Taylor Hill. Lots of them. Seventy-seven that we could count. At 4:12 the soaring began. Fifty birds, buoyed by the wind, circled the roost and left to the west. Then more. We guessed that those leading the soaring group knew about our bonanza and were leading others to roost closer to York Hill so that they could feed early the next morning after a shorter commute. But information centers were supposed to be reliable, stable locations. If we were right, then a raven that missed the soaring display would also miss the information. No ravens missed the soaring that night. The roost was empty when I climbed down to the cold truck. Colleen and I buzzed about the soaring ravens all the way home. It would be hard to sleep tonight.

I met the Maine morning before 5:00 a.m. to confirm that no ravens had returned to Taylor Hill after dark. In the meantime, Colleen and the dogs were at Bernd's cabin, keeping vigil at the food bonanza. It was clear, windy, and −3°F as I climbed the spruce to glimpse the roost. The roost was indeed empty. The same could not be said for York Hill. Colleen was in a sea of ravens by sunrise. Sitka and Topper stared out the windows, looking at the early morning raven extravaganza as if there was an invasion in progress. We could not be sure these were the same ravens we watched soaring the night before some twelve miles away, but we were betting this was the case.

We were pumped with excitement and eager to share our roost stories with our Maine family. Luckily, Lee was having family Christmas, just like Thanksgiving, on December 18. Butch and Nancy hosted us first for homemade eggnog and a gift exchange. We made plates of cookies and introduced our eastern friends to a southwestern treat, a spicy stew of chicken, pork, and hominy called "posole." Lee gave all the ladies a machine-quilted pillow. Henry gave the men each an "old-fashion match lighter" (a rock, so labeled). Butch and Nancy made birdhouses for all. But Billy stole the show. He made every person a custom pair of slippers—thirty-two in all! Each was a different style, color, and type of leather. As the pattern maker for the shoe shop, he had lots of scraps and was able to order exotic leathers to test. We had cow slippers, moose slippers, elk slippers, pig slippers, and ostrich slippers. He had worked overtime to make these gifts from the company's supplies and on their clock. He was, of course, paid for this dedication each week and even got a bonus raise of 25 cents an hour in recognition of his hard work.

After eggnog, we strolled next door to Lee and Henry's for a feast as enormous as Thanksgiving. A Yuletide dessert, suet pudding, was added to the usual fare. This rich delicacy was made with smooth leaf lard from Castonguay's. After-dinner charades carried us late into the evening. We left feeling festive, warm, and grateful to all. Thanks to Billy, our feet would stay warm indoors all winter.

Lee's early start to Christmas allowed each family to have its own celebration as well as the communal one. It also extended the festivities. Butch, Nancy, and their girls Monica and Lindsey joined Billy, Lili, and Aaron for a trek up York Hill with us to cut Christmas trees on Bernd's property. On Christmas Eve we drove over icy roads to North Jay for church services. It was a simple gathering, and when it was over we let the dogs out of the car for a quick bathroom break. Bolting from the car, Sitka ran into the church and up to the altar. We extracted her with little commotion, but our "religious dog" got everyone smiling. We spent Christmas day with the Wojcik clan, celebrating, feasting, and playing with their new Siberian pup, Sky. Our real family remained convinced that we were freezing up in the far north: we received long underwear and flannel pajamas—and an answering machine so that we would no longer miss carcass calls.

The ravens feasting outside Bernd's cabin on December 16 included some of the twenty-four we would later catch December 29. Once in the aviary, they commanded much of our time, keeping us in the observation hut. But even as we began to focus more on aviary experiments we continued to trap, mark, and observe ravens in the wild, to validate what we saw in the aviary. Because we wanted to make sure that the behavior of our captive birds reflected what free birds did in the wild, we needed more marked birds. We trapped birds five more times during that first winter, catching an additional twenty-nine juveniles, five yearlings, and sixteen adults. Initially we trapped atop York Hill, but hauling meat for the trap and the aviary took too much time. And we worried that the nearby wild birds might influence our aviary observations. We established a new trap on the flat between York Hill and Hills Pond, just south of Route 156. This trap was easier to bait and watch, and we could band birds at our one-room cabin in relative comfort. We dubbed the new trap area "Donkey Landing," as our first offering there was a recently acquired dead donkey. Although not as heavy as a cow, it was more pungent. It fit nicely by our new trap and was soon discovered by resident ravens. We christened Donkey Trap on April Fool's Day 1989. As a Barred Owl hooted on a dark, sleety morning, the ravens rushed in to devour the rich, exotic donkey meat. We caught seventeen, including three previously banded juveniles.

The days of driving to roosts before dawn and again at dusk sandwiched around a full day of aviary work would wear on our relationship. We had only one vehicle, and we were always trying to consolidate errands to save time and miles. One day John was distracted as he prepared the trailer for a lung run to Castonguay's. He forgot to snap the hitch on to the

The Donkey Landing trap set for acclimation. Frozen hunks of meat are inside and outside the trap; the door is wide open and fastened to the small tree propping it; and the clothesline is taut from the prop to the blind (just out of view in foreground). As the ravens become comfortable with entering the trap all the meat is moved inside, and the hair-triggered prop is set to be easily dislodged by a swift yank of the line from the blind.

ball and lock it. Fortunately, he had attached the safety chains because when we hit a bump near Wilton, the trailer took off from the hitch. The trailer's tongue slammed into the car and put a nice dent in the middle of the tailgate. I was furious, and I was tired of our crazy schedule. As John reattached the trailer, I told him I wasn't going any farther because it was too dangerous. I started walking the seven or so miles home. John went on to the butcher and then tried to pick me up on the way home. I refused. It was Zetta who came and picked me up, let me vent, and let me sit at her house with a cup of tea to let go of my aggravation. It wasn't the trailer really. It was just the furious schedule of field and aviary research. Sometimes we needed outside help to cover everything that needed doing.

While friends and family helped resolve personal dilemmas, volunteers helped lighten the field burden. In the winter of 1989, we had an outstanding and helpful crew. Its heart was volunteer David Lidstone. Dave, a skilled wildlife photographer on sabbatical from lumberjacking, lived about four miles down Route 156. Quiet, balding, and graying, fifty-something years old, Dave knew the local woods. Although he was planning a summer pilgrimage to Israel with his wife and five kids, he was ready to work ravens for the winter. And he owned a "skiddah." A skidder is an articulated, four-wheel, massive beast of a tractor that woodsmen use to drag felled trees from the forest. Whole. Dave parked his in front of the live bait store on Route 156. We dreamed of using it to skid dead moose and cows through the woods. Dave thought that sounded great. The skidder was first called into action in early April. A farmer called saying he had a freshly dead dairy cow. Colleen and Dave hitched the carcass hauler to the truck and drove to the farm. The cow was indeed dead but not fresh. Its hair oozed off a green, bloated hide. After waiting half an hour for the concerned farmer to move his live cows out of sight of the gruesome scene, into the trailer it went, aided by the farmer's front-end loader. Back near York Hill, Dave's skidder roared to life. Within a few minutes a whole, tenderized cow lay ready for ravens well off the traveled road where we could watch it in peace. With a blind of fragrant spruce and fir, we could even breathe. The ravens, we hoped, wouldn't mind a hairless bovine— or the hairy skid trail that led from the highway to its final resting place.

As we trapped, marked, and released ravens we watched and learned. With Dave's help we kept a series of carcasses under constant surveillance: a moose skidded up York Hill, the cow near Route 156, the donkey, a huge buck deer up Alder Brook Road. Ravens ate them all. Because we had now marked many birds who fed on these carcasses, we were able to prove that a group of foraging ravens was in constant turmoil. Although juveniles predictably outnumbered older birds two to one, this was no stable group of close kin.

Dave Lidstone tows a female moose with his logging skidder in a York Hill snowstorm.

Instead, the fifty-odd birds we typically watched eat their way through a carcass were only a small snapshot of a larger group connected by a communal roost to many feeding locations. When we extrapolated from our observations of marked birds feeding on a carcass on any given day, we discovered that for every one we saw, another three knew the whereabouts of the food. When we didn't see them, they were either waiting their turn nearby or gone for a day or two exploring.

We came to know the individuality of each marked bird. Some specialized on the foods we watched. Seven of the 63 birds we marked were recaptured throughout the winter. Some days most of the birds we watched from our spruce blinds were tagged. On April 10, for instance, we identified eighteen marked birds and guessed that there were about forty to fifty *in toto* feeding on the cow, in addition to some Bernd had marked in previous years and young from local nests that were resighted or recaught. But most birds roamed widely, rarely revisiting a local area within or between winters. These young ravens were true nomads. Sedentary Mainers routinely reported seeing our tagged birds around Ashland, Greenville, Bucksport, Belgrade, and beyond.

The behavior of an individual raven changed dramatically during its tenure at a carcass, just as it did in the aviary. On finding a new carcass, a young bird or even a small group could rarely feed. Typically the territorial pairs, who in our area now wore bold white, numbered tags, chased, pounded, and harassed the young discoverers. These young subordinates begged or yelled vocally, but they rarely ventured within reach of the defended food. The sequence of events at each carcass was similar. As I sat in my airy blind of balsam fir branches in late February, the big deer was disappearing into the thickening snow. I heard two yells to the north, followed by hooting as the yeller moved toward the deer. Twenty-one minutes later a fuzzy-headed raven dropped from the firs to the snow. Begging, it cowered close to the carcass. A Black-capped Chickadee and a Blue Jay ate during the next hour, but no raven did. Instead, I heard soft begging in response to loud gong calls given by a pair of territorial adults. At 7:20 a single, silent crow munched briefly. The ravens gonged and begged but did not eat. A gunshot in the distance at 8:28 spooked the birds, and I snuck out of the blind.

The next day went much the same. I watched from 6:00 to 8:00 a.m. and heard only territorial ravens. A roost awakened in the distance, and I heard a few birds honk and head to the northeast. Perhaps they found another food? I saw Red-breasted Nuthatches, Black-capped Chickadees, Blue Jays, and crows feed, but nearby ravens only growled and begged. It seemed that the resident adults were keeping a few vagrant, younger, subordinate birds from my deer.

The first of March dawned differently. The deer had been ravaged since I had left it the day before. Tracks were everywhere, and the snow was packed tight around the rapidly shrinking carcass. At 6:05 a.m., fifteen ravens were on the snow walking toward the deer—three tagged birds among them. W4 and her mate, the territorial adults, strode in, quorking, and the rush of vagrant

View from a blind. A few meters in front of the blind, glimpsed here through the gaps between spruce and fir boughs, feasts a flock of ravens. The territorial Hills Pond male (wing tagged) commands the prime feeding location atop the rib cage of a cow.

subordinates parted. The quorking king and queen had priority. They called softly to one another, allopreened, and billed but did not chase the vagrants. They displayed to each other and escorted a second pair away from the carcass while strutting in macho regalia. The vagrants fed and the adults fed when they wanted, taking the top spot on the carcass. I estimated thirty birds had fed today by the time I left at 8:30. The crow from the past days fed only when the ravens flushed from the ground.

Mesmerized by the activities and vocalizations of ravens at the deer, we checked in daily, watching closely from our blind for twenty more hours until only a few birds remained on March 11. We were able to track the tagged birds between their nearby roosts and the successive feasts. The same sequence was evident each time, and it was a vocal story. The first few ravens yelled and begged near a carcass but only rarely ate, because the territorial pair gonged and quorked and occasionally physically punished any of the beggars who ventured too near the food. As other pairs arrived, hollow log calls were given by the residents. Trill wars erupted from strutting pairs signaling high aggression and a readiness to fight. I can easily hear them to this day—a vocal sequence etched deeply into my left brain. It was precisely as we saw in the aviary.

We determined that feeding rates climbed steadily in the wild as more and more juveniles gathered. A young nomad fed for less than a minute of every five when fewer than ten birds surrounded a carcass. But nomads fed for four of every five minutes when a larger group formed and adult defense was disarmed. Yelling and begging also plummeted as feeding increased. Sharp yacks and long trills now mixed with the gongs, bells, drips, and woo-wooing of adults. This was the music of a feast. Yells and begs were the music of desperate famine. Subtle gestures were also evident. Mysterious "air calling," which was done with a choking gesture accentuated with spreading wings and tail, was given ceremoniously between strutting adult pairs. We were seeing much more than simple gluttony around a carcass. We were witness to an ever-changing, traveling musical variety show.

Sometimes we would glimpse a tagged bird alone at a carcass. On April 12, a juvenile born just below York Hill the previous summer and tagged in the nest by Bernd was suddenly alone among scattered deer parts and offal. Yellow 14 (Y14) did not yell. He kawed hoarsely, trilled, and chattered, *sotto voce*, like an opera singer warming up. We knew this act and labeled it "talking to oneself." Without the pressure of adults or superior peers, young birds poured forth. We assumed they were just practicing. But suddenly Y14 transformed into an adult pose. Bowing deeply, he gave throaty, territorial kaws, and then he choked the air call display we had previously seen performed only by strutting adults. Another tagged juvenile bird, C2—sporting a faded tag with a black "2"—joined him. She bowed and knocked in response to his air calling. Surely this was a budding pair. Without tags, we would have assumed these were adults. Now we knew that even young ravens were capable of behaving like adults. Social setting, apparently, was a strong modifier that filtered the possible into the acceptable. Juveniles in a crowd would never bow and court with dominant adults strutting nearby, but when alone they could and did. Young ravens dining in a group had to mind their manners.

As we watched ravens ply the snowy mountains and lakes in search of food, we also learned that many succumb to the rigors of their wild life. One juvenile died in a coyote trap in its second year of life. Another was shot seven years later. As our tagged birds roamed across New England and southeastern Canada, they met the destructive hand of humanity. Our own species' curiosity, armed with guns, traps, and automobiles, we would learn, was a major source of raven mortality here and throughout the world.

five

Torment on the Trail

15 October 1988; Colleen's Journal: "We took Brodie, Topper, and Sitka for a six-mile run on the road to Mt. Tumbledown. We had a great run, but Brodie doesn't like to run downhill. Later in the day, Topper managed to tear one of his toenails off as he jumped from the truck."

The many research activities at and beyond the aviary satisfied our biologists' curiosity, but it wasn't enough for Topper and Sitka. Hauling meat to the aviary and logs to the wood pile were surely strengthening them. They enjoyed brief bursts of speed as well. Blistering runs down York Hill and cruising up and down the many dirt and gravel roads that snaked through the woods briefly energized our canine athletes. Long days confined in a kennel or bound to a cable surely bored them. To clear our minds and their kennel fever, we began taking longer fun runs. We hitched our duo behind a three-wheeled cart made from scavenged plumbing pipe, plywood, and wheelbarrow tires that we had crafted in Arizona and hauled across the country. This heavy gig was stable but only crudely steered by maneuvering a side lever forward to negotiate left or "haw" turns and backward for right or "gee" turns. Yelling "WHOA!" would usually stop the dogs, and we would apply pressure to a foot pedal that in turn pressed a plate down on one of the back tires to slow or stop the gig. Craving power and speed for extended forays, we looked to expand our team. We thought about Henry and Lee's

John with the three-wheeled cart we built in Arizona and moved to Maine to train our first dog teams. Topper and Sitka are linked to the cart with the original gang-line designed for a two-dog team. The warm Arizona day when this photo was taken has sapped most of the dogs' motivation.

sleek, black dog, Boo, but traveling to Jay routinely was not possible. The Wojciks' black-and-white Border Collie mix, Brodie, though soft with porch life, had the makings of a sled dog. She got along with Topper and Sitka, and what she lacked in skill, she made up for in enthusiasm. She also had Hilary and Josh as a cheering squad, coaxing her through her paces.

Our three-dog team got some early socialization at the annual Earmuff Parade in Farmington. Chester Greenwood, a resident of Farmington, invented the earmuff when he was fifteen. In 1977, the state of Maine declared December 21 to be Chester Greenwood Day. The city of Farmington celebrated with a fun and funky parade. In 1988, we were asked by the local animal shelter to help with their entry in the parade. Jenn and Hilary were already excited about the parade, but for a more political motivation. The Mt. Blue High School band, for which they were color guards, had been chosen as the best band in Maine. Usually this honor meant an invitation to the inauguration parade in Washington, D.C. But this year the president had ties to Maine, and the high school band from Kennebunk, Bush's summer hometown was invited instead. The Mt. Blue band was planning a protest at the Earmuff Parade in the hopes of attracting the attention of influential politicians. We started making red and green felt earmuffs for the dogs to wear and borrowed some earmuffs for ourselves. The dogs pulled a wagon full of adoptable puppies and generated their own share of attention. The ever-present media and senators and congressmen noted the protestors, and as a result the Mt. Blue band eventually was invited to Bush's inaugural party.

Our hodge-podge trio was working beautifully, but we yearned for more dog power. Answering an ad about a Siberian Husky puppy that we could add to our team led us to the Down East Sled Dog Club. It was not surprising that there was a club devoted to sled dogs in Maine. The International Federation of Sleddog Sports suggests that wherever snow is common, dogsledding likely exists. The mission of the Down East Sled Dog Club was to promote the relationship between dogs and humans: "promoting public interest and understanding of the sport of sled dog racing and promoting the humane and responsible breeding, care, training, and driving of sled dogs." This club sounded well suited to our needs and interests. We passed on the puppy but pursued the club.

Our first club meeting brought us in contact with other sled dog fanciers, none of whom owned fewer than ten dogs. We learned about at least five forthcoming sledding events. With new harnesses for Sitka and Topper, we anticipated many happy weekends of racing, exploring new parts of Maine, and taking a break from raven watching.

Before we raced our dogs, they were working partners in our lives. This sequence is typical of the sled dog–human connection. Native peoples in harsh climates used sled dogs in their everyday lives for survival. Sled dogs enabled exploration of two continents by Byrd, Peary, and Amundsen. Dog teams in Alaska and Canada delivered mail from the 1800s to the mid-1900s.

Endurance and speed were characteristics valued in all sled dogs, so it is not surprising that impromptu races between teams of dogs would happen regularly, a natural reflection of human competition. In 1908, with the running of the 408-mile-long All-Alaskan Sweepstakes, the "sport" of dog racing began. The racers used many northern breeds (defined as dogs having a two-layered, or double, coat of fur), including the Siberian Husky. As early as 1909, exhibition teams were racing in the northeastern United States. Today, teams of dogs that are mixes of northern breeds and hounds and other mixed breeds regularly win races. These mixes provide winning attributes: lungs and legs that provide endurance and speed and a double coat that gives protection against snow, wind, and cold.[1]

19 January 1989; Colleen's Journal: "We've been trying to work the dogs on fun runs instead of just hauling horse meat up the hill. We go to groomed snowmobile trails."

We did not set out to condition our dog team for racing that first autumn, but their strength and endurance seduced us, and much of what we did with the dogs on the gig applied to the sled as well. The difference between the two was that the sled was a lighter vehicle traveling with less friction. Stopping involved taking a foot off one runner and pressing down on a long piece of wood that ran in between the runners. This brake, hinged to the front of the sled, had a metal claw on the bottom that dug into the snow and ice. The whole apparatus was held up by springs attached to the sides of the handlebars. If we wanted to stay in one place, we would apply the equivalent of an emergency brake. The snow hook was attached to the gangline (the main line that the dogs are attached to) and functioned like an anchor on a boat. We would set the snow hook by pushing it into the snow so that as the dogs pulled the hooks dug deeper and more securely into the snow and the team could not pull away. We also carried a sled bag in case we had to carry an injured dog on the sled. Both the snow hook and sled bag were mandatory items for races.

Because the ganglines we had made in Arizona were for two dogs, we needed to make a new three- or four-dog line. There are three parts to a gangline. The first is the towline, which runs from the sled to the lead dogs, bisecting the pairs of dogs on the team. Pairs of two- to three-foot-long tuglines are attached at regular intervals to the towline, depending on the size of the team. The other ends of the tuglines are attached to the back of the dogs' harnesses. Pairs of shorter necklines attach to the dogs' collars and connect to the towline a dog's length in front of the tuglines. The whole system is made of polyethylene rope, the rope used by water skiers. Several hours of measuring, cutting, and braiding with our wire-weary fingers led to a new four-dog line ready for our first Maine race.

Our first race was in Lincoln, Maine. On January 27, we set off with our two dogs and Brodie in our Toyota 4Runner with sled on top. When we pulled into the parking lot that doubled as a staging area for the dog teams we found it full of dozens of trucks with camperlike boxes. Each of these boxes held multiple dogs, usually in individual compartments. The excitement of the dogs was evident in the howling and barking that could be heard for miles. Hay spilled out of the compartments where the dogs had been riding. The dogs, dancing and lunging, were chained on short leads to the chassis of the trucks as handlers doled out water, food, and sometimes a pat on the head. All I could say was, "Jessum Crow!" (a Maine saying that we had picked up). I turned around and looked at our three "sled dogs" that had been asleep but were now peering out the windows to check out the scene. I had never seen that kind of raw energy in our dogs. In our only race in Arizona, there had been maybe ten teams. Here I saw dozens parked in front of me. I was in for an interesting weekend.

The next morning we awoke to five inches of fresh snow. The trail was on a frozen lake. Lake trails are flat and boring. Just ask Sitka. More than four miles of flat landscape, with no change of scenery or "gees" or "haws," do little to motivate a curious dog. We were excited to be finally racing, however. So excited and focused, in fact, that we didn't clearly hear what the volunteers said at the starting line. At sled races, mushers who aren't currently running take turns helping hold other sleds in the starting shoot. Our holders apparently commented on our sled. John thought he heard them say, "I haven't seen an antique sled like that in ye-ahs." A team like ours also was unusual at club events. We were running only three dogs in the four-dog class. Two of our team members were not even sledding breeds. Sitka and Topper were the lead dogs, with Brodie pulling behind them in "wheel" position, or the position just in front of the sled.

Our time was around twenty-eight minutes the first day, and I was the musher. We ended in eighth place out of nine teams. Races are run in reverse order the second day, so big teams (up to twelve and sometimes sixteen dogs) went first, and then later the four-dog teams. Teams are sent out based on time from the first day, so we were the second-to-last team to leave the starting line. Needless to say, after the long weekend the trail was well churned up by all those dog feet and it was streaked brown with loads of dog crap. Good sled dogs don't even stop to poop, they just lift their tails and let it fly as they run full speed. Our dogs were not at this level of expertise. The first 200 yards out the second day of the race was hell. Sitka didn't like to step in poop, so she tried to run on the snow berms that defined the trail and at one point stopped and refused to run. Topper stopped, too. Lead dogs "steer" the team and regulate the speed. My lead dogs had no speed. Brodie kept going, and the gangline tangled. I ended up running in front of the dogs to get them moving. Sitka stopped to add to the poop trail. The whole team did a lot of sightseeing and zigzagging between snow berms while I urged them on with breathless, "Get the birds, get the kitties, get the squirrels!" Anything to get them excited to run. I sweated and pushed, and Brodie pulled the 4.4 flat miles. This was not the human-dog connection about which I had read! Sitka and Topper ambled. The last 100 yards they finally picked up the pace to a trot. Our time was thirty-eight painful minutes, and five of those were in the first 200 yards! The organizers were taking down the finish line when we crossed it. Everyone just wanted to go home. So did I. The best teams could clock times in the fourteen- to fifteen-minute range. We were way behind. I was exhausted from the race and from spending two full days standing around in the cold. We had offers for extra dogs for the next race and a replacement sled for our "antique" one. Oak is a heavy wood for a sled, and ours was made heavier and stiffer by many coats of varnish. Most racing sleds are made of lighter, stronger woods, such as ash, are lashed at the joints with thin nylon rope or rawhide (called "babiche"), and are not so heavily varnished. We were learning.

5 February 1989; Colleen's Journal: "We took the dogs for a long run down the Old Temple Road. We will run them one more time this week before the Bethel races this weekend."

Our second race, in Bethel, Maine, went better. Blind turns, birds, and squirrels on a beautiful, wooded trail kept Sitka interested at lead. I borrowed a strong Siberian Husky, Woody, for another wheel dog to make a full four-dog team. We placed eighth out of eleven teams even though Woody pooped his way around the trail both days.

A dogsled race is truly a partnership between musher and dog team. I often lightened the team's load by running between the sled runners, pushing the sled up hills, and kicking, like a cross-country skier, from one runner as we streaked along the race course. Most of the race we had other teams in sight, which motivated my dogs to chase but challenged us when we had to pass. Slowing the dogs from running up another team's tail or stopping to let faster teams go by was polite but frustrating. At the cry of "trail" from a musher behind me I'd pull over, set the snow hook, and rush to the lead dogs to keep them from tangling with the passing team. As the faster team zoomed by, I would carefully and quickly get back on the sled as Topper and Sitka strained to chase. Usually they would pull the snow hook loose before I was ready, and I would lunge to grab the handle of the speeding sled. I was flirting with

John riding the old oak sled across the finish line
of our second race in Maine. The bib must be
visible throughout the race. The pie plate staked
into the snow marks the trail. Brodie looks tired,
but the other three dogs have their tails up,
indicating alert excitement, not hard work. The
visible lead husky is Woody, one we borrowed
from Margaret Cook.

disaster on each pass, breaking the cardinal rule of dogsledding: never ever let go of the sled. I never lost the team, but it was a scary possibility.

Taking turns as musher, I ran the third race in Greenville, Maine, at the southern edge of Moosehead Lake. This race was billed as the Down East Sled Dog Club Championship. For us this meant nothing—just another race. For others, it was a big deal because of the purse for the winners. All season we ran in what was called the sportsman class. It would be laughable for us to be among the top three, in contention for a trophy, unless everyone forgot to show up (it did happen once). There was, however, another class called the professional class, which had predominately Alaskan husky teams. They seriously ran for money. Some teams came from as far away as Prince Edward Island in Canada. The hilly, forested, out-and-back trail was known to have moose on it, which are dangerous to dogs and mushers. Moose travel most easily on packed, groomed trails, and if chased by dogs, they instinctively turn and stand their ground as they would against wolves. They can stomp a dog team to death with sharp hooves and long powerful legs. Maybe the smell of moose was strong the first day of the races. The dogs seemed to enjoy the trail and did well. The second day the trail was mushy and punchy enough to pull my pac boots off my feet and made Topper grouchy. After several moose delays, race officials had decided to speed up the race by running the sportsman class at the same time as the professional class. The decision was made after the start of the professional class. Officials reminded us that trail etiquette meant incoming teams had the right of way in head-on passing. We were the third sportsman team out, and we encountered some very startled professionals on their way back knowing that every second was important to how they placed. Grouchy, growling Topper was not popular during the head-on passing. One of the mushers of a Professional team complained that we cost him time and therefore placement and therefore money. We got in trouble. Professionals were dominant over the subordinate sportsman class. We were still learning.[2]

A highlight of that weekend was picking out our new puppy. As we watched the four pups from the litter on which we had already put a deposit, we looked for the right shape. We watched them wrestle, waddle, and play in and out of their traveling wire pen. We sought advice from other mushers, who said each pup was sound. We had not read about temperament tests for puppies or what to look for in an eight-week-old sled dog. We just liked what we saw. The sire and dam had been at races, and we liked their working performance and their personalities. The dam also had come from conformation, or show, lines that seemed a good complement to the predominantly working and sledding lines of the sire. Subconsciously, we were using our training in animal behavior and genetics to guide our decision. We knew that build and personality were heritable, but random assortment of traits was also a reality of sexual reproduction. We hoped our pup's phenotype reflected the genotype of a healthy and strong sled dog. We picked the spunky, bi-eyed bitch. Her attitude would serve her well as a lead dog, we reasoned, but the eyes of two colors, one brown and one blue, simply fascinated us. The Wojcik kids were convinced they needed a better Brodie, so they also shopped for a Siberian Husky pup for Hilary's fifteenth birthday present and got one over the Christmas holidays. Any dog may do for sledding, but when there is a need for speed it is the build of a dog that matters most. We learned that a team only goes as fast as its slowest dog. Brodie was slow because her build limited her gait to a trot rather than a long, stretching sprint. We knew we needed more dog power, and we hoped these pups would supply just that.

The final race of the season for the dogs was in Rangeley, Maine. We decided to have Hilary run in the three-dog junior class with Brodie, Sitka, and Woody. Topper stayed behind so Hilary wouldn't have to deal with any growling. The first day Brodie wouldn't work for her, probably because she had eaten some of the carcass down the road from our cabin the day before and was too full to run. We feared for Brodie. Overfull dogs can die from a flipped stomach while running. One of our new mushing friends heard us talking about our dilemma. She asked if we knew about "matching a dog." We

Which one to choose? Kenai (right) and one of her littermates at eight weeks of age. We had to select among these adorable pups and two others based on their potential show and racing abilities.

did not. But shortly, and with some skepticism, we had inserted the sulfured end of a match into Brodie's anus. The temporary irritation was supposed to cause contraction of the muscles and stimulate a bowel movement. Three matches later, we were in business. Brodie was lighter on her feet and ran well the next day. We were all still learning!

Another lesson learned was that we needed a lighter, more flexible sled. Woody's owner offered her Moody sled for the summer so that we could copy it and build our own. We took pictures, made plans, and scavenged for air-dried ash. It took us most of the next winter and summer to cut the wood.

The Moody sled we borrowed as a template for new sleds we would construct.
Notice the sleek look relative to our old oak sled. This sprint sled is made of ash.
Our dog kennel is in the background.

Precision is important with mortise and tenon joints, so we took our time. We
even made the trek to Rochester, New Hampshire, in February 1991 to meet
Ed Moody, the sled's creator. Normally it took over two years to get a real
Moody sled because of the demand for them: Ed made the sled that won the
Iditarod (a 1,000-mile race across Alaska) in 1973. An eighty-year-old army
veteran who trained troops for winter battle during World War II and who at
the age of sixteen accompanied Admiral Byrd on his Antarctic expedition, Ed
was a legendary American craftsman. His simple workshop had steaming
forms to bend double curved handlebars, elegant runners, and U-shaped
brush bows. Ed's storytelling mesmerized us for hours. Our day with him flew
by, and we left by trading him raw air-dried ash for the bent sled parts we
needed but could not manufacture.[3]

In the meantime, we found a used MacDonald racing sled (named after its
maker) that we could buy if we would also buy the three-wheeled gig that came
with it. We agreed to buy both thinking that now we had enough equipment
for Josh and Hilary to work a small team as well. Josh nicknamed the new gig

"the Deathmobile." An apt moniker, it was flat black and fast. But the darn thing was too lightweight and scared the tar out of us especially going down hills. We tried not to run more than three dogs on it at a time.

After a winter of mistakes, mishaps, and misdirection, we thought we were well on our way to becoming true mushers. Two pups were waiting to be trained. We had new equipment and new knowledge to apply. Spring and summer were going to be busy.

six

Becoming Parents

As we lifted the dirty towels draped across each box, we wondered what we had gotten ourselves into. Ten big, gray-black heads rose simultaneously toward the light and gaped. Wide open, glistening red mouths begged hoarsely; the openings to their windpipes, or tracheas, situated just beyond the thick, fleshy base of their pink tongues, pulsed rhythmically open and closed as they gulped air. The beggars from Vermont had arrived.

Bernd was in a hurry that day, May 2 of our first spring in Maine. He had scooped up ten baby ravens from two Vermont nests a few hours earlier and now deposited them with us for safe parenting. We would raise them like our own for the next eight months to better understand how their voice, diet, and status developed. If they noticed or wondered why their parents were a lot bigger, whiter, featherless, and different sounding than they were, they did not let on. They ravenously gobbled everything we could put in their mouths that first week: one and a half opossums; a red squirrel; a gray squirrel; seven white perch; a robin; a pigeon; twenty earthworms; a pound each of pig liver, pig fat, and deer meat; five pie pans of pig lungs (about a half pound each); three pans of a gruel we custom mixed from raw eggs, soaked dog food, blood, and poultry feed; a pan of chicken starter formula; and a handful of beef heart.

Our first day as raven parents was anything but usual. The ice had just left Hills Pond and the loons were back, challenging all comers with ethereal yodels and cries. Maybe it was these sirens of the lake that lured Topper and

Sitka from their cable tie outs. Somehow they broke free, twisting and wiggling just the right amount to spring the snaps holding their collars to the earthbound cables. They were finding their inner wolves when they crossed paths with a local porcupine. Judging from the size of the quills in Topper's face, it was a big rodent and must have fared better than the canines. Quills spread beardlike from the dogs' faces.

After we fed the baby ravens, I headed to the vet, Dr. Robert Patterson, in Farmington. Because I had made an after-hours call, Dr. Patterson asked me to assist and insisted that now was the time for Topper to be neutered. I watched as he deftly handled the hot scalpel and in just a few minutes used a well-practiced hook shot to make Topper's testicles sail across the room into a metal bowl. A quick suturing and removal of quills left Topper with a face that looked "like raw hamburg." Sitka, having already been spayed, was spared further surgery.

Fortunately, the husky pups, our "Teeco's Bi-eyed Kenai" and the Wojciks' "Dancing Sky Wolf" (each of the kids contributed to the name), were not yet confident enough to join the older dogs on this adventure. Maybe they were intrigued with our attentiveness to the strange, young birds. Or perhaps Kenai knew obedience class was starting soon and wanted a head start. In any case, the porcupine experience made us realize that our growing dog pack needed an improved dog yard. We built a 900-square-foot kennel around two sides of a shed between the Wojciks' house and our cabin that provided a secure place to keep the dogs comfortable as we were increasingly preoccupied with baby ravens.

The huge quantity of food we collected, cut into small, bite-sized pieces, and fed to our ten babies was transformed into four basic products: bigger babies, heat, noise, and crap. Growing babies and their associated metabolic heat were the intended by-products of our efforts. Their increasingly loud calls were expected and interesting. But their crap, a slimy whitish-yellowish-green pungent brew of ammonia, rotten meat, and sweet fermentation that howitzered out of their makeshift nest boxes was messy. Its odor called to the dogs, who loved to roll in or, worse, eat it. We knew right away that these Vermonters needed their own guesthouse.

The old gentleman whose cabin we were occupying had also left Tom and Zetta a small, 1940s-era aluminum camping trailer. It was planted like an old sage, green and silver, in the Wojciks' backyard. We were sure it once had many great adventures exploring the wilds of Maine, but now it was no longer roadworthy. It would make the perfect raven nursery. With Tom's help we nudged it from its resting place just enough to easily access its door and cleared an area for a more permanent kennel for the dogs. We lined the aluminum hull and Formica counters of the trailer with blue plastic tarps and moved in two boxes of young ravens full of developing attitude. Cleaning was now an easy daily task that involved removing and hosing off the old tarps and replacing them with those cleaned the previous day.

Another relic invaded our garage. Temperatures regularly remained above freezing, which was comfortable for us but problematic for the mountains of meat needed to sustain growing ravens. A white upright freezer no longer able to serve people now slowly froze bloody bags of roadkill, slaughterhouse offal, and anything else we thought the ravens might eat.

Our two broods were of slightly different ages. Those from Huntington, Vermont, which we would eventually mark with yellow tags, were about one month old. Those from Adamant, Vermont, who would later wear red tags, were only two to three weeks old. The younger, Adamant birds begged from us fearlessly for food. They even begged from the curious dogs. The older, Huntington chicks took to us quickly as surrogate parents, but they never accepted the dogs. Their first reaction to Topper and Brodie was a hoarse scolding. The chicks stretched their necks and pointed their heads down over the rim of their nest box toward the dogs and protested with a series of harsh *kraw, kraw, kraws*. It was a very effective, innate defense. Perhaps our ravens were exercising genetic codes foraged by millennia of close association with

Inquisitive, hand-raised fledglings check out our gear. They speak into the tape recorder and steal our photographic supplies. Their "nest," a box with straw lining, seems of particular interest to two of the young birds.

wolves. The dogs were intimidated and ran quickly back to our cabin. They would sneak toward the trailer later, only to dash back home at the sight or sound of the ravens. The older brood was also extremely curious. They grabbed at the aluminum pans from which we fed them, pecked at the red and green control buttons on the tape recorder, and grabbed at our hands. The younger brood just begged, opened their mouths, and swallowed with pleasant gurgling noises.

Despite their healthy appetites, the nestlings were not willing to eat everything we offered. They relished a young, freshly killed deer but shunned meat from a four-day-old deer carcass (though it was eaten entirely in only a few hours by our older juveniles in the aviary atop York Hill). Moist foods were eagerly taken. Dry, bony items were rejected. Hard, cold fat was quickly and surely spat back into the hand from which it came. But warmed and moistened, it was devoured. Greasy raccoon was never a favorite.

Ten days after we adopted the chicks they started jumping out of their nest boxes. They were beginning the natural fledging process, trying out their wings and legs. In the wild, they would be jumping and flapping from the nest bowl to supporting cliff ledges or tree branches, but here they had only slippery plastic. Anticipating an end to trailer life, we had built a small aviary next to our garage. It was sheltered under a large, old fir and included a covered shelf and smaller tree for roosting, two large perches, and a great view of a small, unnamed brook. On May 12 the broods moved in. We were glad to be past the frequent feeding routine in the dank, smelly trailer. The older birds immediately began walking about their new digs. The younger birds spent two more days in their box before fledging. A midafternoon rainstorm gave them all a good cleaning. By May 16, only two weeks after joining us, all the ravens were roosting together on protected perches. They were quickly becoming independent.

Their appetites increased with their mobility and outdoor life. Feeding time was a circus. We would walk in the aviary with a tin of meat or gruel and be mauled by ten screaming, flapping, sooty-black babies. Their eyes were still gray-blue and their mouths bright red. They would jump on us, scratching with sharp, excited claws. But we loved it. And the Wojciks were enamored: Zetta helped to feed during the day, and Josh and Hilary hurried from the bus to feed right after school. Many an afternoon feeding was delayed until the bus dropped the kids across from Hills Pond. From our shoulders, knees, or head the ravens would take chopped moose, deer, lung, and liver. When full, they would cache what remained in our shirt collars, pockets, hoods, or even our ears. They untied our shoelaces, picked at buttons, and snapped at anything we wore that was red.[1]

On May 17 Hilary and I introduced the fledglings to a pan of water. Four of the ten were immediately interested, even dipping their bills, spoon-like, to drink. Then they tried bathing. Their behavior was innately accurate. All

Colleen intent on feeding our brood of ten raven
fledglings. The young birds clamor about and on her,
begging when hungry with quivering wings as
demonstrated by the bird in the right foreground.

their wetting, shaking, and preening actions were identical to those of older
birds. But they were clumsy and eventually ineffective. The pan of water was
dumped, and the cleansing bath soon became a dirty mud-wrestling scene.

The pair of wild ravens whose territory included Hills Pond noticed our
increasingly noisy gang on May 21. The male, whom we tagged as W52 earlier
in the winter berated the intruders with territorial quorks and resonating calls
that sounded like an Amazonian Indian smacking a hard stick against a hollow
log. The babies immediately froze. Silent.

This reaction was the same one we were getting from nestlings in the wild nests we were following. We wanted to tag as many local nestlings as we could that first summer so we would be able follow their use of carcasses during the coming winter. By early May we had nestlings ready to mark at Bernd's mother's farm, at the Graham's dairy down the Weld Road, at Mt. Blue State Park, and at the local Hills Pond territory. Unlike those who lived in cliff nests in Vermont, these ravens nested in pine trees. Bernd, Dave Lidstone, and I climbed to each nest, most fifty to eighty feet high in the lower canopy of white pines. We banded nine nestlings, one to four per nest. Brood sizes in Maine were a lot smaller than in Vermont. Both nest site selection and brood size in ravens are variable, reflecting local site characteristics and food abundance, respectively. Here in Maine, cliffs were not abundant and apparently neither were winter-killed deer and moose.

Climbing to our nests was a challenge. Most nest trees lacked low branches, and the few that were near the ground were often dead or not much bigger around than a pencil. But they were amazingly strong; if I climbed swiftly, they held my weight. Getting to the nest was often easier than getting around and into the nest itself. (Raven nests are often two feet from top to bottom and a similar distance across.) Hanging on to the tree while reaching from below to grab the screaming young was acrobatic and unnerving given the parents' continual circling and alarm clucking. Occasionally, the parents protested from a nearby perch or dived toward me, but mostly they circled above the nest tree, flapping their wings rapidly with shallow beats. Once I grabbed the chicks, I placed them in a small backpack and lowered them safely to the ground with a thin cord. Waiting for the ground crew to band, tag, measure, and take a blood sample seemed like an eternity, but at least there were fewer bugs at the nest than on the ground. After the ground crew had tagged and measured the babies, I hauled them back up to the nest and returned them to the soft moose hair that lined the nest cup. Then I slipped back down the tree and left the territory, hoping to see the wild broods later in the winter.

Mid-May 1989; Colleen's Journal: "John went to Montana for a week. It rained for two and a half straight days and flooded our driveway. When it finally stopped raining, the babies were moved into their new aviary."

Raising baby ravens and husky pups was always interesting. Kenai had been pushing the puppy envelope. Just like the baby ravens, she was hungry and often tried to steal Sky's food. She treated her plastic bowl like a toy, and she destroyed the rugs. She refused to sleep in a dog crate and vocally protested anything she found disagreeable. Adding Mother Nature to the mix pushed the limits beyond interesting. We had to feed the chicks every two hours, even in torrential rains, such as those we encountered in May 1989. The tarps would not dry, and the nest boxes were soggy. Hilary and Josh provided comic relief with their banter as they helped feed the ravenous brood. At least the trailer leaked only slightly. The last day of the deluge the plastic culvert under our driveway was out-classed. The water from the storm eroded away the surrounding soil and freed the culvert to rise out of the ground, like a giant caterpillar, just before it was swept away. We now had a canyon in our front yard. Our car was on one side of the new ditch, and on the other side in the garage was the carcass trailer. Could life get any more complicated?

I was maxed out by the storm on May 17 when Bernd stopped by unexpectedly with another brood of five Vermont birds. Sustaining our ten, plus the adults and twenty juveniles in the aviary, and monitoring the local wild nests was all I could handle. Getting five hungry babies and seventy-five pounds of thawed meat that needed repackaging and freezing at 10:00 p.m., especially when John was away, was unreasonable. Bernd was always pushing to get as much as he could out of every effort. He had planned to take this brood back with him in a few days to be raised in his aviary in Vermont, but his zeal clouded diplomacy on this visit. This interaction would be the first of many instances when our expectations clashed with Bernd's.

As we think back on this time and our more recent experiences, we can see more objectively why we felt underappreciated and why Bernd felt justified in his actions.

The postdoc-technician-professor interaction is often tense. This tension arises because the postdoc is new to the system, ready to make a discovery, whereas the professor already knows the system and wants mostly to confirm suspicions and maybe explore new directions. Bernd had worked on the raven project for years before we arrived. His insights and hard work had set us up for success. He expected us to work only with aviary experiments, not to reinvent his understanding of the entire raven winter social system. Because of his prior investment, he expected us to be at his disposal whenever he visited from Vermont. We had a debt to pay and a role to fill, but these obligations were not clearly communicated. We followed our scientific senses and chased ravens in the field and watched them in the aviary to fully understand if and how they shared winter foods. It was unproductive to watch only the ravens in the aviary; fieldwork broadened our perspective and filled gaps when aviary experiments were not possible. When Bernd visited, we looked for intellectual stimulation, field assistance, and appreciation. We got plenty of the first but none of the last. Bernd was put off by his perception that we were ungrateful. We were miffed about Bernd's understanding that I, as his technician, was a proxy for his direct contribution to field work. We never understood why he saw our efforts in the field (not the aviary) as superfluous to his prior investment. It had been part of our proposal to the National Science Foundation. We were productive in executing the majority of the daily labor, planning, organizing, and creative thought, so it was hard to appreciate short visits and a thankless press to do more in the aviary. Now having postdocs and technicians of our own, we understand the need to balance appreciation for current work with recognition of past investments. But after a long winter, severe flood, our first encounter with blackflies, and new duties raising ravens, that balance eluded us.

1 June 1989; from our favorite tourist shirt: "Blackflies don't bite, they suck."

As the fledglings began to eat on their own, we spent less time feeding; by late May we were down to twice-daily feedings. Zetta gave us permission to turn and plant a small plot in front of the cabin for our first Maine garden. We even had time to climb Bald Mountain with Josh and all the dogs, although the blackflies kept us from lingering and enjoying the view. The oldest birds started pecking on their own at a hunk of frozen deer on May 29, and by June 8 all were completely self-sufficient. And just in time. Hand-feeding was becoming impossible because ever-deeper scratches on us from these powerful birds and ear-piercing begging at close range were becoming intolerable. Gathering assorted road kill in the wet Maine spring, known as mud season, was increasingly unpleasant. The dead quickly bloated, and the unpaved roads were impassable. We thus dragged and carried much of what we found, and the blackflies, mosquitoes, deerflies, midges (no-see-ums), and mooseflies, were unforgiving.

We went from mud season to bug season. Colleen's lymph nodes were swollen in response to fly bites. So when we were invited to venture with some fellow Audubon Club members to Monhegan Island, a small forested hunk of granite off the Maine coast accessible only by mail boat, we quickly agreed to go. We had heard that coastal Maine was relatively bug-free. Hilary and Josh agreed to care for the baby ravens. Sitka, Topper, and Kenai eagerly joined us. The island was a real bug-free treat. The dogs were a huge hit at the community dining hall and got rewarded by strangers many times for waiting patiently outside as we ate. Returning home on Memorial Day, we wondered why so few people were outside on a beautiful day—fewer and fewer as we drove farther and farther inland. When we stepped out of the car at our cabin, we understood: the blackflies were overwhelming!

My notes from June 3 recounting the collection of a hard-to-find dead doe include a squashed mosquito. After butchering a roadside moose on June 16, I counted ninety-six insect bites on one of my hands. We had taken to wearing long sleeves, light gloves, and head nets whenever we had to observe the birds or walk the dogs down Alder Brook Road. We would sit in total darkness at night before going to bed so that the no-see-ums would not be attracted to the light and come through the screens. The bugs slowed, but didn't stop, our enjoyment of New England's wondrous parade of migrating warblers, thrushes, and tanagers. Our life bird lists swelled with our bites. The young ravens were less sure about our new gear. When we first entered their aviary donned in protective netting, May 25, they flew away in fear. Plastered to the aviary wall, they would not take food. When we were disguised, they did not recognize or accept us. But they learned fast. On June 2, they ate from our hands again, despite the head net. Apparently the birds recognized our faces, which the netting obscured, for when we entered wearing sunglasses, they did not flee. When my parents came near the aviary, the birds flushed again to the wall in fear. But some strangers were immediately recognized as trusted friends. When Ebo Gwinner joined us for dinner June 23, he walked up to the fledglings and talked softly as he often did to his German ravens. Our birds were calm and allowed him in the aviary. Ebo truly spoke ravenese.[2]

6 June 1989; John's Field Notes: "The birds woke us up at 5:00 a.m. as usual."

The hoarse begs gave way to loud, clear, harmonic yells. Just as our older juveniles in the aviary yelled when hungry, so too did our now nearly two-month-old fledglings. Yelling develops from begging and serves a similar, proximate, purpose; the indication of hunger. It motivated us to leave more food in the aviary each night so the birds could feed themselves. Quietly. And it worked. With food available on June 7, the birds were quiet until 7:30. We could catch up a bit on our sleep.

The ravens explored their small world. They chased butterflies and snapped at the biting flies and mosquitoes. They wrestled with each other over favorite toys. Two birds played tug-of-war with a fresh leaf—each rolling from side to side as they lay next to one another. These games were very common throughout June as the birds tugged over sticks, cardboard, bark, and meat. On June 19, one of the birds landed on my back as I entered the aviary. In a flash, it was out the door and quickly well up the old fir. I could not entice him back into the aviary but did manage to chase him into the low puckerbrush along the small stream across the road from the aviary and catch him in a few hours.

Through June and July, the birds developed clear dominance hierarchies. On June 11, the birds were not aggressive and never advertised their status with postures of raised feathers. On June 29, we heard the first growling over food. It was not really fighting, but a hungry bird advertised its status by approaching a feeding bird, crouching, arching its neck up toward the prize, and uttering a growling beg-like call. On July 11, we observed the first fights over access to high and central roost perches. On July 28, we noted more aggression, and the birds were starting to "pouch" their food. A morsel of meat was quickly gulped to take it from others, but it was held in the throat and not swallowed. Later, when others were not near or challenging for the food, the owner would pop the meat back out and properly shred and eat it.

Just as the birds were working out hierarchies, so were the new pups, Kenai and Sky. Until July 5, they had been doing well together, wrestling with favorite dog toys as will most pups. That day we heard a growling coming from their new kennel that sent Zetta and me running. The pups appeared to be fighting, so we tried to separate them. Sky seemed to be gripped tightly to Kenai's neck, and we couldn't loosen her. The fighting intensified. We could now see that Sky had somehow managed to get her lower jaw stuck under Kenai's collar, and Kenai was choking. Both appeared more frightened than aggressive. With some dancing to keep the tension off Kenai, and calling out for a knife, we managed to separate them. I got a deep puncture wound on my palm from Kenai as a souvenir and a trip to the emergency room for a painful tetanus shot. There was tension when I had to explain to the doctor that Kenai didn't have her rabies shot yet; it was ironically scheduled for the next day. My hand healed, but Sky and Kenai were never very comfortable with one another after that, and each always contested the other's relative dominance status.

As soon as the birds began to feed on their own, we started recording their responses to novel foods. Over the next several months we would learn what foods young ravens feared, if they learned to eventually eat these items, and who first tested the items. Bernd would test his brood in Vermont; we would work with the birds in Maine. But we still needed help. Billy Adams and Harry Wycoff, a local builder, were eager to join the research team. Each built a small aviary at his house, dedicated freezer space to science, and agreed to house two or three of our birds. On July 19, we split up the Huntington brood, leaving three with Billy and two with Harry. As we caught and removed the birds from the aviary, the others scolded us, but no grudge was held: they all ate from our hands July 22, even those at Billy's and Harry's.

23 July 1989; John's Field Notes: "We are getting short on food—three bags of moose, a few squirrels, a turkey, and a raccoon. Dwight Cram called at midnight with a moose up at Madrid. The '300-pounder' turned out to be a 150-pound calf, but at least the police at the site of the moose-car collision were unconcerned about our lack of trailer tail lighting. Butchered and fed most of the calf to juveniles and adults up the hill at the aviary. Still in the shower when Mike Pratt brings a buck deer over—as big as a moose! Butcher it for freezing and leave carcass along Weld Road. Hills Pond ravens quorking as we finish. Freezer full again."

We began systematically investigating fear of food in all four groups in August. We offered red and gray squirrels, whole deer, woodchucks, raccoons, rabbits and hares, porcupines, all sorts of eggs, freshwater clams and crayfish, smelt, perch, sunfish and mackerel, shrimp, big snakes, little snakes, frogs, sea urchins, cats, mice, skunks, grouse, tomatoes, chiles, apples, pumpkins, hot dogs, grated cheese, bananas, robins, turkeys, kingbirds, beans, zucchini, squash, mallard ducks, salamanders and newts, blueberries, gulls, a calf, and two skinned foxes from nearby furriers. Our ravens feared medium to large whole birds and mammals. But they learned to overcome this fear. They had no fear of fish, invertebrates, and amphibians. They were absolutely, innately attracted to and fond of eggs. And they were positively unwilling to approach large snakes.

The first egg our birds saw, other than those in their birth nest, was from a Common Loon. We found it abandoned on the shore of Hills Pond. Now we knew why the loons, which delightfully awaken us with their gay but haunting calls, raised only a single young this summer. Apparently one of the normally two eggs laid failed to hatch. By candling it—shining a strong flashlight into the egg in darkened room—we could see that it was infertile. We put the dark, rough egg, a bit larger than a hen's egg, into the aviary on August 14. Before we could get out the door, the birds were on it; the largest and most dominant fledgling immediately picked it up and carried it around. There was no hesitation, no fear or apprehension, just an immediate grab of the egg. The fledglings gathered around the elliptical prize and rolled it about for five minutes. When we checked an hour later, the egg, shell and all, was gone.

We got a better look at how eggs were eaten the next day. A brown hen's egg was received by the ravens just as was the loon egg. As the dominant fledgling paraded it around, it slipped from his bill and cracked slightly. He began to chip away at the crack, eating the shell flakes. Opening a small hole in the top of the egg, he delicately ate the liquid protein, all the while defending the meal from the others who crowded near. After eating a bit of shell and most of the yolk and albumin, the dominant bird left the egg, and the other fledglings raced in to devour every bit. Bernd's, Billy's, Harry's, and our birds ate most eggs in this manner. Some eggs cracked fully when fumbled so that the runny contents mostly soaked into the aviary floor, one appeared to be purposely smashed to the ground, but most were incidentally cracked or pounded open. Fully cracked eggs were not defended; all nearby birds tried to get a mouthful of the runny mess before it became mud. Eggs that could be slowly eaten from

Hand-raised babies testing a new food item, a hard squash. Typically one bird, the most dominant, touches the item first, before others get over their neophobia and join in the fun.

a smaller hole were defended. Hard-boiled eggs were securely defended and never shared.

The size of the egg mattered little to our ravens. They immediately grabbed and ate whole robin eggs. Similarly, they attacked small balls and round fruits and veggies. And even ostrich eggs, larger than the average softball, were touched in less than a minute. The hard, thick shell of an ostrich egg might have required innovation to crack, but we couldn't take the risk. The only ostrich egg we had was Bernd's prized trophy for winning the annual ten-kilometer race held at the American Ornithologists' Union meeting. We let the ravens touch but not open that one. It would have been fascinating to watch them try because when we gave them a plastic egg, too hard to open, they scraped a hollow under a small log and cached it out of sight.

The difference in the fearless approach to smooth, round objects, such as eggs and balls, and the fearful approach to snakes was striking. Small snakes (those less than six inches long) were readily approached and eaten. But large snakes—even Josh's rubber one—were approached slowly. The first sixteen-inch-long snake was not touched for a full day. The second, an eighteen-inch-long garter snake offered twenty days later, was cautiously pecked three minutes after being placed in the cage but not eaten until an hour and a half later. During the intervening time the birds would sneak up to the snake, pinch its tail, and leap skyward. Their leaps were stereotyped jumps with wing flaps, called "jumping jacks," which we often saw our older birds perform when approaching new foods or a new feeding area. Often after a jump or two, the whole group of fledglings would flush to a high perch and study the snake from afar. They even avoided a snakelike roll of foil. But take that foil snake and shape it into an aluminum ball, and they immediately tore it to shreds.

Initial fear and subsequent learning to eat large animals were obvious when we first put a whole bird into the aviary. The recently dead Ruffed Grouse we offered the gang on June 8 caused them to fly against the far aviary wall. Forty-five minutes later, one of the older birds finally tested it. The birds yelled out of hunger but would not eat the grouse. A second grouse offered in September was eaten after a few hours. A third, a week later, was eaten in fifteen minutes. This was a consistent pattern in all the groups. Large animals were initially feared and eventually touched by an older, dominant fledgling. But with more exposure to the same sort of carcass, the birds learned it was food and readily ate it.

Our birds certainly were learning a catholic diet, but were they cannibals? They had eaten grouse, robins, and an Eastern Kingbird when we slipped a dead raven into the aviary on October 1. The fledglings plastered themselves to the far corner of the aviary. One kawed with an agitated, raspy voice. Others joined in the scolding. None fed and all avoided the raven for the day, even while pecking at a chile pepper. Next week they would eat a wild mallard and a gull with little hesitation. Their reverence for the raven was unique. Our older juveniles on the hill ate the dead raven with little hesitation. Maybe canni-balism is an acquired taste.

Why should young ravens have to learn to eat large, dead animals? Why isn't the recognition of such valuable foods simply encoded in their genes? Learning is especially adaptive in rapidly changing environments, whereas caution would seem to be important when mistakes are costly. Both of these situations characterize the environment around a potential carcass. The types of carcasses available to maturing ravens are likely to change seasonally and from place to place, so ravens must recognize many unique dead animals. Dead opossums might be common along roads, fish carcasses might be ex-pected around a frozen lake or near campgrounds, and whole dead deer are common in some forests traditionally used for wintering while rare elsewhere. Learning would allow a young raven to increasingly accept, and perhaps anticipate, particular carcasses in certain places or at certain times. Many medium- to large-sized animals might also be dangerous when wounded or sleeping. Watching from above, slowly approaching, cautiously pecking, and jumping near the potential meal would allow a hungry raven to be certain its food is really dead. Such patience costs little when one's dinner likely gets more tender with time. Cautious learning is also beneficial for young ravens because other dangers may lurk near a carcass. A dominant, territorial raven may be just out of sight, ready to attack an impatient juvenile. A carcass may actually be a baited trap. Or another predator may be sizing up the carcass. On September 10, as we visited Harry's birds, we were surprised at their silence. When we saw the aviary, we knew why. Inside, on the rabbit we had left the previous day, was an adult Cooper's Hawk. Apparently it squeezed through the door. Luckily, it had not harmed our birds, but it showed how attractive a carcass, even one in a protected place, is to wild predators.[3]

Our birds were just over six months old when we noticed something wasn't quite right. A few had mouths that were no longer pink, but rather "darker than the inside of a cow." Others had black spots on their tongues and black at the front of their mouths. The rest were as crimson-mouthed as the day we first fed them. This wasn't some disease; it was a sign of differential maturity in our birds. The most dominant ravens in each aviary group had entirely black mouths and tongues by their first winter, while subordinates remained red-mouthed. Birds of intermediate status wore blotched black and pink mouth linings. In the wild this same maturation occurred but much more slowly. Probably because of social suppression by territorial adults few, if any, ravens less than a year old obtained black mouths. The most dominant males might start getting black mouths late in their first year but more likely not until their second. Subordinates would eventually all blacken with age and increased dominance. In the aviary, we reduced the influence of adults, and our dominant juveniles quickly matured socially. But our subordinates could not flee dominants' repression and thus remained socially immature. Our discovery of a social control of mouth color suggested that it was likely regulated by hormones and therefore also an honest signal of an individual's social status. Maybe this was why we often saw young ravens "bill" each other: biting each others' beaks, wrestling, and peering inside. In choosing a partner, it would make sense to look anywhere for a reliable assessment of status.[4]

We had challenged our growing birds with quite a range of carcasses through their first summer and autumn. How did this experience compare with those of wild fledglings? With David Lidstone, we watched the nestlings from local nests fledge and gradually disassociate with their parents over the summer. From June through September we encountered the fledglings from Hills Pond, Graham's dairy, and the state park. Most of our time was spent observing them at Mt. Blue State Park, where they often were found together.

22 July 1989; John's Field Notes: "Safari! This morning en route to Lake Webb we saw a moose at the head of the lake, shrouded in fog, two deer, and swarms of swallows. All under a beautiful sunrise above Mt. Blue. Nine adult loons rafted by where only last evening we had seen a bear."

The drive to Mt. Blue State Park was a wildlife safari. Among the patches of evergreen and deciduous woods, fields, and lakeshores, we routinely had to pause for fox and deer to clear the road or simply to gaze at loons or moose in the calm lake. In late June we started consistently encountering the local nestlings we had tagged. They were now fledged and around Lake Webb. Y23 from the closest nest was a regular, fearlessly feeding along the roads. He scared picnickers by stealing from their baskets and coerced one camper to give him most of her London broil. Apparently already on his own, he worked summer complaints and local campers for a diverse, albeit human, diet.

In early July, both fledglings from Graham's, about five kilometers to the southeast, joined Y23 at the lake. The Hills Pond fledgling, Y20, remained closely associated with its father, W52, and untagged mother. The other fledglings appeared much more independent of parental care, either panhandling from picnickers or scavenging dead fish along the lakeshore. We occasionally saw adults with our birds at Lake Webb, but they stayed farther from people and appeared to only loosely guard their offspring. The experiences of the state park and Graham's youngsters were not all that different from that of our hand-raised birds. They lived in a relatively small area, associated closely with people, and ate a diverse diet of human scraps and scavenged small vertebrates.

The rigors of life faced by wild ravens were stronger than those faced by our protected birds. Y23's sibling died, apparently killed in the nest by a predator, before fledging. Y21 from Graham's broke its leg around July 4. We learned from park rangers that barbeque grills apparently were responsible, breaking other raven legs in each of the last three summers.

By mid-August, our tagged birds were less reliably seen. Y23 visited the lake through September, but the others either died or dispersed more widely. Troy Johnson called from Stephen-Phillips Preserve, a campground on Mooselookmeguntic Lake near Oquossoc, to report that Y17, from Bernd's mother's nest spent the summer up there, about fifty kilometers from its natal territory.

The life of a young raven moves fast. After only a few weeks or months on their home turf they move to opportune feeding grounds, often associated with people—and danger. They mix with other broods at this time, feeding and roosting together in small groups, and gradually gain independence from parental protection. As autumn sends campers inside and hunters to the woods after deer, the ravens wander farther and enter their nomadic years until they become dominant enough to win a mate and territory. All connection to the natal territory is not lost during this time of wanderlust, but it may be limited to the most dominant juveniles. Over the next three years Bernd and we would only see three of the thirty juveniles we banded as nestlings. Two of these were very dominant birds, likely males, who had partners. They regularly visited the many carcasses we placed from Wilton to Weld. They also used the large municipal landfill at Wilton. We never saw any of the 1989 wild nestlings after their first summer.

The next February (1989), as cold stiffened the landscape, we moved our hand-reared birds to the aviary on York Hill. We observed them interact with our captive adults and then released them into the wild. In contrast to the wild fledglings, we observed several of our fledglings repeatedly over the next two years. They acted like perfectly normal juveniles assimilated into the dynamic social world of nonbreeding ravens. But we had clearly enhanced their survival during their vulnerable first year and, by restraining them, had also more strongly tied them to their local landscape.

When we left Arizona, we had no plans to raise baby ravens. We did not propose this taxing summer work to the National Science Foundation. It just seemed natural to increase our understanding of young ravens by taking on the role of raven parents. As Bernd would teach us, always put a test probe for the next research project into the current one. This test paid off. Our young birds were true ambassadors, bringing us closer to our friends and neighbors who entered the summer world of the raven. We were able to publish two scientific papers on our unique observations. It also paid off later. We could not have known at the time that our parental experience would actually be a key to our future. Only three years later, by drawing on our knowledge of raising ravens, we won a grant from the United States Fish and Wildlife Service to develop rearing techniques for endangered island ravens. This research would lead us in new directions and ultimately to permanent employment.[5]

Just as we had no plans to raise baby ravens, we never thought we would have more than two dogs. With Kenai and Sky we were now running four dogs, but the lure of easier and faster sledding was strong. Our team seemed destined to continue to grow. And just as we saw the baby ravens disperse and start to explore farther from their natal grounds, so did Colleen, as the world of dog showing opened new horizons for exploration.

seven

Dog Days

Even though most of our time was consumed by feeding and foraging for our baby ravens, we were still raising and training our young husky pups. The dog days of summer were upon us, and it was too warm to run the team, so we focused on basic obedience. Because Sitka and Topper had been reluctantly obedient dogs, we decided to start training Kenai while she was young. She and Sky shared a class at Four-K's Golden Obedience, where Sky was the star. She was the perfect student: she sat, heeled, and came on command. Kenai, on the other hand, had a real knack for ignoring us. Aversive or award-based conditioning mattered little to Kenai. She did as she pleased, when and if she felt like it. A book that we read as we struggled with Sitka's early mulishness defined Siberian Huskies as "stubborn and easily bored." Boy, was that Kenai. Her pedigree included a father that was a great lead dog and a mother that was a champion in the show ring, with no common ancestry. We didn't yet know what Kenai's strengths were, but we knew she was a true Siberian.[1]

Mid-August 1989; Colleen's Journal: "All the primped and groomed dogs were incredible. Poodles with poms-poms on their butts, Pekinese with ponytails, and hair-sprayed Bishon Frises. Ugly to me . . . . It was a long drive to be in the ring for two minutes or less."

An invitation from Kenai's breeder, Margaret Cook, to a show in New Brunswick, Canada, gave us an opportunity to test Kenai's potential as a show dog. I had never been to a dog show, and I had a hard time believing all that I saw. My first impression as I entered the building was the noise: the barking, yipping, and howling. My nose was barraged by a mix of smells: perfume poorly disguising wet dog fur smell. Dog hair floated like smoke in the air. And I saw every type of dog—large and small, hairy and naked—being brushed, combed, blow-dried, and spiffed up by people with aprons covering suits and dresses. I had never seen so many crates and kennels with dogs in them, often stacked four or five high.

The scene was crazy and cacophonous, I could feel the tension in the building. Dog shows are a beauty contest of sorts, and it was this feature that produced the tension I felt in the grooming area. The dogs are judged against a written standard that dictates precise and rather artificial criteria, such as color, size, and shape. The more dogs an individual can defeat relative to the best example of the standard on that day, the more points he/she gets. Points accumulate toward a championship. The dogs are judged on movement but not on running movement or movement while pulling a load. Kenai's training thus far had encouraged a strong working dog ethic and basic obedience. Conformation, in contrast, requires standing still and walking briskly on a leash. A show dog doesn't pull hard, sit, or bother other dogs in the ring. It is polite to the judge, even when its lips are pulled up to allow tooth inspection or its genitals are checked to confirm vitality. Up to this point, Kenai had somewhat perfected sitting nicely at our side if we stopped walking, but she was not going to stand for much of what a judge expected.

The official Siberian Husky standard is complex. It paints a general picture of the ideal Siberian as of "medium size, moderate bone, well balanced proportions, ease and freedom of movement, proper coat, pleasing head and ears, correct tail, and good disposition. The Siberian Husky never appears so heavy or coarse as to suggest a freighting animal; nor is he so light and fragile as to suggest a sprint-racing animal. In both sexes the Siberian Husky gives the appearance of being capable of great endurance." Then the requirements get more specific. Bitches are 20 to 22 inches tall and weigh 35 to 50 pounds. Dogs (males) are 21 to 23.5 inches tall and weigh 45 to 60 pounds. The eyes are almond shaped, brown, blue, or parti-colored. All coat colors from black to pure white are allowed. The feet are oval, not round, and well-furred between the toes. The shoulder is well laid back. The upper arm angles slightly backward from point of shoulder to elbow. The muscles and ligaments are well developed. The skull is of medium size in proportion to the body; the stop on the nose (where the forehead meets the muzzle) is well-defined, and the muzzle is of medium length where the distance from the tip of the nose to the stop is equal to the distance from the stop to the occiput (the bony peak of the skull that is located at the back of the top of the head). Nose color can be black in gray, tan, or black dogs; liver in copper dogs; and flesh-colored in pure white dogs. The pink streaked "snow nose" is acceptable. Teeth have a scissors bite. Neck should be medium in length, arched and carried proudly erect when standing. The neck is extended when moving at a trot. The chest is deep and strong but not too broad. The ribs are well sprung from the spine but flattened on the sides to allow for freedom of action. The back is straight and strong with a level topline from withers to croup. The tail is well furred and of fox brush shape set on just below the topline and carried in a graceful sickle when the dog is at attention. Above all the Siberian Husky "performs his original function in harness most capably, carrying a light load at a moderate speed over great distances. His body proportions and form reflect this basic balance of power, speed, and endurance."[2]

Judges have to qualify to referee each breed. They are initially mentored and then allowed to judge provisionally before they solo. They will have studied the standard and committed it to memory, but many have certain preferences within the standard, so their assessment is a very subjective application of the standard. At any given show a judge has about a minute per dog to assess its conformation to the standard. Classes are divided by sex and age and other variables. The dogs in each class are brought into a square arena where they all line up standing nose to tail. Then the judge walks down the line and individually goes over the dogs. He will check the mouth for a scissors bite and place his hands on the dog to feel the bone structure and muscles as well as the coat. If it is a male, the judge will check to feel for two testicles. He will ask the handler to move the dog up and back and then around the ring. Usually all the dogs then get moved together for a quick comparison. At that point for that class the judge makes his decision. And so it goes through all the classes until he picks best of breed and then on to the next breed.

The groomers and handlers who were showing dogs took the job of showing very seriously. I later found out that many of them were professionals working for owners, and they were paid more if they won. Just as with the professional dog drivers, professional handlers were dominant over straightforward owners such as me. They knew the judges and their personal preferences (e.g., shorter, gray, blue eyes). They showed specific dogs under specific judges to pile up points. They competed against one another yet stuck together. It was a fraternity of sorts; like gypsies, they would travel from show to show with their dogs: bathing, grooming, showing, and then on to the next venue. Like a traveling carnival, they would move to a new location and a different judge and go through the same routine. It was a foreign life to me. I couldn't see devoting my life to weekly beauty contests among dogs. I liked the idea of competing against a standard to show that your dog is what it is supposed to be, but I still questioned why. In working breeds I could understand that form should affect function. But what difference does it make with a Chihuahua, for instance? And it was expensive to prove your point; entry fees and traveling costs added up fast. Judging was inconsistent, varying with the judge's interpretation of the standard. But, dog people tend to like and talk to dog people, so the social benefits of showing sometimes outweighed the costs.

The first judge I met was not impressed with a sitting dog or with Kenai's overenthusiastic "walking" around the ring. She placed second behind her mother, who was then defeated by a male puppy. We would have to learn a new regimen of training and equipment for the show life because it appeared that Kenai had enough beauty to compete for a championship if that was what we wanted. But as scientists, we had to wonder if the exterior shape of a dog translated to the ability to be a good sled dog like her father? In other words, will function follow an artificially defined form? Anatomical differences of features such as shoulder lay back or leg and back length could result in different gaits and therefore pulling abilities, but the shape of her head somehow didn't seem applicable to function.

My interactions with people at our first shows put me in contact with some of the pillars of the Siberian Husky fancy. Peggy Grant was one of the first I met. I had no idea who she was when I approached her for help at one of my first shows. She took the time to educate me on ring etiquette and graciously congratulated me when Kenai defeated her dog. At the time I knew her only as another Siberian owner. Later, when I came to understand how influential she was in the Siberian fancier community, I knew I had met an icon. She owned the Marlytuk kennel that had been founded in 1958 and had mentored many young Siberian fanciers, including Carol Nash, who was mentoring me. Her foundation dogs were only two owners removed from Leonhard Seppala's Siberians. Seppala was a famous Alaskan musher who introduced New England racers to Siberians in the 1920s. His "little" dogs broke records in every New England race he ran, changing the sport forever. Just as we were meeting some of the founders of animal behavior, here too we were meeting the founding forces behind the Siberian Husky.[3]

I was learning more about shows and the politics surrounding shows. Members of the Yankee Siberian Husky Club recruited me and stressed the importance of being in the club to help further our showing potential. I jumped in with enthusiasm, eager to explore a new area in the world of dogs.

I even gave a skijoring demonstration to the club. I thought this sport, where one or two dogs pull a single skier, cross country, would appeal to Siberian owners not able to take the deeper plunge into mushing. My mentors, Margaret and Carol, kept me in the show loop, warned me of entry deadlines, and drove Kenai and me to many shows through October and November. These beauty contests brought few victories and many defeats.

Show fever was contagious, and soon Hilary wanted to try Sky in the ring. Sky's pedigree was known but included no show champions, and her sledding background was unknown. Sky also had a very different form from Kenai. She was taller and narrower all the way around, nor were her markings as symmetrical. We took both dogs to a show in Portland. Hilary learned that Sky didn't have the form that the show judges were seeking. To us, it mattered not. We loved huskies because, as Konrad Lorenz put it, they were a breed that "retained a wild exterior and thus does not spoil the landscape by its civilized appearance." Besides, Sky was turning into a reliable puller with leader potential. Just as she had been a star pupil in obedience, she was showing the same willingness to learn and take commands in harness.[4]

We thought Sky and Kenai could learn the fundamentals of sledding by watching the other dogs. Rather than starting them off with dragging a tire and learning from our instructions, we let the experienced dogs handle the mentoring. Fortunately, no training was necessary to get them to run and pull. Generations of breeding had predisposed our pups to these traits. They did, however, have to get accustomed to running next to another dog and potentially right behind a dog. Lead dog training had to be done individually, and Sky and Kenai got their share of leadership training. We worked with them on turning right and left, starting, stopping, slowing, merging, and waiting. The mentorship of the other dogs was invaluable, however. The "monkey see, monkey do" scenario was evident. Sled dogs aren't running because they want to chase prey. They are running because other dogs are running, which is contagious to these animals. It seems that their breeding has favored those motivated to run with other dogs so that the social team shares the workload fairly equally.

Carol Nash knew that we were thinking of borrowing more dogs for the upcoming sled season even though we had our two new pups. She called one day to ask if we would like to foster a couple of young Siberians for the winter. We had to discuss this proposal with our landlords, Tom and Zetta. We also had to consider our ability to do it. Could we manage the raven study and train four new dogs? Was it worth it? We were already impressed and intrigued by how rapidly Sky and Kenai had learned to work in the team. If two were that easy, surely four would be even easier. We were caught up in the camaraderie of dogsledders and felt the need to do as they were doing. Tom and Zetta said, "No problem, the more the merrier!" So we added more dogs and adjusted the newly renovated kennel.

On an October day that was far warmer than the month would suggest, I went to pick up our new charges. My mother was visiting, and she got the copilot seat. Neither one of us was prepared for the stench emanating from the two dogs, Buster and Granite, we picked up. We survived the ride home only by rolling down the windows for the entire 100-mile trip. Fortunately, the warm day meant the dogs could be bathed in Zetta's large claw-footed tub. Poor Buster and Granite! Their owner was in transition with a divorce pending and couldn't handle, never mind wash, all of his dogs. They were littermates, about 18 months old and with some sledding experience. Buster had been neutered a few weeks earlier because he was monorchid, which means one testicle didn't descend into the scrotum. He was at risk for health problems if he hadn't been neutered. And because of being altered he couldn't be shown.

Essayon's Buster Brown easily drew attention from anyone who set eyes on him. He had a luxurious gray and white coat with an open face. The white on his face completely surrounded his eerie clear blue eyes. He looked ghostly and actually was spooked by new situations. Essayon's Granite looked like her namesake. Her coat was off white and wolf gray with brown overtones, like the granite stone of New England. She had a mask, like Kenai, where the creamy white ran down her nose and punctuated her eyebrows. Her most striking feature, beside the crook at the end of her curly tail, was her marble-like parti-eyes. Her right eye was mostly brown with blue flecks and her left mostly blue with brown flecks. We could never decide which eye to look at. Both dogs were somewhat shy and needed more socialization with humans. Their dog etiquette was good, although Buster and Topper did some posturing very early that indicated to us that they might not do well together.

After the arrival of Buster and Granite, with temperatures consistently cooler than 60°F, we began running our new six-dog team. Sled dogs cannot radiate heat fast enough to counteract the internal heat they build up if they run in temperatures above 60°F. If their internal body temperatures get as high as 109°F, collapse and even death can occur. Excess heat is dissipated from all surface areas, but fur interferes with the radiation of heat. Panting, which facilitates evaporative cooling from the tongue and mouth, cools the lungs and brains, and sweating through the pads of the feet helps as well, but the pads don't have much surface area.

The difference between this team and our three-dog team of the previous year was indescribable. These animals really moved! A lot of our time was spent trying to balance the team. We had experienced dogs and novice dogs. We had differences in sizes, shapes, and strides. To efficiently use the dogs' strengths, we had to make sure that each pair of dogs pulled equally. Otherwise, the gangline would not be straight and the pulling force would be in opposing directions. If we had an unlimited number of dogs at our fingertips, we could probably come close to a perfectly balanced team, but we had six dogs and six positions, and there were only so many permutations. We also had to account for personality, which meant that Topper and Buster could not run next to one another. Within our little pack, being alpha dog did not necessarily translate to being lead dog. A musher doesn't want fighting for

Colleen and John take a break with the expanded team: Sitka (left), Buster, Granite (still shy), Kenai, and Topper. Photo courtesy of Rob Sanford.

supremacy that would defeat the balance and shape of the team, not to mention stop you dead on the trail. Cooperation and a well-paired team was our goal.

Our trial run came on a beautiful early November day at a Down East Sled Dog Club meeting. Club meetings usually featured hands-on fun runs and food before business. We put Sitka and Buster at lead and Topper and Granite at wheel with the pups in the middle as team dogs. After their collar incident, the pups were somewhat edgy around each other, but when running they were all business and well matched. We finished the four-mile cart race on a dirt trail in the middle of the pack at twenty-three minutes. We were feeling pretty good about the shape of our team.

As our training took us farther afield, we found that additional transportation for the dogs was necessary. We also knew that winter road conditions had a serious effect on our four-wheel-drive truck. Winter transportation issues really put us in touch with local Maine customs. In the southwestern United States, snowy roads are plowed and cindered. The cinders, small gravelly bits of volcanic rock, provide traction and do little harm to the undercarriage of a vehicle. In granitic Maine, sand and salt replace pumice. These materials work well for traction but at a high cost to the body of the car. Salt quickly rusts away any steel. Local residents have a simple cure for the rusty side effects of winter driving. Most parked their good cars for the winter and drove a specially purchased, hunk of rattling rust, known as a "wintah beatah." It was time to shop.

14 August 1989; Colleen's Journal: "John almost vacuumed up the rug as it disintegrated while we removed dirt and most of the floorboard from the new truck."

Five hundred and fifty dollars will buy a good winter beater. For us, it was a 1977 maroon Toyota pickup that we found in an *Uncle Henry's* ad. There was a hole in the gas tank; we could see the ground pass below us through the missing parts of the floor; there wasn't a tailpipe or functional exhaust system; but it came with a great decal on the side of the bed that proudly announced us as the owners of a "New Englander." We were not mechanical, but we quickly learned that it was okay to use an open flame to heat the putty to seal the leaking gas tank. We also learned that although a faulty fuse suggested the need for a new alternator and regulator, all that was really required is a new fuse. But mostly we learned about welding. Our New Englander had been beaten by many a winter, and we resorted to welding in new floorboards and eventually most of the basic frame that supports the engine, cab, and bed. In Maine each car is required to have an annual inspection, where the car is appraised not for its emissions but for its actual roadworthiness. The New Englander was immediately deemed unworthy. That meant that we could not

The New Englander holds the dog box and Mac sled through pounding snow.
Travel accommodations for Kenai, Granite, and Buster are on the visible side; three
more compartments are accessed from the far side. Each dog door is clipped shut
and screened; there is a board that folds up across their base (gray in photo) to help
keep the dogs safely inside while traveling and sleeping.

legally drive it; the inspector feared it would crumble in the most minor of
accidents. We were beginning to wonder if it would do so without provocation.

Car inspections in Maine are relative, not absolute, pronouncements of
opinion. If your beater didn't pass, we were told to try again at a different
garage. Inspectors are also repairmen. We took the New Englander to a new
shop, where we asked the owner to install a new and much-needed exhaust
system. And, by the way, we asked if he also could inspect the vehicle while he
was doing this work. A hundred dollars later, we were driving a legal New
Englander. But even this worker informed us that our pickup was not likely to
pass next year's inspection without a major overhaul of the truck's skeleton.
To us there were other priorities. A few pieces of plywood framed out over the

bed of the truck made a nice "dog box." We divided it evenly by six and installed six individual doors. Special wood and bolt attachments allowed us to put the sleds on the roof. We scavenged some navy blue paint for it. In white, we stenciled each dog's name over a door and "Hills Pond Kennel, Raven Haven, ME" on the back. We felt professional now.

We drove the New Englander all over western Maine. It ran like a champ, even if the radio did not work, the wipers were ineffective, and the heater slow. We took it to dog races. We ran back and forth between our cabin and York Hill. We hauled a lot of dead animals and parts of animals. It spared our good truck from the salts of Maine. We have no record of the miles put on the old Toyota from November to August, but they were many. When our inspection sticker expired, we decided to upgrade. With the help of Tom's brother Dave, we completely rebuilt the frame—welding heavy plates of steel to anything that would not flake away. The New Englander was reborn; a strong beast that we sold for $400. After splitting the proceeds with Dave, we had just enough cash to get a new water pump and exhaust system for our next beatah, a 1984 cherry red, extracab, longbed Toyota pickup. This time we checked the frame before we spent the $700. The long bed required changing the dog box a bit: we put an addition on the back that became our easily accessible storage compartment for gear.

The snow was starting to pile up again. We returned from a show trip in late November to twelve inches of new snow. The time had come to dust off the sleds and get down to some serious fun and training. As our fieldwork continued, we explored more miles by sled. We found groomed snowmobile trails and traveled as far as our finances and time would allow. Most dawns and dusks would find us high in trees or deep in blinds watching the ravens. Some hours during the day were spent in the hut, hauling carcasses, or tracking radio-tagged birds. One or both of us would manage an hour or two with the dogs out on a trail within a fifteen-minute drive of the cabin. Our raven assistants, Hilary and Josh, often accompanied us as handlers or riders. The dogs loved their routine. They expected their run every day around the same time. If we couldn't run on any given day, it usually led to trouble in the form of fights or escapes.

There was so much snow early that winter that our Christmas tree was the top of a very tall tree that we cut on Tom's property. He would use the rest of the tree for firewood in the future. The temperatures were colder than normal, and Topper was having a tough time staying warm. With his well-being in mind we left him snug in our warm cabin as we left for a Christmas party at Billy and Lili's. While we were away, Topper was having a party of his own. The cabin was a disaster when we got home. He sheepishly approached us when we discovered he had eaten all the homemade dog treats that were wrapped and ready to give to our dog friends. Wrapping paper didn't stop him from finding a bag of M&M's in a Christmas package. He ate the homemade caramels that were a Christmas gift, and he had dumped the trash and eaten some coffee grounds (for dessert?). To add insult to injury, he peed on the down comforter on our bed. He looked as though he had swallowed a watermelon! His hangdog look meant that either he felt guilty or he felt awful. Cold or no cold, we tossed him outside. We were afraid he would produce another mess, and we didn't want to find out from which end it would come. After he had served several hours of penance in the cold, we let him back in the cabin. He never got sick.

We began our second racing season in Rangeley in early January. Fortunately, it was not far away so we could go back and forth each day. Josh and Hilary had worked hard training the team and wanted an opportunity to show off their skills. We entered both of them in the junior races with three dogs each. Hilary had Sitka, Sky, and Granite. Josh had Kenai, Buster, and Tilly, a dog we borrowed from Margaret Cook. Topper was too unpredictable for Josh to use. Brodie was happily retired. The Wojcik kids had a lot to contend with in that race. There was head-on passing, Tilly wouldn't run, and Sitka was rammed by a passing sled's brush bow that broke when it hit her. She wasn't very excited about running the second day and even shied away from other teams they met. The kids were also learning about competitive sportsmanship. We were proud when Josh had stopped to help the girl with the out-of-control team that rammed into Sitka. That girl won the race but never thanked Josh, maybe because she spoke only French. Our teams finished sixth and seventh.

After watching the junior races, we could hardly wait to put our six-dog team into competition. We were entered in the Lincoln race scheduled for the end of January and the Gouldsboro race the first weekend in February. We were also considering a race in Newport, Vermont, the second weekend in February. Unfortunately, the excellent snow conditions we had enjoyed earlier did not endure. Races were scratched.

It was probably for the best that races were cancelled. Granite, Sky, and Kenai were all in heat, which made them especially hard to run and very attractive to the males. The estrus cycle lasts about twenty-one days: seven days coming into heat with lots of flirting toward the males; seven days when the females want to breed and will go through a lot to accomplish this, for example, backing up to a male and showing off her genitals; then seven days when the females don't want to breed and will snap at all dogs. None of these parts of the cycle were particularly appealing to deal with during a race.

Finally, the weather improved and we were able to run our team at the Sabattus Lake races. The first day was cancelled because water was on top of the lake ice. The temperature plummeted overnight, however, so the race was on for Sunday. John ran the 6.5-mile flat course in twenty-nine minutes with no borrowed dogs. The wind was blowing with a wind chill of about $-36°F$. Every inch of John's body was covered in black clothing except the tip of his nose. He looked like Darth Vader. The dogs weren't very happy about the cold, especially Topper, who was reluctant to leave his warm box and get harnessed for the race. When we finally got them out of the boxes, they did a

Colleen (with sunglasses) handles our expanded team (Buster and Kenai at lead; Sky beside Colleen at swing; Topper behind Colleen; Granite and Sitka at wheel) in preparation to move to the starting line. John is in bib 21.

little dance trying to keep their paws off the ground. We realized they were doing this to prevent their moist paws from freezing to the snow and ice. Similarly, some of the mushers had trouble with their intact Alaskan husky males who had little hair on their scrotums. When the dog would lie down on the ice on a day like this the skin would freeze to the ice like a wet tongue on a cold flagpole. A few solved the problem with a rabbit fur jock strap that insulated the dogs' testicles and kept them safely away from the tenacious ice.

We had hoped that our team's improved time would qualify the huskies for a leg on their Sled Dog Degree. Purebred Siberian Huskies could earn this title, which is attached as a suffix after their name (e.g., CH Joe Dog SD), even if they are spayed or neutered. Earning a leg was not easy. Your team had to finish within 1.33 times the average of the top three teams in your class (or in the top 50 percent if fewer than six teams compete). Some professionals ran their second-string teams in the sportsman class, so the average was very fast, and we couldn't qualify. It was hard to compete against Alaskan huskies, even if they were scrubs or too young for the first team. Alaskan huskies are not a pure breed. Northern breeds like Siberians that are double coated have been bred to dogs with longer legs and deeper chests (such as whippets and greyhounds) to achieve greater speed. The deep chest allows for more lung volume and the longer legs can cover the distance more easily. Their form is very different from a Siberian's, but Alaskan huskies' overall function is more efficient than a Siberian's. Modern racing sled dogs are the fastest animals in the world when they are running a distance of more than 10 miles. The cheetah sprinting at 70 miles per hour or the antelope dodging at 61 miles per hour cannot sustain that speed. Alaskan huskies are the marathon athletes. The longest races require these dogs to maintain a 3.2-minute mile speed while doing the equivalent of five marathons a day for ten days. Just when we thought we were getting fast enough, more speed was needed. For us, it would be impossible to achieve the 100 miles of qualifying time spread over at least five races needed for the degree. We just had to set our sights on enjoying the ride.[5]

Josh accompanied me to the Greenville Race the first weekend in March. John was at academic job interviews. Our two-night stay bunking on the floor with Margaret and Carol wasn't restful. The course was slushy, and Sitka wasn't putting any effort into the race, perhaps because of John's absence. I wondered why we bothered to come. It didn't seem to bother Josh. He sang all the way home to make up for the lack of a radio in the dog truck.

The following weekend we ended our racing season where we had started, in Rangeley. Josh ran the six-dog team 7.5 miles in forty-two minutes. As the day progressed, it got warm and the snow melted. The trail was covered in

Hilary (left) and Josh sprint to the finish line of the final race at Rangeley Lakes. Sitka and Sky lead Hilary on the Mac sled. Buster and Kenai lead Josh, who is piloting the old oak sled. Running side-by-side always elicited fast times from our competitive dogs.

puddles that Sitka at wheel chose to avoid. Josh had a hard time keeping her moving and steering the sled. The second day they shortened the course to three miles to speed up the race and to avoid the now-bare areas. The team did it in nineteen minutes. Josh was disappointed because Margaret ended up beating him by the thinnest of margins: thirty-eight seconds over the two days. The season had started out to be promising, but the weather just didn't cooperate.

With racing over, we continued to work the dogs for fun and prepared for more shows. At one of the races, Margaret had suggested that I have Kenai's and Granite's eyes checked by a veterinary ophthalmologist. Siberian Huskies have three hereditary eye problems—juvenile cataracts, cornea dystrophy, and progressive retinal atrophy—that can be detected by an exam. I made appointments for both dogs. Hilary, who was very curious about the procedure, rode with me to the eye clinic in mid-March. The doctor put dilating drops in the dogs' eyes and then looked closely in to the pupils with a special light. Granite had what was termed clear eyes or "not affected." There was no evidence of any of the three eye diseases. Kenai, on the other hand, was declared to be "affected" with juvenile cataracts (bilateral posterior cortical/polar cataracts). This condition can cause opacity of the lens of the eye, allowing less light to enter the eye, and might lead to blindness. Juvenile cataracts differ from senior or old-age cataracts in that they are inherited.

I was devastated by the doctor's pronouncement. I cried all the way home, thinking that Kenai would be blind any day. Ethically, we couldn't breed Kenai and have her pass the juvenile cataract gene to her offspring; we had to have her spayed, ending her show career. Margaret offered to take her back because she sold her to us with a guarantee of sorts that she could be shown. Kenai was a member of our family and she could still pull a sled, so as far as we were concerned, she was staying. Her cataracts never led to blindness. She chased moving objects like leaves, and her depth perception was not too good, but she lived a long life. Several years later, when we were ready, Margaret sent us a replacement show pup even though we kept Kenai.

Which parent passed this gene to Kenai? Or did both? Margaret, in a subsequent phone conversation, explained that Kenai's mother had cleared her eye exam. Her father had never been checked because he was from sled lines, and there was a misguided belief that this line of dogs didn't have any of the hereditary eye problems. Our research has showed that there was some evidence that juvenile cataracts were a recessive trait: to exhibit the cataract, a dog needed to inherit the recessive allele from both parents.

An allele is a molecular form of the DNA coding for a trait, or a variant of a gene. Because Kenai's mother did not exhibit the cataract trait but Kenai did, her mother must have been a carrier, technically heterozygous for the trait, having one recessive allele that was not expressed (likely "covered" by a

Colleen and Kenai share a quiet moment before
the hectic hook-up to race begins. Photo
reprinted with permission from the
Bangor (ME) Daily News.

dominant, sound allele). Her father was at least heterozygous and might have
been affected, or homozygous recessive (having both alleles for the trait from
his parents), like Kenai. Even today the exact hereditary mechanism for this
disease is not known. Researchers at the Animal Health Trust in England
continue to investigate this disease. It appears to be caused by a recessive
allele, but there is also the possibility of incomplete penetrance or polygenic
inheritence.[6]

143

In Kenai's case, simple inheritance explains how she got the trait. If her father didn't have cataracts, then it is likely he was heterozygous. By random chance, when two heterozygous individuals breed, 25 percent of their young will be homozygous for the recessive allele. In fact, in the litter of four pups, three were clear-eyed and only Kenai had cataracts. This result is identical to that discovered by Gregor Mendel in his breeding experiments. Mendel, a monk, pioneered the science of genetics by crossing peas of various characters (smooth versus wrinkled seeds, for example). By measuring the occurrence of the parental characteristics in the pea progeny, he deduced the basic laws of inheritance, noting that traits are rarely blended but rather are inherited intact in precise proportions. The pups in Kenai's litter would not have partial cataracts; some would have none, others would have a full dose. Following Mendel's laws, by random chance one pup in four would get the recessive allele from both parents and have cataracts. Kenai was the unlucky one.

Considering that Kenai had not been the result of close line breeding, we were surprised that she ended up with cataracts. Close inbreeding, which is what line breeding is, increases the chances that both parents will have similar genetics (often a single dog may repeatedly show up in both the sire's and the dam's pedigree), and if this result includes recessive, dangerous traits like cataracts, then line breeding increases the chances that similarly heterozygous dogs will breed and produce unlucky pups. Line breeding is a common practice in the purebred dog world, as it is in any domestic species, because it maintains the distinctive and valuable traits valued in a breed. But this selective breeding can lead to hereditary problems, especially if a recessive allele doesn't kill its carrier quickly. Nonlethal but dangerous traits can remain in the gene pool and be expressed when relatives breed. Kenai's parents were unrelated for at least six generations and quite different in form. Her sled dog sire was more line-bred than her show dog dam, but they had no recent ancestors in common, so one would not have expected them to have similar genetics. The chances of them both hiding the recessive allele for cataracts was small, but because of generations of line breeding to make a Siberian Husky fit its standard, the chances were all too real for us.

After a winter of fostering Buster and Granite, we were attached. Their owner decided to sign over their papers, making us the owners of five dogs with a full schedule of training and fieldwork ahead of us. Because Granite's eyes were healthy, I could start showing her as soon as I felt she was ready. I found myself caught up in the show world and wanted to continue exploring that path. Our summer training could continue, and we would renovate the kennel to make Buster and Granite comfortable for many more seasons.

We had finished our second season of mushing and attained speeds of five to ten miles per hour. It was good to travel fast because we had much to do that winter other than run dogs. Our second season of raven nights was anything but slow.

eight

A Second Winter of Ravens

Ernie, the master of the New Vineyard dump, had been seeing small groups of ten to fifteen ravens each summer weekend as he manned the small shack perched aside the one-acre pit of garbage. It was September 18, 1989. We were retracing familiar routes, checking on roosting and foraging activity while preparing for a second winter of research. The progress of science was often tedious because we needed to confirm our observations. Discovery was exhilarating, in part because it is rare. We were confident in understanding how ravens used attractive sounds, such as begging and yelling, to home toward large animal carcasses. But there were nagging questions, especially about the mechanics of longer-distance recruitment from the roost. Did naïve ravens simply follow knowledgeable birds from the roost? Could naïve birds without roost mates find food? Were there any recruitment signals that we could witness in our aviary? It was these details and a better understanding of how the behavior of roosting and foraging birds varied with the sort of food they exploited that we sought to gain this second winter. We began excited with our past discoveries, comfortable in our new land, and sure confirmation would have a modicum of discovery. Then Ernie's partner emerged from the heap of warm garbage.

I never got the assistant's name. His scarred face and rural beard blended well with the dirty habitat. His clothes might have been scavenged earlier that very day. Bathing was not routine, and this thin man clearly had no time for dentists. He lived a corvine existence, flitting among small jobs, scavenging as needed, communicating and listening for useful information. My talk of ravens intrigued him. I spoke from the academic tower, proudly explaining how we had carefully figured out that the yells and begs of young ravens attracted others to a feast. He interrupted my lecture. Yes, he knew all about this behavior. His Grandpa Dyer taught him how to call ravens decades ago. He cupped his hands around his mouth and belted forth a yell that cleared the green air. The call was a perfect rendition of a raven's yell. Two or three ravens milled about, clearly interested, just as grandpa had said. If I hadn't seen the yeller, I would be looking for the king of all ravens that surely had just bellowed. We had a great chat, and I listened and learned. I can't help thinking that this waif from the New Vineyard dump spread the word at his roost that evening about those clean but somewhat backward scientists spending all their time trying to figure out what any good woodsman already knew. I guess I coaxed the New Englander home wondering the same thing. But secure in knowing that most scientists just quantify the obvious, and hoping that repetition and experimentation would unveil interesting new details and unknown motivations for the ravens' behavior.

7 October 1989; Colleen's Journal: "While I was showing Kenai; John, and Bernd were hosting a pig roast on the hill. Big turnout. I guess no work makes more people want to come."

Through late September and early October the ravens were settling into a familiar roosting routine. Numbers at the Taylor Hill roost varied, and most days the entire group headed east to the dump. Observing at the roost in the evening and morning, Colleen and I confirmed the scattered arrivals and unified departures evident last winter. We saw many marked birds from our previous trapping efforts, so we began to resolve the comings and goings of the birds with more detail. Bernd was coming from Burlington on the first weekend in October and could stay most of the week. This was a time to enjoy the fall colors and friends. We roasted a local "weiner" pig and had a big turnout for the annual raven fest. This time it was all eating and talking, no cage building. With full bellies, we planned a field experiment that would prove how discovery and exploitation of food cause changes in the roost.

I had been piling cow lungs at Donkey Landing, trying to entice ravens near our favorite trap along the Weld Road between our cabin and Bernd's. On October 7 we got a dead moose from Mike Pratt, and the next day I added all but one hindquarter of the beast to the cow lung pile. I built a blind and kept close check on the bonanza as I traveled between our cabin, the aviary, the Taylor Hill roost, and the scattered dumps from Weld to Strong to Wilton. No ravens fed at the moose for the next two days. Twenty or thirty birds that typically fed at the dump occupied the Taylor Hill roost. On October 9, from the observation tree I could see the birds heading into the roost. It seemed warm to be watching birds in the roost (40°F). Clouds doused the sunlight earlier than usual. Suddenly, a group of twenty ravens left the roost heading west toward Mt. Blue. They soared briefly, perhaps just swinging around to another nearby roost. I hoped they were moving closer to the moose. I saw a tagged bird, either G23 or a left-winged white-tagged one. I couldn't be sure. A few returned shortly, and I climbed down to the truck, guessing that only five birds slept in the roost that night.

At 6:00 a.m. the next morning a few birds flew from the direction of the roost to the New Vineyard dump, where I waited. From Ernie's shack I saw them briefly scold a singing coyote. I identified a few of our tagged birds, and the number of ravens at the dump slowly grew to thirty, along with ten to fifteen crows. Maybe those I saw leave the roost last night had snuck back or didn't really go that far. I guessed they hadn't gone to the moose. But at 9:30, as I crested the height of the land and rolled past Donkey Landing, I saw a crowd of ravens. I eased into the spruce and fir blind to see twenty or more birds feeding. They were busy with the moose all day, and at least one sported a red wing tag that I glimpsed as it crossed the highway. Over forty feasted the next day, including three red-, one white-, and one yellow-tagged bird. They seemed oblivious to my excitement in the blind. One landed on the log supporting my cover, not twenty inches from my face. It seemed to look right at me and trilled, crane-like and aggressive, but did not spook. The lure of moose was strong. Bernd and I decided the feast would also be erratic.

Our plan was to keep the moose, the roost, and the dump under constant observation, counting ravens and identifying tagged birds. As we watched, we would challenge the ravens by alternately concealing and revealing the moose. We expected the birds would respond to the loss of the moose by returning to the roost and there use knowledgeable birds to find either a new carcass or reliable garbage. A large, blue plastic tarp was the only sophisticated tool we needed.

More than forty ravens were devouring the moose on October 11. They had descended from a roost new to us, just across Alder Brook, within earshot of the carcass. Bernd, high atop a tree by his cabin, saw no birds from Taylor Hill come to the feast this morning. Only five roosted on Taylor Hill that night; the foraging gang was ensconced in a bivouac far from Taylor Hill. After dark, we trekked to the moose, wrapped it burrito-style in the blue tarp, and secured the tarp with a bit of brush. At 6:18 the next morning the black masses arrived, but finding no moose, they quickly scattered. Only a few ravens drifted by all day, even those who had made meaty caches in the forest did not seem inclined to seek them.

For the next two days, no ravens visited the moose site, but up to fifty waded among the garbage at the New Vineyard dump. The numbers roosting on Taylor Hill also swelled: thirty on October 12 and thirty-five on October 13. The group on October 12 soared widely above the roost—to the west, the north, and back to the usual grove of conifers. Imagine my delight when I peered through the waning daylight toward the roost and saw the last of the sun's rays flash off a red tag we had put on a raven's wing. Several tagged birds were at the dump, including R131, whom we saw the day before at the moose. This juvenile, small and with a scraped beak and head when we tagged it last April, had more than repaid our efforts; we could confirm our suspicion without a doubt—the foragers from the moose had returned to the roost and nearby dump because a more distant feeding opportunity had been lost. Our experiment also seems to have worked; faced with a loss of food, the ravens returned to a traditional roost and advertised this change in roosting location with conspicuous soaring.

As fifty ravens sifted through garbage, we uncovered the moose on October 14. Immediately, ten birds were in the vicinity yelling loudly but unable or unwilling to feed. These birds apparently did not commute back to the traditional roost. At Taylor Hill that evening the scene was bare. Only six ravens roosted. It seemed the word got out before the birds joined the roost, but we saw no obvious roost near the moose either. Where were they? Apparently nearby: a large hungry crowd dropped in to the moose early on the morning of the fifteeth. Twenty-five or more were in the area, including three that Bernd saw with red wing tags. I climbed the tree atop Taylor Hill that night and marveled as the setting sun washed the golden-leaved hills in purple. A glowing, red, full moon rose. I counted only five ravens. On the sixteenth Bernd headed back to Vermont, and Colleen took over in the moose blind. She confirmed that R131 had returned, having completed a round-trip. The moose bivouac roost was again full, but this night there were also many ravens at Taylor Hill. And they soared, some obviously arriving from the direction of the moose and departing again. Ten remained at Taylor Hill—maybe these were dump addicts or super wimps unwilling to follow the others to compete over a dwindling moose? We covered the moose again mid-morning on October 17. The ravens scattered, and at least fifty roosted in three separate groves on Taylor Hill that night. None soared. All went to the dump the next morning, the most I had ever seen amidst the trash. Fresh snow, like powdered sugar, coated their treasure and softened my view. We completed our experiment by uncovering the moose a final time on October 19. At this time, the trapped warm air and confining tarp had beaten the moose. Most of what remained wiggled. Soon this moose, now transformed into maggots, would itself be capable of flight. We added cow lungs to the decaying moose and again attracted ravens away from Taylor Hill. Only one or two roosted this night—most likely the resident pair.

Our simple experiment taught us much: soaring at the roost plays a role in coordinating recruitment. But questions remained about the timing and function of the soaring displays. Clearly, many ravens return to traditional roosts like the one atop Taylor Hill, when rich but ephemeral foods are exhausted. And they just as clearly leave these traditional roosts to bivouac near distant discoveries. Soaring seems to advertise or coordinate these roost shifts, but it can happen at the departure from or return to the traditional roost. We had to watch more.[1]

We had no way of knowing the identity and foraging history of each bird in a roost, yet to support the idea that roosts serve in part as "information centers" we had to clearly demonstrate that a specific raven learned about food by joining a roost. To test this notion directly, we devised simple field experiments that used the ravens we had caught, tagged, and released. Our aviary had been attracting small groups of ravens, which we had succeeded in catching a few at a time—just the right ingredient for experiments. We fashioned a small blind alley of chicken wire, like a cattle chute into a corral, along the aviary's right arm. Wild ravens attracted to our captive birds drifted into this dead end, and if we bull-rushed them from Bernd's cabin they simply went deeper into the dead end. Breathless, we only had to block the entrance, reach in, and pull out our ebony prizes. What a nice bonus as we traveled up and down York Hill to feed or observe the aviary flock!

On October 18 there were seven to ten wild birds visiting the aviary, and I managed to corral two in the drift trap. Colleen and I measured and marked them, NV-A and NV-B. We kept them calm in pet carriers during the day and flipped a coin to determine their fate. NV-A won the toss and was going to be released into the Taylor Hill roost that night. NV-B spent the night in the dog crate and was going to be released the next morning at the dump. Together, they tested two simple hypotheses. NV-A would test the notion that a naïve bird finds food by following knowledgeable roost mates: a central tenet of the information center idea. NV-B would show us if a bird finding food on its own can join the feast, or if freeloaders that have not participated in the roost are somehow recognized and shunned. This would help us understand the importance of reciprocity.

The trees on Taylor Hill were coated in ice and snow as I struggled up my sentinel pine, NV-A in tow. At 5:15, perched atop the tree, I could hear ravens grumbling in the roost grove. I pulled NV-A from my pack and set him free at 5:25. He flew directly to the roost, kawing three times as he flapped. He landed in the conifers, and I saw him yell ten times. The roost was noisy! Birds were flying about, switching among the three groves we'd seen them using during our tarped moose experiments. I slid down the icy pine at 6:25, estimating a total of fifty birds, including NV-A, were in the roost. I expected them to descend on the New Vineyard dump in the morning.

NV-B and I arrived at the dark, cold refuse pit just after 6:00 a.m. Ravens began arriving from the roost at 6:28. The first twenty-five birds were on the ground feeding by 6:42 and clearly visible. None sported tags. NV-A certainly did not lead to the dump, but did he follow? I scanned, waited, and hoped. I was emotionally overinvested in these experiments—their outcomes were crucial tests of our knowledge. I ran over the reasons why this experiment wouldn't work. Why would a bird captured, tagged, hauled, packed, and plopped out into a new location do anything approaching normal behavior? But he had naturally joined the roost, despite our insults. He was of moderate size—a survivor. In my mind, I was convinced he would follow his roost mates to food. It had to work! And then at 7:05 I saw him. Clear as gin, he had followed others to the dump and now pulled at a lung scrap I'd seeded into the garbage. Like the other pink-mouths in the group, he was attacked by a strutting, dominant black-mouth. But he was there. Hypothesis 1—confirmed!

My companion in the shack was getting restless. At 7:10 I snuck the diminutive, and therefore likely female, NV-B out the door, and she joined the others in the dump without hesitation. She was ignored by the busy birds. As the group ate, I recorded interactions: NV-A displaced NV-B three times in just a few minutes, as expected given their size, and likely gender, differences. There were no lasting friendships in this society. Each raven was on his or her own, yet as our release experiments had demonstrated, they collectively supported one another, even if only by passive toleration and mutual attraction.

On October 22 and 23, we replicated the release experiments with NV-C and NV-D. Confirmation! A bird that joined the roost found food the next day, and even those not in the roost could join a feast. But what if we let a bird go at a location away from the roost and the dump? As it got dark on October 24, we released NV-H alone, two miles north of the dump along Route 27; similarly, we released NV-E two miles east of the dump up the Anson Road. These birds were whoppers: pink-mouthed juveniles but among the largest we'd caught. Males, I reasoned. At the dump the next morning I enjoyed seeing NV-C, NV-D, NV-B, and five other tagged birds in a group of fifty exploiting the trash. Neither loner had found the dump. Without roost mates to follow, or foraging birds to parasitize, a single raven remained alone. A few hours later I observed NV-H where I had released him. He had not found the bonanza at the dump. He was either not motivated to search alone, unsure where he was, or ignorant about the nearby feast. Either way, the benefits of joining a roost were clear. The power of a simple experiment, under field conditions, was equally clear. Excited, I headed home to tell Colleen the good news and to catch more drifters.

For the next three days, we saw neither NV-H nor NV-E at the dump. But as expected, NV-I, released into the roost on October 27, arrived at the dump with about fifteen others the next morning. NV-K did likewise. NV-L, released alone 1.7 miles from the dump, was a no-show. And so it went, through twenty-nine releases scattered among the second winter of field and aviary research. In total, all fourteen naïve ravens released at the roost used the group to find food, up to six or more kilometers distant—quite a benefit of communal roosting. Only four of fifteen released alone found the feeding group the next day. And despite being released within two kilometers of a reliable food source, for example, a dump, only two more found their way to the riches within two days.[2]

Watching roosts and dumps was providing answers to some of our puzzles. Most important, it appeared that the locations of profitable feeding opportunities were freely shared among mixes of birds that happened to spend the night together. But the more we watched, the more we also questioned. When did individual ravens decide to leave one feast in search for another? What motivated them to do so? When did they return to traditional roosts to seek recruits or necessary knowledge? We planned to tackle these questions in the aviary and field using old approaches and new technologies. But first we needed room. The main aviary was full of our original juvenile flock, our home aviary held the summer's hand-raised babies: something had to give. We were ready to release the gang from the main aviary, but we needed to determine each juvenile's gender. We had strong guesses from a year of intense personal observation. We had to be certain of their sex so that we could relate this important moniker to the other data we had collected on individual status, size, foraging rate, and associations with other ravens. Surely our top ravens were males. And RYR must be a female. Birds of intermediate status might include both sexes. We had to be sure.

We knew from others' works that male ravens tended to be larger than females, with especially stout beaks and exaggerated throat plumes, but these features weren't absolute. To be certain, we had to perform a delicate operation, known as a laporotomy, on each living bird. Bernd and I could carve a cow with a pocketknife, but slicing the paper-thin skin of a raven with a scalpel and peering into the heaving chest of a live bird for a glimpse of its gonads wasn't our strong point. My surgeon brother sent supplies: scalpel, rib spreader, and a lighted ear scope that would brighten the inside belly of a raven. We had done our homework, and we were prepared.

We started with a dead bird and pictures of bird innards. The books contrasted male testes, small white pea-like structures, with female ovaries, which were indistinct, granular organs. Males had a pair of testes, one on the right side and one on the left. Ovaries were only on the left, a neat adaptation to reduce weight and better enable flight. Both organs were nestled against the posterior end of the kidney. We thawed a frozen raven, found dead years earlier. Simulating our impending operation, we cut between its ribs and peered inward. It was like looking into a roiling volcano. Organs, tissues, bone, and cartilage glistened. We saw vivid red lung, drab intestine, magenta kidney. But no gonads. We opened the entire chest, as a medical examiner might do to conduct an autopsy. No gonads were evident. Perhaps the bird was not fresh enough, or as a nonbreeder its sex organs might be regressed. Needing another specimen, we grabbed Bernd's .22 rifle and headed to the New Vineyard dump. It was hard to pull the trigger in a place and on animals we knew well, but scientific progress has costs. The ravens we had held so long in captivity would contribute less to interested scientists and citizens unless we could accomplish a laporotomy and determine their sex. We did not want to diminish what the ravens had already sacrificed. A raven fell at the report of Bernd's shot, and I rushed to get it. A good shot, but he hit it right in the 'nads. We saw nothing in the splintered bone and ragged flesh. Our confidence waning, we decided to work with two live, newly captured ravens that drifted into the main aviary corral. We prepared scalpels, lights, and anesthesia—and found out why neither of us had considered a career in medicine.

Anethesizing the bird was effective. A ketamine-soaked cotton ball dropped into a box with the patient did the trick. Cutting into the heaving chest, we spread the ribs and came face to face with cellophane. At least that is what the bird's air sac (part of standard avian respiratory system) looked like. We didn't think we should puncture the sac. Peering, poking, we saw a blurry lung, kidney, and blood. The tiny hole in the raven's chest afforded only a glimpse. And each breath seemed to reshuffle the view. There, perhaps that was a testis. We imagined but were unsure. Frustrated and afraid for the patient's health, we pulled out and closed the wound. No stitches were needed. No antibiotic. Resilient, the bird survived without incident.

We studied more and asked others for advice. The procedure, we were told, is routine. Just practice and you'll be fine. We tried again on our surviving patient. Again, we thought we saw testes. His survival increased our surgical confidence, but our inability to confirm gender was frustrating. We needed hands-on instruction.

Patty Parker Rabenold was collaborating with us to determine the kinship of sharing ravens from the DNA in blood samples we had taken from each captured bird. During her studies of social scavenging in Black Vultures, she had done hundreds of laporotomies on wild birds. She would be glad to come out and help, but being a busy professor and mother of two, she wouldn't be free until the end of the semester. It was early October. December seemed years away, but we were grateful and happy to wait for real expertise. We would split time between detailing the social dramas of the birds in the aviary and those in the wild. We'd placed a buck deer and bear up by New Vineyard, dropped a dead cow by the trap on the Weld Road, and discovered a trapper's coyote lure while sledding the dogs along the base of Tumbledown Mountain. The cow started to attract a crowd.

For the first two weeks at the cow, only a few juveniles, begging and cowering, dodged the aggressive Hills Pond pair. Each day we checked. We found twenty or more at the dump, but only two or three begging at the cow.

The weather was unseasonably warm, 60°F and calm, at the roost on Halloween. Three days later, heavy snow was falling, and the ravens soared from Taylor Hill to the deer and bear a few miles away. Twenty to forty birds devoured these snacks in a week. I saw tagged juveniles and adults at the bear. On November 9 they were soaked by the wet snow. Two landed on my crude blind, and I could feel their heft sag the fir branches onto my back. As this feast was consumed, the roost numbers grew, as expected. We kept vigil at the roost, dump, and several carcasses. Colleen watched the trapper's bait. Billy was at the cow. I had the bear and roost. Bernd watched morning arrivals from York Hill and rotated in and out of the cow blind. He had also brought help. Rick Knight, a professor and raven specialist from Colorado State University, was visiting our field site. Rick loved the blind, but only a few ravens entertained him this morning. The real show was a few days away.

The wind picked up November 12, and I hung on, as sailor atop a mast, as my roost observation tree bucked and wheeled in the raging snow. The ravens soared the next night and flew westward. To the cow? You bet! The bear and deer were abandoned. Only thirteen were at the dump. But as I crossed Alder Brook, I saw fifteen to twenty flanking the cow. Taylor Hill was quiet, and the bivouacs again formed around York Hill, near the cow, just as they did a month earlier in response to the moose. R131 returned from New Vineyard. Twelve days later, the crowds peaked as fifty or more feasted at the cow. My eyelashes were frosted shut by the −9°F temperature.

As hundreds of ravens scoured the Maine woods for cows, deer, moose, the offal and bait from hunters and trappers, garbage, and nearly anything else that didn't move, they confirmed and refined our insights from last year and those made previously by Bernd. Territorial ravens or a few vagrant juveniles are the discoverers. Small groups of 10 or fewer, usually only 3 to 5, vagrants beg from defensive adults, thereby assembling a small party over a few days at any new discovery. Recruitment from roosts swell the foraging party two- to fourfold, and the sounds of begging and defending transition to periodic fighting and chasing. Feeding rates of juveniles soar as everyone scrambles to get their fill. Group size continues to increase until 40, 60, or even 100 ravens swarm the carcass. This November, we estimated our cow was fed on by 120 ravens; once feasting began, it took only a month to reduce the huge dairy cow to scattered bones.

With our aviaries full, we trapped, tagged, released, and watched ravens move from roost to carcass to carcass. Our experimental releases at roosts and dumps, the wild nestlings and tagged birds from past years, as well as eighty newly tagged ravens opened our eyes a bit wider. We could now absolutely confirm the extreme vagrancy of juvenile ravens. Our tagged birds did not stick together as a flock. Instead, they flitted from deer to cow to dump to bear, sometimes within a single day. They moved between bivouac roosts near new foods and traditional roosts atop places like Taylor Hill, just as they did during our covered moose experiments. Soaring at the roost signaled a shift, either to a newly discovered food or a return to the traditional site from a bivouac.

November slid into December. Patty Rabenold led us through the laporotomies. Bernd and I quickly learned we were too timid in our initial internal explorations. We should have probed deeper, toward the intestines, and shamelessly through both sides of the air sac to find the gonads. Patty cut right in and expertly brought the posterior end of kidney into view. There were the small peas we couldn't find. This big bird was a male. The next one had no testis, but a granular ovary. A small female. It took only a day to "lap" all our birds. We'd been caring for six males and fourteen females. Our suspicions were confirmed. The largest birds were males. All six males were dominant. Only two females were dominant; the rest were subordinate or of intermediate status. As we expected, RYR, the partner of the alpha male, was one of the most dominant females. The budding pairs of preening partners were indeed male-female associations. The birds that give rattle and knocking calls were females. Males gave the strange air calls.

The drama of the laporotomies was amplified by a drama unfolding at our cabin. Our weekend with Patty included gathering colleagues for dinner at our cabin. The night before Patty's arrival, I discovered what I assumed was a louse on Topper. Like a good scientist, I collected the critter and took it to the vet the next morning for identification. Dr. Patterson confirmed my suspicion: chewing lice typical of livestock. I supposed that Topper, the carcass king, crawled into the trailer to check his stockpile only to come away with an extra passenger. The vet said I had my work cut out for me: wash all human and dog bedding, sprinkle or spray pesticide on what could not be washed, and vacuum everything. I had to treat any animal or area that had contact with Topper, such as Brodie, Sky, and even Zetta's cats. At the same time Kenai had a vaginal infection that required medication.

I stopped at the hardware store and asked for pesticide. The attendant gave me a funny look—it was a cold December, not bug season—but got me powdered bug killer. Once home, I started washing bedding and spreading the pesticide. I took a break to deliver lunch to the surgeons in the cabin and to fill John in on the new dilemma. When I got home, I found blood-stained snow and chaos. It was apparent that Buster and Topper had been fence fighting, grabbing what they could of each other through the wire wall of the kennel. Usually they only strutted, barked, and postured, but today they upped the ante. Buster had managed to rearrange Topper's nose, the source of the blood. I threw Topper in the truck and prepared to go back to Dr. Patterson, but a quick check on Buster revealed only an empty kennel. I had forgotten to lock the gate, and both Buster and Granite were gone. Frantic, I banged their food bowls together, and like Pavlov's proverbial dog, they came running. I made sure the kennel was locked and headed to town. Ten sutures, a few tranquilizers, and some antibiotics later, Topper was discharged and would be okay.

Hilary and Josh helped me finish up pest eradication. We changed all the kennel straw, applying liberal amounts of pesticide (only powder worked in the freezing temperatures). Finally, the job was done, and just in time. The surgical crew arrived for dinner and, exhausted, we all shared our zoological tales.

It was with great relief that we began to discharge our first aviary flock in mid-December. We'd cared for, watched, and learned from them for a year. They had all survived, and now ten waited in burlap bags for a final measurement and release. Colleen and I conducted the final exams. Topper and Sitka watched. Young Kenai seemed especially interested, and when one of the bags leapt off the deck and, powered by an internal raven, zigged and zagged into our front yard, Kenai, instinctively a predator, gave chase. Her prey drive was intact if blurry from her cataracts, and she pounced, fox-like on the bag, killing the raven we knew so well. For us, the loss was personal and devastating. RWB, the raven now limp in our hands, was an individual; its blood would be difficult to scrub from our skin. We could blame only ourselves and learn to keep tighter reins on our growing menagerie. We released the rest of the birds without incident. They appeared in no hurry to disperse and joined with wild birds around York Hill, feasting on the remains of the cow and discovering the trapper's bait later in December. Their social status was stable in the wild; even among new ravens our dominant males and females retained their titles. They joined others traveling to New Vineyard and beyond.

In mid-December 1989 temperatures stayed below zero. The ravens cared not, but our stints in the uninsulated blinds shortened out of necessity. Throughout this second winter we demonstrated the consequences of status and how this tempered the benefits of flocking for vagrant ravens. At large carcasses, such as the cow, dominant and subordinate ravens benefited from increased feeding opportunity as group sizes increased from one to thirty birds. This increase occurred because adult defense and juvenile neophobia, the fear of new situations, both declined. As group sizes swelled beyond thirty, foraging rates declined as competition among the many juveniles for limited places at the carcass increased. The increase in group size beyond thirty—often to a hundred or more—at a large animal like a cow or moose was costly to those ravens already at the feast. Their feeding rates dropped, but group size continued to increase, because from an outsider's perspective it was still better to join a big group than to venture alone in search of a new, and likely defended, carcass. Selfish ravens joined the feast, and those at the feast suffered competition. The existing flock did not cooperate to keep intruders away and optimize group size because flocks were not of stable membership. A flock member at the cow today might be a latecomer at a bear next week. If she excludes at the cow, she would be excluded at the bear. Ravens at a feast live by the Golden Rule. Those who are not at a feast do what is best for themselves. They control the group dynamic with their decisions. While ravens appear to cooperate—groups of vagrants collectively win access to defended food and soar to attract roost mates to a feast—much of what we observed was the collective sum of competitive, individual, selfish decision-making. Small groups formed at carcasses as searchers orient to the submissive begs of vagrant discoverers. Roost mates were recruited to soaring displays, perhaps actively by vagrants unable to access food, but also as selfish individuals naïve to the location of food parasitized this public information. Groups grew large because of selfish decisions by ravens outside the group.

It is very common for animals to live in groups that are larger than expected based on simple economics. Wolves, for example, achieve their greatest per capita feeding rates in packs of only two animals, yet routinely they live in packs of ten, twelve, or more. Wolves control who joins the pack, so they should, more than ravens, be able to keep numbers low and closer to the optimum. That they do not may reflect the high degree of relatedness among pack members. Certainly ineffective young hunters should be allowed to remain with their parents in a pack—this extension of parental care boosts the parents' fitness by increasing their pups' survival even if it costs some meat. This kin benefit would not apply to ravens; our analysis of their DNA shows that few ravens that share a moose also share genes. It turns out that the benefit to kin of pack-living wolves also is minimal. Kin benefits cannot explain prolonged tenure in the parental pack. It seems that wolves live in large packs because by doing so they lose less meat to other scavengers—most notably to ravens. It is better to share with other wolves, including capable relatives, than to share with ravens. Considering ravens helps us understand wolf pack size, and considering wolves helped us understand raven group size. Because ravens cannot control the entry of others to a feast, group size is controlled by those seeking to join not by those already present. Under this situation ravens, pigeons, finches, and many other animals live in groups larger than an economist might expect.[3]

The consequences of competition are most apparent at the carcasses of small- to medium-sized animals, such as deer and bear. Here dominants enjoy moderate feeding rates regardless of group size. Subordinates, however, are quickly excluded in groups of fifteen or more, and their feeding rates plummet. It is likely that these subordinates will be the first to leave the group and search for new options. Their strategy should be to dine, dash, and discover. A dominant has little to gain by leaving and everything to gain by waiting for subordinates to discover and recruit a small group to the next feast. Unraveling the influence of social status on exploration, discovery, and recruitment forced us back to the aviary and suggested new field experiments that required us to try our own wings.[4]

29 December 1989; Colleen's Journal: "A weasel got two ravens on the hill."

Our aviaries were never empty. In early December, weeks before we started freeing our original captive flock, we had begun to prepare their replacements. In the peripheral aviary of Raven Haven, the cage at the end of the long, left tunnel that was not occupied by our defensive adults, were eight newly captured, blue-tagged juveniles. Colleen and I observed them each morning, scoring their dominance. In a few weeks we had an accurate graph of their social relationships. In the adjacent left arm of the main aviary we held our five lowest-ranking original juveniles. We hypothesized that these wimps, now in control of a nice pile of cow lungs, might advance in status in the company of new "recruits." To simulate recruitment to the lungs, we simply had to open the door that sequestered the blue-tags and observe their interactions with the wimps. Knowing the history of arrival and prior status of each raven allowed us to detail the social dynamic that we could only glimpse in the wild. This would test one phase of our overall hypothesis concerning subordinate ravens that, we reasoned, should dine, dash, and discover new foods. We wanted to know if dashing to make a new discovery could improve one's status. The wimps would quickly tell us.

We often came face to breathless face with Maine's impressive bevy of native predators. Every black bear excited us. We spent many days with short-tailed weasels in our blinds. Fisher, coyotes, and cats dined on our baits, often within a few bounds of our blind. One day we learned why many farmers support predator control: two of the blue-tagged ravens lay dead beneath their roost. Their skulls were gnawed open and their brains mostly gone. The small tracks in the crimson snow belied a weasel's rampage. We were edgy and feared future raids by the deadly mustelid, but fortunately as our experiments progressed and fewer birds were on the hill, no more were killed. We remained strong advocates for native predators, but we had now some inkling of the stockman's hatred of the wolf.

On January 2, 1990, we opened the door separating the blues and the wimps. It was quiet for an hour and a half, and then all hell broke loose. GYG, a wimp, flew into the blues' aviary with her ears up and pants down. She trilled and for all the world looked like a territorial adult. She attacked B55 and the fight was on. Only a few feathers flew, but aggressive trilling, chasing, posturing, and poking showed us clearly that every blue bird ranked below every one of our former subordinates. The magic of priority and the advantage of leaving one group and founding another hit us in the face. Being first at a new food bonanza, which we had rigged for our wimps, elevated the status of even the lowest, lowly vagrant raven. It could pay to dine and dash.

High status is not easy to maintain. The next day we added B71, a juvenile of average size that we assumed was a female, to the mix of wimps and blues. She took over the group, never backing down. It appears that the heightened social advantage that a subordinate might attain by moving can be adjusted as new, truly dominant vagrants find the new feast and join the party. Two weeks later we confirmed this by adding another known dominant, one of our hand-raised babies. Y1 rocketed to the alpha position. We kept mixing new members into the group, and while some ascended the hierarchy and others did not, the response to a newcomer was always the same: social upheaval. Vocal trill duels and postural displays were immediate as the newcomer was challenged by the highest-ranking ravens in residence. Because of this, most interactions in the group occurred shortly after we added a new bird, and they were between that bird and those already present. On February 2, for instance, we recorded fifty-seven interactions in standard, random scans of our flock. Forty were between newly arriving birds and established group members. The remainder of the interactions occurred either among the new arrivals or among the ravens who had long resided in the aviary.

Staking one's position on the social ladder is the first business when a recruit arrives. Even familiar birds must reestablish their positions when they change location. On February 8, we captured seven birds from a wild feeding group of about twenty-five. When transported to the aviary and allowed access to a new food, they immediately trilled and scrapped—setting the new hierarchy—before feeding. A new situation meant new opportunity. With each mixing or adding of new recruits, we saw the same dance. The new recruits had to fight their way into the hierarchy. Apparently the importance of status

Y4, a hand-reared fledgling, in a dominant, territorial or courting posture that accompanied "air calling" (bowing and spreading of the wings with soft clucking and choking noises). The object of the display has taken a submissive, fuzzy-headed posture.

display has favored the evolution of unique calls, such as the crane-like trill, and postures, like the erection of head and thigh feathers, in ravens. Each individual carries these signals at all times but shows them only when challenged. Like good poker players, ravens do not show their cards until called.

The ability to change one's relative status within a group, even if short-lived, would seem a powerful motivator of the comings and goings we glimpsed in the wild. Because all ravens are not socially equal, and because social status is not simply a property of an individual but is a joint product of an individual and a given place, a raven flock is forced into constant turmoil. Individuals acting in their own best interests must dash when they are subordinate and crash a good party when they are dominant. High status may be less malleable than low status—it can be backed up with a strong peck or chase if needed. In this way, perhaps older and larger juveniles are always dominant to the fresh-man class just a few months out of the nest. But the place-bound, contingent nature of low status means that vagrant groups of ravens should never be stable—subordinates have little to lose and much to gain by reshuffling the deck.

We worked out the pattern of priority and status over three months with three groups of captive juveniles. We also watched each new group respond to recruits in times of need and at times when recruits were simply competitors. When we added recruits to small groups unable to access food from our territorial adults—groups in need of assistance—nothing special happened. Such recruits were treated just like others in the group. They were trilled at, chased, and forced to show their social status first. They were welcome to join the group, but only after demonstrating their place in the social hierarchy. As we made the groups larger, they were able to overpower adults and gain access to defended foods. Recruits helped, but we saw no active recruitment of group members. We simply confirmed what our first flock had taught us. Dominant juveniles were usually the first birds to venture into the adult aviary when no other feeding options were available. They were attacked relentlessly by the adults until the dominant juveniles cowered and begged. In response to the commotion, other juveniles swarmed in to the adult territory, which eased the adult attack and enabled all to eat. We could see no unique recruitment call in the aviary, though it seemed one would be so efficient and useful—and it could so easily be uttered by the verbose raven. But at the scale of our aviary, they would also have been redundant with the highly attractive, albeit differently motivated, begs. Perhaps the aviary was just too small to study long-distance recruitment. Or maybe the collective actions of selfish ravens appeared only as coordinated cooperation. We were making progress, but the conundrum of deciphering the selfish from the cooperative remained.

The aviary was ideally suited to study group dynamics. What about kin-ship? Might siblings team up to recruit or help one another? We rotated our hand-raised siblings in and out of groups of wild-caught juveniles to test this idea. On February 27, we let R92 into the aviary that held two of his sibs and twelve others. Those fourteen had already settled their relationships, so when R92 was introduced he got a lot of attention: thirty interactions in the first hour, nearly half of which found him on the losing end of a scuffle with a sibling. No brotherly love among these ravens.

The turmoil we now understood from the aviary groups explained what we often saw when wild birds approached the aviary. Outsiders attempted to gain access to the food enjoyed by those within, setting off trilling and displaying by the dominant juveniles in the group directed at those outside the cage. A dominant always plays its ace. It faces each challenge with its best display. Each arrival of a new bird at a feast sets off a rigid chain of display, and the ensuing turmoil makes watching ravens day in and day out fascinating. It is ever-changing as new scores must be settled. And while dominant ravens strut, subordinate ravens rush in to eat and eventually decide whether to dine or dash.

Throughout April and May we focused on the raven's dilemma—to stay at a known food or leave in search of the next. All we needed was a small carcass and patience. A dairy calf and a few hours each morning in the hut, after our rounds at the dump, trap, or carcasses in the field, would do perfectly. I put the calf in with the juveniles and watched. They ate, mostly with manners dictated by the social hierarchy—dominants first and at the choice openings, subordinates dashing in taking the scraps, milling around the edges. Each day I put the calf in, watched, and then removed it. After nine days, when the calf was mostly skin and bone, I put a fresh pile of cow lungs in the far, undefended aviary, out of sight but available to an explorer. When I put the calf in on the tenth day, I opened the arm to the left aviary and wondered who would be first to leave the calf and chance upon the lungs. None did. As two birds were cautiously easing down the arm, a juvenile goshawk rushed the aviary and sent all the juveniles clucking in alarm for the safety of their roosting

Colleen (foreground right) and the extended family gather for an Easter feast at
Henry (head of table) and Lee's home.

shed. The risk of venturing off alone was real, and the innate alarm calls of
young ravens were equally effective. Safety in numbers was another benefit of
group foraging. As I returned to the aviary the following day, April 8, I could
hear the birds yelling. They were hungry. And motivated to explore, I hoped.
Lee's Easter feast was later that afternoon and that was one feeding bonanza I
didn't want to miss. I returned their calf and watched. The dominants worked
deeply into the bony carcass. They had been the only birds to get much of
anything to eat in the last few days. The subordinates yelled plaintively.
Finally, three subordinates and one of our hand-raised babies of intermediate
status wandered into the aviary arm and toward the lungs. Again the goshawk
rushed from outside the cage, and the birds flushed. But hunger was a strong
motivator, and they finally got to the food. They did not call in the others, but

as they flew about with bloody hunks of lungs, the others chased, followed, and found the new bonanza. I headed off to Lee and Henry's before I would have to chase Butch, Billy, and Tom for ham and pie.

The same story unfolded in the next group of eleven juveniles captured in mid-April. We learned that dominant ravens have more on their mind than accessing food at a feast. Again, the dominant was the last to switch from calf to lung, but for good reason. He had a partner, another motivation to challenge newcomers and join a feast. Although our research revolved around decisions faced by ravens as they sought food, a group served many purposes from protection to mate acquisition. We had to try to understand each if we were to fully understand group life.

When the thawing rain washed away our second winter at the aviary, we had run thirty-seven new ravens through a series of experiments. They showed us how important social status is around a carcass. Status is paramount to a raven because it determines how much food one gets and in turn how long one stays at a feast. Social inequity and the potential of improving status by discovering new foods keep a raven party in flux. Displaying status supplies much of the noise that defines and attracts others to a bonanza. And display has multiple functions, among them wooing partners and intimidating rivals. Ravens at a carcass are on stage, serious participants with complex themes that make the show curious and interesting to watch. Just like many of our own gatherings.

We moved through the second winter of research with a blend of field and aviary investigation. Our field efforts were often driven by the need to fill the aviary. But as we moved flocks of juveniles in and out of the aviary, we also found our aviary efforts driving a new set of field experiments (see appendix 1 for a schematic of the timing and composition of the aviary and field experiments). Could we learn more about long-distance recruitment by following ravens after they finished their stints in the aviary? Newly available radio tags could help in that effort. When we set each bird free, we could add a radio tag

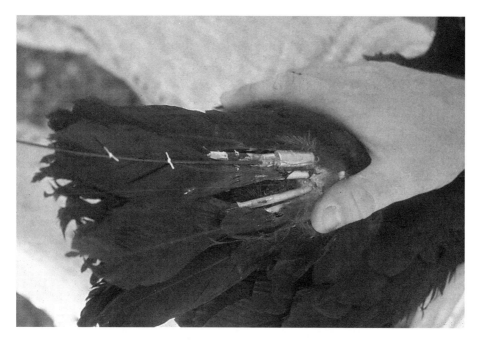

A radio transmitter (silver canister) affixed to the tail feather of a young raven. The antenna is tied using dental floss to the feather shaft for stability.

enabling us to track it from carcass to roost. What might happen if we released it directly at a new carcass? Would it eat? Would it share? Might it join a roost and recruit others? We were unable to resolve these questions in the confines of the aviary, so we gave it a try in the nearby forests.

January 4, 1990, seemed balmy: 40°F. I was sweating from dragging a fresh deer up Cherry Hill Road. My heart raced as I looked at B70, in Kenai's puppy crate just beside the deer. I hid the crate with a light covering of spruce and fir boughs, crawled into a quickly cobbled blind, and grabbed the clothesline I had attached to the crate's wire door. I paused and gave B70 thirty minutes to adjust. It was late afternoon when I tugged the line, squeaking open the door. The raven preened, then pounded the side of the cage and walked out as though he owned the joint. He sidled right up to the deer and began to eat. I had kept him on limited rations for the previous two days, and he was now gorging and caching. I watched the sky, listened for other ravens, and hoped the concealed cage, my presence, and previous experience would not cause my anointed discoverer to lose confidence and fly wildly into the forest's shadows. Twenty minutes of freedom was met with raspy kaws right above me. The Hills Pond pair? A single bird joined B70; silent and without a fight it disappeared. Perhaps the camouflaged crate bought my friend a bit of time. Drizzles of rain froze to the snow cover and encrusted the trees. All was quiet as I slid from the blind at 4:10. My radio receiver picked up a signal from B70, roosting just up Cherry Hill. Alone. Quiet. Selfish.

The first experiment was set. I knew only B70 and the territorial pair of ravens had discovered my deer. Before B70 left our aviary, Colleen and I tied an aluminum cylinder holding a small radio transmitter, or "tag," to his central tail feathers. The transmitter seemed big on the young bird. It weighed over thirty grams or 3 percent of B70's weight. A black wire antenna extended from the tag about a foot. We mounted the canister near the raven's body and stitched the antenna to one tail feather, allowing the wire to extend a few inches beyond the tail. B70 paid no attention to this contraption. To us it was a godsend—we could know where B70 was anytime we pulled out our receiver and dialed in his tail frequency.

I was back in the blind at 6:15 the next morning. Seven minutes later, I heard calls from a nearby raven that sounded like two short rapid knocks. I knew this was the territorial female. She flew in to perch right above the deer. W52, her mate, joined her minutes later. They hesitated, dancing between ground and tree. All three of us could smell the deer. I held my breath as the pair settled in to eat. At 7:50, B70 flew from his roost to reclaim his prize. Predictably, W52 attacked, causing B70 to cower and beg. Despite the defense, the juvenile snuck a few mouthfuls of wine-red deer. In the next hour, another juvenile edged in, apparently attracted to the sounds of begging and chasing. This bold bird was trilling, trying to exert its dominance. Immediately it begged as W52 exerted himself. Both juveniles were chased by the adults. The newcomer challenged B70 with loud trills and quickly learned its place in the stretching social fabric. B70 attacked and dominated. The discoverer was the top juvenile at this deer. Despite the abundance of machismo all four birds were able to eat this morning, and by 10:00 I could sneak away undetected by the satiated group.

I checked from a safe distance every hour, gloating on how complete my knowledge of the scene was. It was a perfect test: I had defensive adults, a known discoverer whom I could follow, and already one recruit attracted from the local area by the fighting, chasing, and begging calls exchanged between discoverer and defenders. All I had to do was wait, check my radio signals, track B70 to the roost, and watch him recruit his army. Tomorrow was going to be grand.

I was horrified to hear snowmobiles at 2:15. It was the Mosher family ferrying supplies to their cabin, two miles up Cherry Hill Road. They had not been there all winter, and now they parked two trucks on the road near the deer and disappeared for the rest of the day. I hoped the disturbance would not spoil my experiment. The environment beyond the aviary was unpredictable. B70 abandoned the deer and roosted alone, several miles away, nearly in Weld.

The deer remained unused, and B70 continued to roost alone between Hills Pond, Donkey Landing, and Weld. The snowmobilers departed, but the deer seemed forgotten. Frustrated, Colleen and I prepared another radio raven for release at two calves up the Carthage Road. On January 8, I repeated the process of staging the discovery of food by a lucky raven, this time B71. He kawed and attracted a second passing juvenile shortly after stepping out of the crate. They trilled and fought, attracting a third juvenile. The quickly assembled trio scattered, black wings against a coal sky. I appreciated the availability of the radio and used it to track B71 to a large nearby roost. Perfect! Surely he would recruit this roost to the calves tomorrow. But I worried that there was no soaring tonight. Bernd and Colleen confirmed that there had been no unusual roosting activities anywhere in the area.

Bernd had brought his winter ecology class from Vermont to help survey our growing number of tagged birds and known carcasses. We learned little as B70 continued to ignore the deer and feed with a few juveniles at the trap. B71 taught even less. He boogied, leaving us to wonder what he and his roost mates could have found. Damn, two good releases and hope for recruitment from the roost, but nothing! Obviously other factors, for example, human disturbance and perhaps other known foods push and pull ravens in a roost. Each discovered food is not the immediate object of recruitment. But some are; we've seen it, and I'm sure with patience we'll see it again—from the eyes of a radio-tagged bird.

I moved the deer from Cherry Hill a few miles to the Alder Brook Road just above our cabin. The students released a wing-tagged, not radio-tagged, bird at the deer, and we watched the roosts, our other radio-tagged birds, and the known foods. As if to rub salt in our wound of bad luck, we saw ravens soaring above their roost near the trap on the morning of January 13. They descended to the newly positioned deer. We got recruitment from the roost, but without a radio-tag we could not tell what role our discoverer played in the movement. We did learn that B70 was a recruit, because he joined ten to twenty others in a deer feast over the next several days. I wondered if he recognized his old buffet.

I was anxious to locate our second discoverer, B71. Tom, having just earned his private pilot's license, was eager to help. For a few hundred bucks we could rent a plane and search widely and efficiently for our AWOL radio. I was told radio tracking from a plane was great. You just mounted the antenna on the plane's wing strut, ran the coaxial cable from the antenna through the window to your receiver, and listened for the magic beeping radio signal from the copilot's seat. Colleen had experience with this technique in Arizona, tracking her squirrels, and I was game to give it a go. We taped the antenna on the plane, fired up the engine, and banked off into a clear but breezy sky. The H-shaped antenna began vibrating, spinning like an eggbeater in the prop wash. I couldn't hear a thing except engine and static. We landed, remounted, and reboarded. I was a bit overzealous and broke the window handle trying to close it on the coaxial cable, but duct tape solved that problem, just as it solved the antenna mounting issue. Taped in, we reclaimed the sky. We were cruising, and I was listening when I noticed the ends of each of the four antenna elements slowly loosening. Helplessly, I watched one of them break through the tape connector and hurtle to earth. I prayed no ice fisherman was below. We returned to base and left the rest of the flying to the ravens.

24 January 1990; Colleen's Journal: "We got a call early this morning— 4:15 a.m.—from a dispatcher telling us that the game warden would arrive in 15 minutes. Dwight came right on time and told us of a dead cow moose 'up to Carthage.' He'd help John tie her to the truck bumper so he could drag her all the way home without anyone knowing. Afterwards, seeing the drag trail leading up to our driveway, he changed his mind. The old timers, he said, would know."

B89 became our third radio discoverer on January 15. Same story: local recruitment and following others from a roost to a distant, but not our, food. B90 took his turn on January 25. We allowed this lucky raven to find a moose near our trap. A heavy rain seemed to wash him away, and he followed roost mates toward Weld, the opposite direction from the moose. Bernd and I split time between roosts, moose, and following the radio ravens. Both B89 and B90 circulated among the various carcasses we had stashed from Carthage to Alder Brook. Nothing was happening to the moose, but we had the key ingredients well mixed: known roosts, known discoverers, and potential re- cruits, some of which even carried radio tags. We watched and hoped.

Chasing our dreamy field ideas pushed again on our tension with Bernd.

He needed results, and the experiments were slow to yield substance. We were deep in the chase, thrilled by the prospect of a result. His actions during this winter screamed displeasure; he remained aloof but tolerant. His semester break was ending, and he watched the moose for an hour and half on Sunday, January 28, before heading back to Vermont.

Nothing happened at the moose during Bernd's watch. His notes tersely state: "only chickadees." He was well on his way to Burlington when I checked on the moose an hour later. There sat B90 with four other ravens. Did he lead them there, or did he hear others near the moose? We could not know. Thankfully, it mattered little. A small flock assembled around the moose that day. But that night it was different. Ravens were soaring. A group from the east, twenty-two that I could count, circled the area joining the local birds, including B90. A roost of more than thirty formed just south of the moose. B90 was there, and soaring had organized distant groups at a new location. The next morning there were twenty-five ravens all over the moose a few minutes after I climbed into the blind. B90 was one of the first birds out of the roost and on the snow. He played a hand in recruitment; I am not sure he soared last night, but I know that a discoverer at least plays a role in recruitment from a roost. I wished Bernd could have seen it.

My apprentice-mentor relationship with Bernd was especially delicate during this second season as I began to apply for my next job. Certainly this was expected, but the task of searching through journal ads and compiling my application materials was a bit distracting for me. I suspect that the uncertainty of knowing when Colleen and I might leave Maine was trying for Bernd. Most jobs might be postponed until our three-year commitment was done, but for a postdoc, when the right job comes up, you have to think about moving on. That winter I sent my credentials in response to advertisements from New Mexico State University, the University of Montana, Chico State University, the University of Rochester, and the University of Arizona, possibly others I don't recall, and I also submitted several applications to private consulting firms. Bernd had to write a letter of recommendation to support each application. He was eager to put in a good word on my behalf, but it was a distraction for him just the same. It also put a fine point on my need to keep things productive between us; my career literally depended on a good, respectful relationship.

Most universities never responded to my application. Some thanked me for my effort and wished me well elsewhere. But in late February, New Mexico State called wanting to know more. The search committee for their professorship in biology wanted to interview me by phone. That interview went well, and shortly afterward they invited me for a two-day, in-person interview and visit to the campus in Las Cruces. I would compete for the job with two other hopefuls. The job interview was amazing. The location was like going home. I was a westerner, and Las Cruces offered the huge scale and rugged openness that is found only west of the 100th meridian. Colleen was excited at the prospect as it was close, but not too close, to her parents. The teaching assignments and research opportunities dealt entirely with birds and behavior. Chihuahuan Ravens were everywhere and calling for my attention. Everything clicked. I saw that my efforts in Maine were leading to the job Colleen and I wanted. Then a former professor from Montana called to tell me that the University of Montana, my undergraduate alma mater, was also interested in my application. Could I fly to Missoula from Las Cruces before returning to Maine? Hell yeah, I probably wouldn't even need a plane!

Nobody needed to sell me on the merits of a professorship in Montana. This was really my dream job. My reception in the Big Sky Country, however, seemed stiff. Maybe my former professors didn't yet see me as a colleague. Or did they remember my bad habits as an undergraduate a long way from home? During these interviews I met with each faculty member and various student groups and discussed my teaching and research vision in formal and informal settings. I was overly nervous at Montana because many on this faculty had shaped me. But ravens intrigued everyone, and, as in New Mexico, my seminar about our adventure was well received.

The "job seminar" is key to success during the academic interview. A good seminar draws on the discoveries one makes during graduate and postdoctoral research. The feedback I got was that we were doing exactly the right thing—mixing detailed field and lab observations, using new and innovative experiments, and testing new technologies. This combination excited the search committee, potential colleagues, and students. I was sure my postdoc would take Colleen and me beyond the lure of the raven to a real job.

I was anxious when I returned to Maine in early March. I waited for the phone message offering an academic post. I imagined what it would be like to start my own research projects, mentor students, and teach classes. The phone never rang. Finally I had to call the search committees. Others, more advanced and productive in their training, got the New Mexico and Montana jobs. I learned just how intense the competition was for the few jobs in my field. I was dejected and mad. My skin was getting thick as moose hide. For Colleen it was a roller-coaster ride: one day imagining life back in the Southwest and the next thinking of mountains in Montana. She wanted to continue our life in Maine, not just for the ravens but because she had fallen in love with the people and culture. While we had to apply and plan for the future, we were thankful our funding was secure for the next year. The roller coaster leveled quickly; we were too busy with the dogs and ravens to brood for long.

We released three more radio discoverers through March. They all stayed around the food for a few days. Two recruited a small force with local begging. None revealed any roost magic. But we were more determined than ever, and Bernd seemed much more supportive of our combined aviary and field approach.

As we replicated and watched, we learned how variable roosting was in the wild. Our radio-tagged birds used at least ten roosts scattered among the ridges and pine groves between Wilton, Weld, and New Vineyard. Use of a particular location was unpredictable to us. We guessed that birds in a roost might collectively know of several feeding options on many nights. How did they decide which to exploit the following morning? Was there discussion of the options during soaring? We could only wonder and order more radio tags for our final winter's work.

It was late March, and spring was pushing winter away. Rain one day was snow the next. Barred Owls hooted as I followed radio-tagged birds between roosts. Short-tailed weasels and red-backed voles joined me in the blind— predator and prey both trying to survive to breed again. Winter Wrens sang. And on March 25 the pair of wild ravens on Graham's farm carried a stick high into a thick pine. Our attention turned to the breeding season and finding nests. We didn't have to go far. Our captive pair completed renovation of their roosting shed the last week in March. It now held a growing nest. We gave them all the sticks, sheep wool, deer hair, grass, and bark they wanted and settled in to watch how professionals raise baby ravens.

We would be on our own this spring. The years of hauling meat and running marathons had sidelined Bernd. He called in early April to tell us he ruptured a disc in his back, and in his words, "he is stuck horizontal." He needed surgery, and he was glad we could run the project while he recovered. We were all comfortable that the research would roll along. Our nesting pair of adult ravens had guaranteed as much.

nine

Dating and Mating

Living year-round with a mob of ravens drew us into all aspects of their world. Our proposal had been to unravel the mystery of food sharing, and we felt well along toward understanding how aggression and status shaped their winter feeding habits. But as days lengthened and snows receded, our ravens revealed their softer side. February and March are winter in Maine, but the small increases in daylight these months bring are precisely sensed by special receptors in the raven's eye, brain, and pineal gland (a small gland atop a bird's brain that functions as a biological clock pulsing melatonin in concert with the day-night cycle). Unbeknownst to us, these organs were setting forth neural signals from the brain of the raven to its pituitary gland, where hormones were being produced that swelled the testes of the males, stimulated sperm and egg production among the mature birds, and incited a riot of new behaviors, including courtship, nest building, incubation, and parental care. In short, we were looking at a cage full of horny ravens.[1]

We took advantage of these changes to extend the connections we were making between a raven's ability to find food and its chances to survive the vagaries of winter. For an animal to succeed in an evolutionary sense, it must not only survive but also successfully pass its genes to the next generation. A raven has to find scarce foods in snowy forests and also breed successfully and produce offspring that survive. We could better understand what it takes to reproduce successfully by watching our caged ravens choose mates and raise young. And we might further our understanding about why both young and old ravens invest so much time preening one another, strutting, fighting, and showing off around their dinner tables. Could, as Bernd imagined, raven winter feasts function in part as avian singles bars, where unmated birds hooked up? As the reproductive hormones of our ravens surged, we adjusted, watched, and devised new experiments to test this intriguing hypothesis.

23 March 1990; John's Field Notes: "RYR drops in to eat the dead pony, and she seems to have a mate. Yes, it is C1. They allopreen, duet, and stand atop the pony. Their mouths are now black, and they display just as would a territorial pair. They had a strong preening partnership as members of our first captive aviary group only a year ago."

Mate choice has interested biologists for centuries. Darwin wrote a sequel to his *On the Origin of Species,* in which he argued that mate choice was important to animal evolution. He reasoned that competition among males was evaluated by choosy females and the result, which he termed "sexual selection," led to the evolution of bizarre secondary sexual characteristics such as long beetle or antelope horns, fancy fish fins, a rainbow of bird feathers, and punkish crests capping bright monkey faces. He wrote at length about how this force of competition and mate choice complemented or conflicted with natural selection to fashion familiar differences between men and women: our muscles, beards, and attitudes. Since then, thousands of scientists have researched and theorized the ways that hormones, life histories, relatedness, early rearing conditions, prior experience and past performance, physical stature and appearance, and even the marks biologists affix to animals affect the battles among and between the sexes.[2]

Nobody had suggested how sexual tensions might act on ravens or even what cues might influence the process of mate choice. Surely such investigation was possible. Mate choice was often a decision of a lifetime because pairs remained together until one partner died. Selecting a poor mate—one that lays few eggs, cares poorly for offspring, or cannot defend sufficient territory— dooms a raven to evolutionary obscurity. But how do they do it? There are no obvious flashy feather adornments, such as the peacock's tail. Males do not sing or dance to impress females, as do mockingbirds and grouse. It seemed possible that feather sheen (a bruised greenish purple hue that flashes promi- nently from adult ravens in the sun) or the feather hackles that beard a male's neck could cue a potential mate. Maybe the amazing acrobatic chases and flying stunts of a raven serve to advertise skill and prowess. Attributes such as these could reliably indicate the size or health of the owner. In practice, ravens likely use multiple cues to choose a mate because the cost of making the wrong choice is so high. But we focused on a single reliable and assessable cue—one we would use to pick our mate if we were feathered. We began experiments to determine if social status—dominance—affected mate choice.[3]

Young ravens bluff and fight a lot, but we noticed that they also sorted themselves into curious partnerships. Pairs and sometimes trios of birds al- lopreened conspicuously, choosing to sidle close together on the maze of perches available within our aviary. Our laporotomies taught us that preening partners were typically of the opposite sex, so we naturally saw these as budding pair bonds—the lifelong partnership of a mated male and female. Those preening most often were dominant birds—both males and females. My past work with the extremely social Pinyon Jay indicated that corvids seeking a mate could passively advertise their wares through their ordinary, daily social interactions. We reasoned males might do this, while females watched, remembered, and later selected. Active female choice of males is typical in many animals because females usually invest more in reproduction than do males—forming large eggs and nurturing demanding offspring. But because both male and female ravens invest heavily in reproduction—females lay and incubate eggs while males provide food and guard duty—we also thought males might actively choose their partners. We seemed to see these processes working in the aviary. Not every attempt to preen or sit beside another raven was accepted. One bird might rebuke the advance of another with a sharp jab or simple flight away.[4]

We had one problem: our birds seemed to have already made their choices. Immediately upon closing the aviary doors, we saw preening partnerships among our young birds. We could describe the pattern of male-female partnerships, but this told us little about the actual cues used to produce the pattern. Our colleagues who studied mate choice did experiments. They colored their birds, shortened and lengthened their tails, and infested them with parasites. They changed the cues they hypothesized were driving mate choice and then observed pair formation. If tail length was a cue in mate choice, they reasoned, then changing it must affect partnerships. We wanted to know if a male's status affected female choice, and so we would have to manipulate a raven's status.

We knew male status was pliable, so we focused on males rather than females. In fact, we thought that a raven's ability to improve its relative status, even if only temporarily, might motivate the comings and goings around a carcass. Subordinate or moderately ranked birds might leave a carcass to join a smaller group or find a new carcass where they could magically assume the role of dominant. In the aviary, we were amazed at how quickly our second-, third-, fourth-, and fifth-ranked males took on the alpha role when their superiors were held offsite or even just behind a screen door unable to exert their power physically over their minions. In ravens, it seemed that male status was completely set by the social milieu of the moment. Although this situation might reduce the reliability of status as an honest signal of male quality to a female, it certainly seemed to us an important part of the signal and, more important, one we could influence.

In early July, we rounded up the six females in the main aviary and took them down York Hill to our home aviary. While the females lived with us, we set about reorganizing the male hierarchy. We had six males at the time, and we herded the three top-ranked birds (RG, WBr, BrGr) into the isolated aviary at the end of the left arm. The lower-ranking males (Y1, Y4, and Br) remained in the main aviary, where we expected them to assume top status. Y4 quickly did so. After a month of this arrangement, we then gradually introduced the formerly dominant males back into the main aviary. We expected these past kings, now relative newcomers to a group, to drop in status relative to the current residents. BrGr was first to rejoin those he had dominated. He came in on fire, strutting, and seemed to reclaim his alpha position. But the next day, he was clearly below Y4, who shadowed his every move with ears up and pants down. WBr was next, joining the group on August 15. Y4 met him as he entered the main aviary with trills and then attacked. Kicking and biting, the two amped-up birds wrestled wildly. Y4 remained top dog, but fighting was much more common over the next week and WBr seemed not well integrated with the group. The consequences of social turmoil were evident; a less cohesive social group would be vulnerable to predators and other threats. RG, the former alpha male, was returned to the main aviary last, on August 23. Y4 dominated him, forcing submissive begging.

On August 28, the male hierarchy had stabilized, and, as we had planned, it was different than it had been. The original hierarchy had been scuttled. Y4 and Br had risen from mediocrity to top of the heap, while WBr and BrGr had fallen to nearly the last rungs of the social ladder. Before their fall, these males were clearly attractive to the females. They were often preened, and WBr was consistently associated with one of the females, GBG. If the preening partnerships we observed led to mate choice, and if male status influenced this choice, then Y4 and Br should now be much more interesting to the females, and WBr and BrGr should be much less so. On August 29 at 10:30 a.m., we brought back the females, popped a couple of donated hams into the aviary, and settled into the hut to watch the show.

It was an interesting but unexpected performance. At first, the males and females fought as they ate their smoky pork. We did not see any preening among the males and females, but we at least thought the newly established dominance hierarchy among the males should be evident to the females. The former king, RG, who had been demoted only slightly, just below Y4 by our experiment, maintained his partnership with RW. Over the next month, however, he really worked at it, often approaching her to preen, and it was clear she controlled the situation, choosing to either accept the advance or rebuff it with a sharp beak. The former dud, Br, was more attractive to the females after his status rose. In August and September, GBG and he formed a strong partnership and preened as frequently as did RW and RG. The former studs, WBr and BrGr, were now perceived as duds by all the females, only occasionally getting preened and never consistently by one female. Changing dominance did affect some males and some male-female partnerships as we expected. Indeed, it seemed males and females chose whom to preen and whether to allow preening. Female status was important in this respect because dominant females preened with males more than did subordinate females. But nearly two-thirds of all preening we observed in a revised social world were among partners of the same sex. Females that we had housed together often preened each other, even when reintroduced to the males. And the sibling pair of males, Y4 and Br, remained a tight pair, preening and bathing together despite the social upheaval.

Watching the females showed us they assessed the status not only of the males they lived among but also of each other. Only the top-ranked females formed partnerships and regularly preened with males. I had previously interpreted a female's status mostly as a consequence of the males with whom she preened. That interpretation revealed more about my male bias than about ravens. Isolating males and females allowed me to see that females had their own, albeit often overshadowed, hierarchy that determined preening. Increased preening by dominant females may belie older age, greater size, or greater social and mental acuity. Someday we may know, but for the time being I saw the new and subtle importance of females to the goings-on around a meal.

The preening partnerships that so intrigued us may in fact be a stage in the courtship that eventually bonds a male and female raven for life, but they also have immediate benefits. We would be unable to study the long-term possibilities within the confines of the aviary. In the short term, however, we could be sure that partnerships among nonbreeding ravens indicated familiarity, future pair bonds, and foraging alliances. Female choice may encourage brash threat displays among males. And male dominance and choice provide a dividend to dominant females who eat peacefully in the demilitarized zone that surrounds a high-ranking male at prime eating spots around a carcass. This may increase female survival. Preening partnerships indicate the complexity under the chaos one sees when watching a flock of ravens scramble for food.

We supposed that many of the males and females that regularly preened in our aviary groups went on to form pair bonds and obtain territories, but we had no such confirmation. RYR and C1, whom we observed at the pony carcass, certainly seemed to be carving out a territory, but tracking such highly mobile birds throughout a long vagrancy was beyond our means. In fact, what little we knew about pair formation in wild ravens, and it was extremely meager, suggested that this is less determined by the past than by the random nature of the future. Instead of a familiar pair of young birds traveling together for years before establishing a territory together, it seems that ravens are more likely to obtain their first territory by filling in a vacancy created when one member of an established pair dies. The surviving bird quickly repairs with a local and likely familiar, but unmated, individual. Chance may have more to do with pair formation in ravens than suggested by theory. I guess we shouldn't have been surprised. Although ravens may use several criteria to narrow the field of suitable partners and perhaps form initial bonds, nature often constrains choice. A recent widow may present a territorial opening to a young male but not his favorite preening partner, or the chance location of a dead moose may keep a perfect pair from ever crossing paths.

Bernd's analogy of a raven flock as a traveling disco might not be far off the mark. Young ravens interact at a carcass like young people do at a disco, showing off, impressing, and observing. Our experiments showed that it matters how they behave. But raven status displays are much more practical than those of kids. Ravens interact for immediate benefit at accessing contested foods. The social bonds among young ravens may last long into the future, allowing a pair to enter the breeding population intact, but few probably do. This is still unknown, but it is unlikely in the natural world where chance events constrain personal choices. Come to think of it, that really isn't all that different from teens at a disco!

Topper and Buster, our two male dogs, also seemed to be under the spell of longer days and rushing hormones. Although both were neutered, they became increasingly hostile toward one another. One day in April, Buster managed to rip Topper's nose (again) through the kennel. Often they strutted along the kennel fence just like ravens. Mostly it was all show, like trilling ravens, but this time Buster pushed his snout through the fence and grabbed Topper. At least it took only two stitches for Dr. Patterson to close the wound this time.

23 June 1990; Colleen's Journal: "We drove down to Boston for the Yankee Siberian Husky Club meeting. We stopped and visited Ed on the way."

After a long second winter we were looking forward to a less frantic pace during the summer months. I had found myself drawn more and more to the good friends, intriguing culture, and the dog side of our experience. The Down East Sled Dog Club elected me assistant to Carol Nash, the treasurer. This post required that I attend all races and outings sponsored by the club that Carol could not make. I was popular as I was responsible for paying out the purse to the professionals placing in each race. My increased involvement in the Yankee Siberian Husky Club led to a "wolf spot award," which meant that I had led my dogs through three activities—skijoring demonstrations and meeting events, three races, and three confirmation shows in a single year. The award is named after a dark spot of fur on the Siberian Husky's tail, a vestige of the precaudal gland at the base of a wolf's tail. In the wolf, this gland releases pheromones that impart to its owner an individually distinct scent used in pack recognition. These activities took me away from the aviary part of the time, but between my frustration over my role on the project and facing another black fly season, it was healthy to get away occasionally.

1 May 1990; Colleen's Journal: "Today is May Day—almost 60°F and misty. I bought flowers to brighten things up. John is off looking for the Hills Pond raven nest."

The dogs consumed my summer and fall. Ravens had been my primary focus for two years, but now I began to withdraw my allegiance to the research and focus my thoughts and time on the dogs and what the future might bring. I was frustrated with Bernd and my role as his technician. The more that I complained about it to John, the harder it was on us as a couple. John was caught in the middle, trying to keep me happy and trying to be a productive postdoc for Bernd. My solution was to distract myself and do things I enjoyed: I sought solace in the dogs. The organizations we joined were outlets for volunteerism that was valued and appreciated. Again, I seemed to be in Konrad Lorenz's world, following his dictum, *"When I am fed to the teeth with brainwork . . . then I decide to 'go to the dogs' "* (emphasis in original).[5]

The future was unknown, but the possibilities were exciting. I researched all the places where John applied for jobs and encouraged him even when he received rejections. I carried out my duties as a technician but tried to separate that from our life as a couple. Envisioning a future in New Hampshire, Virginia, or Alaska provided a release from built-up tensions and kept us both sane. Zetta hired me for a few hours a week as an office assistant, which expanded my computer skills and added a few dollars to our stretched bank account. Gas prices had spiked to $1.42 a gallon from around a dollar a gallon, and our research and recreational travels meant more time on the road.

Although we had only a glimpse of the process of mate choice in ravens, our mated pair taught us much about raven parenting styles. I was eager to build on Ebo Gwinner's descriptions of breeding displays of captive ravens and our knowledge of when and where wild birds nested. We knew virtually nothing about the extension of parental care beyond the nestling period. And yet this information was vitally relevant to our winter research because many of the birds we captured and observed were fresh from parental care. What had they learned on their home territory? How long did parental care persist and when did it transition to territorial defense? The pair just beyond our observation hut started providing answers.[6]

20 March 1990; John's Field Notes: "Adults have worked on nest for three days. I add straw and two dead squirrels to the aviary."

We had no idea how settled our pair of territorial ravens was until their second spring in captivity when they started to build a nest. As they developed new roles, so did we. Raven nests are bulky structures consisting of a large woven stick basket, about a yard in diameter and up to a yard deep, filled with a lining of progressively smaller sticks, rootlets, grass, and animal hair. The inner cup of a nest is woven exclusively from animal hair and is twelve inches in diameter and half that deep. The carcasses we dragged up to the adults would provide plenty of hairy hide, so we needed only to start piling nest-sized sticks, grass, and straw in the aviary and see what the prospective parents would do.[7]

It took our motivated carpenters only ten days to fabricate a typical nest, which they built within their roosting shed. They wove the larger sticks between the shed's fixed perches and soon had a big, secure nest foundation. Their nest was thinner than most we saw in nature but otherwise typical. Both the male and female crafted the nest and lined it with grass, sheep wool, and deer hair. They took turns sitting in the growing structure, settling, spinning,

The nest built by our captive ravens in their
roosting shed.

and chest-bumping a cup into the soft fur lining. While building, they often
gave loud raspy kaws to vocally defend their territory from all other ravens
who passed.

The female was flat on the nest on March 27. And silent. Even when
external birds passed, there were no loud calls from the shed. The male was
also quiet, occasionally grunting soft air calls that sounded like *hiccup* as he
guarded the nest from a perch just outside the shed. Wild male ravens act the
same way, looking for potential predators and, more important, interlopers
who try to breed with their mates during the fertile egg-laying period. Suddenly the female came to life, slipping off the nest to stretch, defecate, preen,

and cough up a pellet of undigested bone and fur—residue from yesterday's dinner. In response, the male immediately went to the nest and sat low upon it. Could our pair have eggs?

We watched from the hut, afraid to unduly disturb the pair at this sensitive time. The same ritual replayed for days. The male guarded. The female sat low on the nest, presumably incubating eggs. Although the male briefly sat on the nest when the female did not, a male can't truly incubate. His feather cloak surely helped retain some of the heat provided to the eggs by the female, but she alone has a brood patch—a portion of her belly that responds to reproductive hormones by shedding feathers to expose a rich network of blood vessels that traffic their warm cargo just below the skin each breeding season. This rubbery patch settles around the eggs, imparting the constant warmth required by a developing embryo, much like a warming oven. Incubation is costly to the female. Producing this heat in addition to maintaining herself requires her to obtain extra food. Also, sitting on eggs exposes her to predators and the vagaries of winter. In the wild, these costs of incubation can lower a female's life expectancy, but in the aviary where food was plentiful, shelter provided, and predators mostly excluded, this extra burden was slight. The male shares little of the female's burden. He is basically only tinfoil, keeping a warm dish from cooling too quickly, and saving the female the cost of reheating eggs every time she returns to the nest.

Tinfoil wouldn't do on March 31 as temperatures dipped below freezing and five inches of new snow covered York Hill. The male rolled and bathed in the powder snow and provided room service, carrying fresh moose to his female who begged from the nest. In the wild, males typically bring food to their mates during incubation, but in the aviary, where food was always nearby, this behavior appeared to be necessary only on extremely cold days.[8]

We glimpsed the clutch on April 8. It had warmed up, and we needed to see what our birds had produced before the eggs hatched and they disposed of the eggshells. Female birds remove and often eat the shells from hatched eggs to recoup some of the calcium that has been drained from their blood and bones during egg formation. Five light turquoise blue, brown-speckled eggs bejeweled the nest. The adults remained calm as we entered the aviary and shinnied up to the nest. Their reaction was subdued, relative to the harried alarm clucking that greeted us at a wild pair's nest. Our birds were cautious, but tolerant, perhaps looking for the deer or bread treat that we might bring.

As it neared the time when the eggs should be hatching (the typical incubation period in ravens is twenty to twenty-five days) the parents became more vocal. A curious wild juvenile was confronted with a coordinated chorus: both male and female gave raspy kaws, they mixed hiccup (male) and knocking (female) into a duet, and they honked and gave those resonating hollow log calls we had often heard. The female dropped from her nest and tore at her wire wall attempting to get a mouthful of the juvenile who had edged close to the border fence.

Twenty-three days of incubation did the trick. We noticed the adults bending into the nest to feed chicks on April 18. We climbed up for a count eleven days later, and found 4, pinkish-gray, fist-sized, and helpless baby ravens. One of the eggs was a dud, which is not uncommon even in the wild. As the birds grew, they begged loudly and hoarsely from the nest. Both parents were diligent, feeding the noisy crew a few times each hour. These parents were much more fastidious than Colleen and I could be with our trailer broods. The female touched the anus of her small nestlings after feeding and received a steaming dollop of feces for her efforts. But the waste of a young songbird is neatly encased in a rubbery sac, which allows the mother to keep a sanitary nest, deftly pitching fecal sacs from the babies to the ground beyond the nest. Older nestlings backed up to the nest rim and whitewashed the outer nest sticks. The female also cleaned these, picking off the chalky uric acid and probing deeply throughout the nest to catch, remove, and eat insect larvae that might dine on the bare bellies of her growing nestlings.

It was still snowing in early May, but it was warming and the chicks were increasingly able to generate their own heat. Despite snow and high temperatures that only reached 40°F, the parents no longer insulated their offspring.

The feathered mass of four fat ravens was an efficient heat machine in no need of the external warmth provided by a brooding parent.

By mid-May, migrant songbirds were returning to begin their breeding season. I saw my first-ever Rose-breasted Grosbeak—a striking black-and-white beauty with a vest of crimson—in the maples just outside the hut. The arrival of these South and Central American wonders reinforced the unique breeding habits of ravens. The timing of our birds' nesting was absolutely typical. Ravens nest early when snow thickly blankets their northern realm. Nest insulation and a generalists' diet enable early breeding. Shaky fledglings with much to learn have the benevolence of a long summer, including the eggs and nestlings of later-breeding birds, like the grosbeak beyond my window.

When the nestlings were nearly fully feathered, we measured, banded, and wing-tagged each one. We were surprised to find only three nestlings, whereas two weeks earlier there had been four. One had apparently died, a victim of "brood reduction." This phenomenon is common in birds and serves a variety of functions. In nature, brood reduction aligns the number of fledglings to available resources and selects for rapid nestling growth, vigorous begging, and combative disposition. Perhaps our missing nestling had become ill, was handicapped in some way, or was a weak beggar and easily outcompeted by its siblings. We guaranteed that the parents had sufficient food for all four. Theory suggests that the survivors would be stronger for the loss. But where was the missing bird? We never found it. Either the parents removed and hid it, ate it, or fed it to the other nestlings. We suspect they recycled it, just like eggshells.[9]

The parents paid little attention to the bling we affixed to their babies' legs and wings. But for us, tags meant that we could watch the individual trajectories of each new life. YA5 was first to jump ship, "fledging" on June 5. Two days later, all three fledglings were on the ground, walking and waddling like arrogant ducks. They leaned forward, flapped their wings, flashed their red mouths, begged, and chased after their parents. Both male and female stuffed bite after bite of squirrel, moose, deer, and grouse into the bottomless pit that

Three nestlings about twenty-three days old that were reared by our captive pair. At this age, they have huge red-lined mouths, pale blue eyes, and feather vanes emerging from a coat of natal down.

is a baby bird. After only three days, a hailstorm savaged the aviary. All fledglings survived, but they were grounded, unable still to fly up to the roost shed and elevated perches. They were fearlessly pecking at a whole deer carcass. We saw no apprehension as they approached novel foods—they simply followed their parents. This behavior was a striking contrast to the fear last summer's hand-reared babies showed toward anything new. This wisdom —what to eat and what to avoid—is an obvious advantage of parental care. But learning appeared passive, young ravens imitating their parents rather than actively receiving guidance and instruction.

Si Bachly, a local resident who had pitched in watching ravens whenever we called, threw his coat over a lone baby raven up by Lake Webb. He immediately headed for our house, knowing we could always use another bird and fearing that his prize would never survive in the wild. In hindsight, we should have returned the young raven to its natal grounds and likely parental care. But this recent accident of a strong night windstorm presented a unique opportunity. She was the same age as our captive brood, so we brought her up the hill to the aviary. The thin fledgling hopped right into our captive family and began to beg from the male who was feeding at a deer carcass. The male reacted, attacking the hungry visitor, pinning her to the ground and bruising her with quick jabs from a strong beak. The demonstration of kin recognition went on for three minutes. The other fledglings watched silently. Calm returned for forty minutes until the male again demonstrated his discrimination ability. I slipped from the hut into the aviary, broke up the fight, and took the outcast to our home aviary. We had no problem raising her and eventually integrating her into upcoming experiments so she could be returned to the wild.

When dog shows or class took away part of our pack, the others were integrated into the research routine. Topper and I were in the hut June 9 when the fledglings were playing tug-of-war with chunks of deer. Raven versions of football games broke out spontaneously, as all the fledglings chased and tackled the one that had a hunk of deer. I was fascinated by the innate social skills the siblings showed during their first two months of life. They preened each other, played with objects alone or together, and used their limited vocabulary, begging with varied duration and intensity, to solicit food and peace from their parents. Topper was more interested in the red squirrel that was now living in the hut, darting in and out of the wood pile. He sniffed, cocked his head to listen like a coyote hunting a subnivian vole, but was quiet and patient. Kenai was more active. Like a young raven, she explored and chased everything. Walking up York Hill on June 18, she surprised and caught a snowshoe hare. She proudly carried it up to Bernd's cabin, whereupon we transferred her prize into a fresh feast for the growing raven family. That would be as close as our birds would get to their ancient profession of scavenging from wolves.

We noticed the first signs of parental intolerance in mid-June. The male rarely fed the fledglings now, and he occasionally chased them or reinforced

The three parent-reared fledglings plan strategy.

manners with a sharp poke of his beak as the family crowded to eat a small meal, such as the woodchuck I presented them on June 19. The female still occasionally fed a begging fledgling, but often the male would interfere. The bond between mates was strong—it seemed much stronger now than the bond between parent and offspring. We also noticed subtle changes in the voices of the fledglings. Their hoarse begs were strengthening and transitioning into harmonically complex yells. A young bird might start begging and end yelling as it approached food. This was the same vocal ontogeny we saw in our hand-reared birds last summer. Young ravens did not need an adult tutor to learn their socially important calls. One month after fledging from the nest, just as these young birds were perfecting their take-off, landing, and flying skills, they were already accomplished socialites. They begged to aggressive parents to dampen an overt attack, and they yelled among themselves reinforcing a dominance hierarchy and signaling a confident approach to food. These skills would be crucial during their first winter.

When I began observing the family on July 12, it seemed the parents were ready for the fledglings to disperse. There was a lot of chasing and fighting. One of the fledglings was especially aggressive. I assumed it was YA4, the clearly most dominant sibling, but then I got a good look at its tag. It was YW, from our first aviary cohort that we had released only three months ago. He now had a black mouth, signaling dominance, and he was *in* the adult aviary. I hustled out of the hut and through the aviary door to scoop up the prodigal with a fishing net. The previous night a coyote, skunk, or coon had dug into the adult aviary to scavenge deer. That breach of security left an open portal through which YW must have crawled. I rolled a boulder into the hole and headed home to take a closer look at him. He weighed 1,210 grams and looked to be in top form. He had been a dominant bird in our first cohort and was the largest bird of the bunch. We decided to hold him at home until late September when we would radio-tag him and release him again, this time as part of our experiments testing the reactions of released birds to foods we allow them to discover.

29 July 1990; John's Field Notes: "Stan (Roth) helped identify frogs in the area. No bullfrogs. What I thought were bullfrogs are technically green frogs. Also we have northern leopard frogs, pickerel frogs, and mink frogs up in Tumbledown Pond."

YA5, the first to fledge, was in trouble. We noticed her limping. Stan and Janet Roth were visiting from Kansas, and being biologists, they were eager to help diagnose the injury. Stan had been my high school biology teacher, and his passion and knowledge were applied to any biological riddle. His mentorship and drive to get his students into the field, catching and watching any plant or animal they could, was the reason I chose the career path Colleen and I were now following. We easily caught the gimpy raven and saw that her leg was bowed, but not broken, from the thigh down. Perhaps we had failed to provide some necessary nutrient or, more likely, she had dislocated or strained a joint. We guessed she had caught her leg in the aviary wire somehow, like the wild fledgling from Lake Webb who injured itself in a picnic grill. We left her with her family. She was eating, and we felt the beneficial socialization she was getting would contribute to her future survival in the wild. Her parents were indifferent at this point, rarely attacking or feeding their increasingly independent brood.

The aviary family did not want for food. The Grahams' freezer failed in early August, and their spoils were the ravens' riches. T-bone steaks, geese, roasts, and chickens supplemented a steady wild diet of roadkill. We also spiced meals with softened dog food kibble and chicken feed, just in case our offerings lacked some essential vitamins or minerals. Abundant food and protection from the dangers typically faced by a young raven in nature seemed to be helping YA5. Her leg was not worsening, and her powers of flight, while well below the other fledglings' abilities, were improving. We rooted for her success. Natural selection, however, was impatient: on August 18, the canid, coon, or skunk that opened the aviary earlier in the summer returned. The scavenger turned predator on this visit, killing the gimpy fledgling. Nature doesn't care for the underdog.

As our baby ravens expanded their knowledge of the aviary, we expanded our experiences with the nature of Maine. John and I sometimes switched off aviary duties as he traveled to scientific meetings and I went to dog shows or club events. More often, Hilary and Josh, Dave Lidstone, Billy, or other friends would volunteer to feed, water, and check on the birds so we could steal away together for a moment or two. John fished as many lakes and rivers as he could. It was easy for him to track down raven sightings or scout presumed nest sites while casting flies from the canoe we borrowed from Henry and Lee. My parents visited and really pushed us to look at the places where my father's ancestors had settled. We made a special trip to Deer Isle to visit the historical society, to do research on my ancestors, the Sanfords. Dad and I found documents of land ownerships and marriages relating to some of them. We copied all the records we could find and sent them west to my uncle, who had been researching our genealogy.

As Dad and I dug into his past, Mom and John found blueberries. Lee had taught us about raking the wild, low-bush berries. When they found a hillside loaded with small berries, they used their fingers like a rake to quickly fill a small bag with the juicy fruit. That was when the shouting began. John thought the berries were there for the picking, like our more familiar western huckleberries. The landowner reminded him that they were on private property, specifically his property. He had been patiently waiting for peak ripeness and was not at all happy that we were stealing his prized crop. John and Mom apologized, sprinted to the car, and fled with tails between legs.

Entertaining our steady stream of visitors kept us exploring Maine. One trip to Casco Bay led us to Eagle Island where Admiral Byrd of Antarctic exploration fame had a house. A smaller, adjacent island was used to summer his sled dogs. I wished we had an island like that. It would have been much easier to allow the dogs to run freely than to keep them captive in the kennel.

By the end of August, we were ready to allow the residents of our aviary to start mixing. We wanted to better understand how social pressures and bonds influence the dispersal of fledglings from their natal territory into the nomadic life that defines their first winter. Around Lake Webb, Hills Pond, and Farmington wild raven families were disintegrating. We had tagged two nestlings at the nest on Bernd's mother's property and three more in a patch of woods near the Irving fuel station in Farmington, but now we saw only the adult pairs. The Hills Pond pair was also usually alone, their single fledgling only occasionally in tow. The young ravens either had been killed or had dispersed into the social world of vagrancy. Our adult pair was increasingly defensive. The male often chased and attacked his most dominant offspring, YA4. On August 31 we opened the door that had barred the fledglings from leaving their parents' world. Now they could either remain with their parents or move down the aviary arm that led to the twelve juveniles in the main aviary. Two days later, the fledglings made a choice. The increasing aggression from their parents pushed them into the aviary tunnel, where they crowded near the gate eyeing the juvenile gang.

Rather than open the main aviary to the fledglings at this stage, I caught each and dispersed them to the vacant left aviary. Here they had food undefended by their parents and could roam the length of the left arm, building strength and confidence before joining the masses. Immediately, YA4 poured forth a rich repertoire *sotto voce*. His vocal abilities, a signal of maturity, had apparently been suppressed by his dominant parents. Four days later, there was ample whitewash on either side of the gate separating the left arm from the main aviary, suggesting that the fledglings and juveniles were interacting frequently. The pull to join other young ravens seemed strong. I gave it a few more days, thinking the social skills the fledglings practiced among themselves would grease their entry into the strong hierarchy of the gang. I opened the gate September 11, and with the usual fighting and posturing the fledglings immediately cast their lot with the juvenile group.

Peers were clearly attractive to young ravens. We saw this phenomenon daily as wild juveniles investigated the aviary, displayed to captive birds, and did their best to join the mix. This attraction to each other, and the prospect of a meal that a group signified, caused juvenile flocking. Repulsion as meals were consumed forced their vagrancy, often for years before they secured a territory. But for newly fledged birds the option to remain on, or return to, the natal territory may delay the assumption of a fully vagrant life. In the wild, our infrequent sightings of tagged fledglings suggested that during dispersal they might occasionally return to familiar turf before fully integrating with wild juveniles. We decided to lift all six aviary doors to better simulate this natural situation. This action would allow us to observe the yin and yang of opposing forces: the pull of familiarity, parental care, and peer association versus the push of parental defense and peer competition. For the first time, the adults could travel freely throughout the aviary complex. The juveniles and fledglings could move into the adult territory or continue to roam their familiar grounds.

Despite the open travel corridor, the adults stayed put. The boundaries we had enforced with impenetrable gates seemed deeply engrained. The male ventured only a few yards down the arm toward the main aviary and announced himself with husky territorial calls. When the adults finally broached the main aviary, they were not overly aggressive. Clearly they were dominant at shared meals, but they regularly returned to their aviary and roosted there every night. The bulk of the juvenile group similarly stayed within their familiar main aviary. But the two fledglings belonged to both worlds. The subordinate fledgling returned each night to roost in her home territory just outside the shed where she was hatched and within a few feathers of her parents. The dominant fledgling did likewise, but not every night. Usually he remained with the juveniles and roosted in the large communal shed far from his home turf. The complexity of dispersal we could only glimpse in the wild was laid bare in the aviary, as were the unique pressures placed on subordinate versus dominant young ravens. Our subordinate fledgling could not integrate into the socially structured juvenile flock. She was clearly at the bottom of the social ladder—the last to eat and the victim of aggression from both her parents and her peers. In nature she would travel more widely, perhaps finding food on her own or entering a communal feast in the company of a more dominant male preening partner, but here she could do neither. These social tensions in part explain why female birds in general disperse farther than do their brothers. The early aggression we witnessed between the male and his dominant son and the son's ability to integrate into the juvenile hierarchy hints that males may disperse sooner, yet remain closer to home, than females. Unfortunately, we could not test this hypothesis more completely in the aviary.

On September 24, the subordinate female was dead, the victim of fierce peer competition. The social network, perhaps unusually rigid in the permanence of the aviary, could be breeched only by a dominant disposition.[10]

Over the course of the summer of 1990 we learned much about the usually hidden world of young ravens and their parents (see appendix 1 for a visual summary). Most ravens die during their first summer and autumn. Our birds were no exception. Birthing one raven into the juvenile flock was a stellar accomplishment by our pair, right on par with the annual success rate of wild ravens around the world. This success was a direct result of the social skills learned by young ravens, first from their parents and siblings and then from their peers. Learning over the first month or two of life seemed mostly a result of young birds passively watching their experienced parents and playing with each other. They learned what to eat and how to act at a communal meal. It seemed very robotic, not as nuanced as we might expect from one of the world's brainiest birds. Resource defense demanded aggression. Innate social signals—the begging calls first uttered by nestlings and continued by fledglings—dampened aggression. Young ravens first learn those skills by interacting with their parents in an initially safe environment lacking in aggression. They then use these skills to survive parental intolerance and hostile peers. Social status that was set mostly by gender enabled a male, but not a female, to successfully join our juvenile flock. Luck as manifested in gender determination, accidental injury, and untimely raids by hungry predators was also an important determinant of our raven pair's success. This force, we suspect, is even more important in nature where wire fences, roosting sheds, and all the deer one can eat do not shield young ravens from the teeth and claws of the north woods.

15 September 1990; Colleen's Journal: "Tonight we are off to our third pig roast at Candy Goodwin's. Billy's band will be playing. It's hard to believe that we are beginning our third year here."

Letters were flying back and forth between Bernd and us. Having recovered from his back injury, Bernd visited us in August but stayed only a few days, saying he was bored and anxious. We adjusted our scheduled experiments because of his absence. Bernd's anxiety was heightened by the distractions of our life. When he visited, we wanted a break from the daily tasks captive animals require. He knew what we were up against but wasn't very sympathetic. His own intensity in research had cost him two wives. He was also frustrated having to deal with a steady stream of paperwork required of any federally funded project: permits, annual reports, and hassles over a meager budget. He felt unneeded and unwanted in the field and retreated to Burlington.

The real tension underlying our deteriorating relationship with Bernd manifested itself in concerns over authorship. This tension is nothing new in science, and it shows the selfish nature of driven researchers, including Bernd and us. The data we had gathered during our first two years was suitable for a series of publications in standard scientific journals. Bernd and John had worked diligently to communicate their work to colleagues in printed and oral venues. The National Science Foundation required such communication, which has been stoked by the culture of science and human ego. They had five papers in the publication pipeline. Tangible product showed Bernd and our supporters that we were doing our job. What was controversial was the order of authors. It seems silly, but senior authorship is a big deal among scientists. Readers of a paper often perceive that the first author listed has contributed most to the research. John and Bernd had agreed early on that they would split senior authorship. The first five papers were tilted toward Bernd as the senior; John was senior author on only one, and Patty Rabenold was senior on another that appropriately dealt with her genetic analysis of foraging ravens. I was an author (never senior) on only one. As the work unfolded and we lived and breathed its every aspect, John felt more and more that he should be senior author on most of the papers we were writing, and that I should be a coauthor. All the work reported in those first five papers involved our observations and experiments. I had made significant contributions to the design, implementation, and analysis of the data, which meant I should be an author. But paid technicians often do not get such just rewards. Bernd saw me as his investment in the research, and as such his claim to authorship. More important, he felt his pioneering groundwork on the raven project demanded senior authorship on some of our work. As he put it, he had dug the mine so we could pick up the gold. Anyone could pick up the gold. We respected Bernd's prior work, but the gold was heavy, and we were doing the vast majority of the hauling.

Bernd, John, and I communicated our frustrations over authorship frequently in autumn 1990. This debate was healthy if painful. We were told this was not a "Marzluff et al." production, referring to an authorship scenario where John, Bernd, and I would be ordered thus on forthcoming key papers. My subservient position given to help John was reinforced. It was made clear that I served at the discretion of Bernd. He told us he would rather be here doing his own work, and he would do so if need be. Given the current arrangement, he at least would be assured of equal representation on publications. We countered that current investment was most important in determining authorship on a particular paper. We were starting to act like hungry ravens around a small carcass.

We entered the final winter in need of critical evidence that would prove or disprove the use of roosts as information centers by vagrant ravens. Our findings would be reported in a paper we all envisioned as a major accomplishment, one that was expected by our proposal to the National Science Foundation. Bernd was responsible for that expectation because he was listed as the grant's principal investigator. John's career hung on productive and collaborative research. We knew of each other's concerns, and we continued to chew on them. Authorship was not settled, but it was in the open. The ravens called, and we dug in for a final year of discovery about ravens and ourselves.

ten

Radio Waves

The raven twenty meters away was double the size of the busy crow. One-on-one, this size advantage guarantees the raven the ability to take what it wants from its lesser cousin. Today, the raven I watched was intent on stealing a red rubber ball from a dump-diving crow. He easily intimidated the crow, then pecked at the ball, rolled it, and tried to crack it like an egg. Unable to eat it, he cached it in the litter. Such antics were not uncommon in the dump, where ravens find playthings among food. This September, the raven's game had awakened me from more abstract thoughts that scurried along the synapses of my brain as I sat for hours in a cardboard box that once housed a new refrigerator. The box was perfect camouflage in the ocean of trash in the Wilton town dump. But today it was warm and the air ripe, so I focused inward.

I was thinking about the final field season and was bothered by an inconsistency in understanding how ravens share what they know about newly discovered foods. Last winter the ravens we dropped into roosts easily found new feasts. They simply followed their bedfellows. Although this ability is central to the hypothesis that roosts are information centers, it was insufficient for us to make our case to skeptical colleagues. In our experiments we had completed a lot of the legwork for the naïve birds: we got them to the roost. But as we watched roosts and tracked birds, we learned that roosts often change location from night to night. It seemed change happened just when the roost would be most valuable as an information center: the night of, or day after, a lucky few birds returned with news of discovery. The big, traditional roosts we watched were often abandoned, or nearly so, after a distant discovery. Abandonment might be cued by conspicuous soaring, but I knew many ravens down on their luck would miss the display. Why didn't all the ravens return each night to a traditional roost site, divulge their secrets, and then share the spoils the following day? Bees did it, so why were our brainy ravens so inefficient? The birds in the dump before me were part of the answer. They could count on food, even if inedible balls distracted them each day. The certainty of refuse must temper the uncertainty of finding the next moose. Perhaps it also buffered the need to track every shift of the itinerant roosts.

Our strategy heading into our final winter was not new. We were stubborn in repeating our approaches from the previous winters, hoping to gain a deeper and broader understanding of the interplay between roosting and feeding sites. This repetition was standard in our field. As Niko Tinbergen had expressed fifty years earlier, "I am not exaggerating when I say that I have watched the courtship of the Three-spined Stickleback hundreds of times, and still I am seeing new details, some of which contribute to a better understanding of basic problems."[1]

I had to witness information coming in and flowing from unpredictable roost locations and then tie this knowledge stream to the shuttling of ravens between garbage and nature's deceased. The only way to do that was to know what ravens knew and prove how this knowledge affected their actions. This proof would demand more radio telemetry as well as watching our growing populations of tagged, free-living ravens. We would follow the knowledgeable to learn when and where information was provided, and the naïve to learn when and where this information was used. As we released birds, we would tag and follow them as precisely and for as long as possible. With an increasing mass of wing-tagged and radio-tagged birds revealing their roosting locations and daily foraging paths, we were primed for discovery.

In late September 1991 YW, the prodigal son who shimmied into the adult aviary last July, was whacking at the door to the dog carrier. He was the first radio-tagged bird we released this season, and knowing his habits, we wanted to ensure he had reason to stay away from the aviary. We had dragged a huge cow up a short logging road between our house and York Hill, and that day I popped the carrier door open by pulling the line from my blind and set the big male free. He burst forth and dug right into the cow. Over the course of the next two days, he fought with the Hills Pond pair, and the squabbling attracted a small group of vagrants—six to eight of them that seemed poised to recruit from their night roost. YW had eased right back into the wild society from which he came, and now because of the radio transmitter glued to his tail we could follow him. Unfortunately, the Vining boys, local loggers, had just decided to thin the exact patch of forest that concealed our cow. They pushed the cow deep into the puckerbrush and ran their saws daily for the next several weeks.

The cow quickly dissolved into the warm Maine autumn, fertilizing the forest and sending YW further afield. Our ruined experiment left YW naïve and in need of information. He was not a gambler. He turned to the small but consistently stocked Weld dump. He fed daily in the dump with a small group of other nonbreeding ravens. And he roosted within a kilometer of the dump with these like-minded birds. The Vinings had essentially repeated our covered moose experiment. My initial frustration with the disturbance vanished as YW's shift to reliable dump fare confirmed what we had seen two years ago, with new details that only telemetry could provide.

We had a second release experiment ready to go in two days and we headed south to Bernd's mother's farm with GY and a whole pony. No loggers here, just a swarm of turkey vultures. The warm weather kept these scavengers from migrating, and they descended onto the pony. Twenty-five of the hissing, bald undertakers dominated and quickly stripped the equine bones of anything a raven could swallow. Again, there was only time for a small group of ravens to join GY here before nature changed the scene. GY headed to the Wilton dump. Like YW, she was no gambler. She stayed with the pony until she and a

Ravens (note wing-tagged bird in upper left) and crows (smaller birds mostly in foreground) mix it up at the Wilton dump.

few other vagrant ravens were excluded by the larger and more numerous vultures, then she went for a sure thing. She first roosted near the pony and then shifted to roost next to the dump. Neither GY nor YW searched the evening skies for soaring ravens. They stayed where they had found food, just like the other birds we released outside the roosts last year. Now this strange behavior made sense. A displaced raven would waste energy looking for a roost that has likely moved. A smarter strategy in this situation was to wait and then follow the natives to a sure bet. Here that meant to the closest dump.

The connection between using traditional roosts when eating nearby reliable refuse was confirmed by these first two releases. As deer hunting season approached, YW taught us about bivouac roosts. Despite eating at the Weld dump at least some of each day, YW had been roosting in a variety of locations from Hills Pond to Lake Webb. These nocturnal forays were linked to new feeding discoveries. On October 18, I tracked YW down to a fresh bear carcass by Tumbledown Mountain two and a half kilometers from his previous roost. He was not alone. There were about eight others with him, including a couple we had wing-tagged last winter. The Weld dump was vacant of ravens. The same story repeated ten days later. Successful deer hunters were leaving gut piles in the forest. The ravens were enjoying the hunt and had mostly abandoned the dumps. YW was missing. I drove in search of a signal and got a faint one by Lake Webb. Adorned in blaze orange so even the most trigger-happy deer hunter "from away" might recognize me as something other than a deer, I hiked along a ridge, down a gully, over a hill, down another gully across a stream and up another ridge. There I saw YW with a few other ravens finishing up a gut feast. I could not find his roost that evening, but he was not near the dump or in any of the usual places. He was bivouacking. As the deer season progressed, YW moved wildly each day to a new place of slaughter, but I could not find him every night. He was unpredictable, on a grand feasting and camping trip.

The Maine landscape has rich ephemeral foods like deer guts and dead animals and consistent, but likely low-quality, foods like garbage dumps. This exotic mix of the human and the more natural drove foraging and roosting decisions. Dumps appeared to be reliable fallback options for naïve young ravens. Some, like the dominant YW used dumps rarely. Others, like the subordinate GY were real dump addicts. Adults occasionally visited dumps, but most of the birds there were young nonbreeders biding their time. From these stable, but low-quality feeding sites, ravens searched for rare riches. The shots from hunters' rifles drew them deep into the forest where gut piles could be found. From there, new roost locations were forged and potential feeding locations explored. Sometimes knowledgeable birds with which they roosted must draw them to hidden treasures. Our insights on this key point were only inferential. We saw the interplay among roosts, dumps, and deer, but we still had not glimpsed the actual exchange of information. GY and YW were followers. We needed a leader to show us how knowledge was carried in and out of a roost.

It was Halloween, and Bernd was present for our next round of raven releases. From the blind, Bernd heard a single raven fly over and give raspy, territorial kaws. R73 retorted loudly from the pet carrier, his door not yet sprung. As dusk settled, Bernd pulled the door open and freed R73. The raven preened and drank next to a mountain of lungs and meat scraps but did not eat. I was up a tree at the crest of an overlooking ridge, watching and monitoring the airwaves for radio signals. We were up the Byron Road, not far from the Weld dump. YW was nearby on Blueberry Mountain; few other ravens were evident. There was no soaring. The dark woods just behind the Weld dump now held both R73 and YW, roosting for the night. I was nervous, desperately wanting our experiments to succeed. We were learning that success came in many forms. Nearly anything the ravens did helped us understand their world, but I wanted some consistency. I was ready for a home run: clear recruitment from a distant roost. Although I wished for it, I couldn't force it. The ravens would have to show us the truth. We figured they would dine at the dump in the morning.

November 1 was clear, calm, and 30°F at 5:45 a.m. Both radio-tagged birds were still in the dump roost. I watched the release site meat pile from a shabby spruce blind and heard a murmur of wings and yelling ravens heading right toward me. At 5:58 a.m. my ears were blown out by the radio signal particular to R73. He yelled, others fought, and a black mass boiled through the limp conifers and stiff birches down to the food. Finally, we had a leader! R73 had recruited his roost mates to his secret stash. YW was also here, very close, but he did not show himself. Only his radio revealed that he followed R73's information. As the day wore on, YW retreated to the dump. There he could eat without contest. R73 fought for his food at the release site. We staked out all the usual suspects that evening to see how this crowd spread its new knowledge. It was a full moon, and there was no soaring above the Byron Valley. Bernd saw only four ravens at the distant Taylor Hill roost. Colleen chased the radio birds, confirming that R73 and the others from the meat pile formed a bivouac roost nearby, just across the gray gravel road. YW was out of this information flow, roosting in his traditional site behind the Weld dump. Perhaps he knew this good thing wouldn't last. Sixty ravens devoured the meat the next day. Colleen, Bernd, and I cheered the home run.

Early January 1991; Colleen's journal: "We released a radio bird last week and on Saturday John and I went to find the bird since the signal never seemed to move. We found the raven still being eaten by an owl!"

Our success ebbed through the heart of winter. We released six more radio-tagged birds in the next three months. None of these birds were leaders. One followed others from a roost to the site of a dead deer. Another remained near the site where she was released and attracted a small group as she begged from defensive adults. The others hightailed it for parts unknown. A large male didn't get far. His signal was booming from a thickly wooded area toward Dixfield. We crept in anticipating a feast of moose or deer only to feel a silent Great Horned Owl whizz past our heads; it had been dining on our bird.

The survivors, however, were painting a detailed picture. They led us to three new and regularly used roost sites. Fortunately, human recruits arrived just in time to help monitor these new discoveries and the growing number of erratic radio signals that needed following. Bernd developed a winter ecology class, whose members filled Camp Believe It to capacity. The students spent two weeks with us catching, tagging, releasing, and chasing birds. Stan Roth returned with his son, Jim, late on Christmas Day to see Maine in its winter plumage. They spent the next six nights hanging on to treetops watching for roost signals and rising early the following morning to record tagged birds from cold blinds. Stan seemed to blend into the trees from which he eyed ravens. His lanky frame hugged the contours of the evergreen trunks, but his pipe glowed red and was easy to spot high in the lookout tree when dark sent the birds to bed. I was delighted to share a cramped blind with Stan and Jim as we eavesdropped on the wild society of the raven. To see Stan beaming with new knowledge and experience, as I often had under his tutelage, warmed the cold mornings.

With all these efforts we obtained details of the daily movements and decisions of many individual ravens. It was clear that no roost was used every night. Pine groves were typical roost locations, and the ravens often shifted the few kilometers—unpredictably from our perspective—between nearby ones. Occasionally more distant shifts occurred either to short-lived bivouacs or to oft-used traditional roosts. Although we had no further documentation of radio-tagged recruiters, we nailed down the dynamics of soaring. Our total efforts produced a sizable sample. During 175 nights, we found soaring sig-naled roost shifts just over half the time. In contrast, there was less than a one in ten chance that soaring would occur when roosts did not shift location. We were overjoyed to listen to the beeps of a radio signal in a soaring kettle of ravens on seven separate occasions. In all but one, the soaring radio-tagged bird shifted to a new roost site. Soaring was a clear signal enabling ravens to track nightly changes in roost location, but it was not the signal used to recruit. Often it followed, rather than preceded, food discovery.

16–17 February 1991; John's Field Notes: "At dog races during days. Evening radio checks show three birds together at East Shore roost, about 1.5 miles from Weld."

Dog days and raven nights merged on winter weekends. Weather initially postponed our plans for a full sledding season with our now well-trained six-dog team. We planned on an early season thirty-mile race set for the end of December in Lee, Maine. Freezing rain on bare ground cancelled the race. The freezing rain caused the cancellation of the first regular race of the season in early January as well, even though snow had started to fall the day before. Water over the ice on a lake cancelled the next race in January. We were still running and training at home but becoming increasingly frustrated with weekend conditions at the racing venues. Our likely last winter in Maine was not starting out the way we anticipated.

Training runs replaced races. Instead of head-on passing with other teams, we would pass snowmobiles and cross-country skiers and occasional loose dogs. Sometimes the dogs were crazy fast, and we noted that they seemed more energized after we installed a new exhaust system on the truck. Fresh air in their mobile doghouses meant clear lungs and heads and greater speed. On one run, the dogs were so fast that John hit a tree with the sled on a tight turn, broke the brush bow, and snapped the line just behind the wheel dogs. He scrambled to catch the free team and came back to the truck with a big knot in the gangline and the brush bow in his hands. His grin was a mile wide because of the fast ride. His high was somewhat dampened on the way home when the truck boiled over. We redid the line, repaired the brush bow, and paid $80 for a new water pump for the truck. It would have been easier to go to a race.

31 January 1991; Colleen's Journal: "The dogs and I got a trophy this weekend."

Finally we were able to race. John was in Boise for a job interview with a consulting firm, and I went alone with the dogs. It was a tough lake course with a barely discernable trail in clear, cold conditions. Kenai led like a pro, although she took us off course on the first day when she followed the sticks used by ice fishermen to mark their fishing holes instead of the sticks officials used to mark the trail. Perhaps her juvenile cataracts clouded her view, but even I could not distinguish the fishing and trail markers. We startled more than one fisherman before we got back on the right trail. The second day Kenai stayed on the correct course but wasn't quite sure what to make of the hound team that bayed its way up behind us and passed. The chase increased our speed. We slid through the thirteen-mile event in an hour and "placed" second, only seven and half minutes behind first place. We were actually the third team across the finish line, but the second finisher was driven by a junior musher who beat us by eleven seconds and got his own first-place junior trophy. There was no third-place winner. He didn't finish the race. Our second-place trophy would have made a great hood ornament for the truck.

Early February had warm and balmy weather for more than a week. Much of the snowpack disappeared. Brodie and Topper took advantage of the softened carcasses in the raven trailer in the driveway. Brodie threw up all over the Wojciks' house. Zetta called and said she had cleaned up at least twenty pounds of vomit. Topper kept his illicit meal down a bit longer, but it too was a problem. When he started retching, he kept heaving until he was throwing up blood. We gave him medicine for the indigestion, but he got worse. We finally called Dr. Patterson, who suggested that toxins from the rotten meat probably were poisoning him. The prescription was a quarter of a cup of mineral oil. Luckily Zetta had some on hand, and Topper surprised us by willingly drinking it from a bowl. John and I wondered what the inert mineral oil would do if it met with no obstructions. By 2:30 a.m., we knew. It passed straight through without Topper being aware. It cured his problem, but it was smelly and messy. Within two days he was back running with the team.

Winter was back, refreezing the carcasses and putting the races on schedule. John ran the dogs in West Bridgton, which was close enough for us to commute to the start line between raven radio checks. The dogs sprinted faster than ever—more than fourteen miles per hour the first day—but slowed the second day mostly because John had to change lead dogs midway through the boring, six-mile lake course. Our dogs had gelled into a competitive amateur team. What a transformation from our first race three seasons ago!

Back at the aviary, between races and field experiments, we settled into a familiar, yet faster-paced routine. In the past two years we had observed two groups of ravens in the aviary and currently held the mixed group of hand-raised, parent-produced, and wild-caught juveniles that had taught us so much about mate choice and parental care. By housing each group for nearly a full year, we knew them well, and they revealed to us aspects of their social and sex lives that we could not see in the wild. We were amazed at their plastic social status, their rich vocal repertoire, their crazy reaction to new foods, and their hot-and-cold relationships with their parents and each other. In our final year, we aimed to run as many new groups as possible through a set of aviary tests to confirm that our findings were not somehow peculiar to our three well-studied groups. We were able to move four new juvenile groups in and out of the aviary from October to April. As soon as we could catch a group and get it into the aviary, we would score each bird's status and then observe it discovering foods defended and not defended by the adult pair, test their reaction to recorded calls, and observe their comings and goings through the life cycle of a carcass. (Appendix 1 provides a visual summary of each aviary flock.)

We confirmed our previous findings. Social status was the critical determinant of access to food. Subordinates fed least and in the least-preferred locations. In our aviary, this caused them to search widely and often discover the next feeding opportunity. When defended foods were found, the begging of the young discoverers stifled the defense of the territorial pair and attracted a rapid swarm of backups. These local recruits came from within our aviary and often from afar, drifting toward the aviary from Weld and other wild places, just as they did in nature to our field experiments. Those already at a feast challenged recruits, but they were able to eat. Recruits often enabled the start of a feast. These details complemented what we saw less clearly in nature.

Looking back and forth between nature and the aviary was a powerful one-two punch into the mystery of raven behavior. Our need to move more birds through the aviary trials and our recent experiences with single discoverers abandoning the rich foods we provided convinced us to start letting loose small groups of ravens for our final experiments. We packed two dog carriers with five ravens (a radio-tagged dominant, a radio-tagged subordinate, and three others with only wing tags) and started pulling two strings for each release. Right away we were rewarded. Our next two experiments provided the replication that science demands. In both cases, the radio-tagged birds we released joined wild roosts and recruited their associates. It took days—three at first, then seventeen—just like the glimpse we saw last year, but it worked. Both leaders were dominant young ravens, in contrast to the subordinate who led her roost toward Byron Road earlier in the autumn. Each of our released birds showed us the competition for information that must daily flow in and out of raven roosts. Only three of the forty radio-tagged birds eventually recruited others to their grand discoveries. Two of these leaders also followed roost mates prior to leading them. Ravens in a roost must routinely choose when to follow and perhaps when to lead. And often that was just the half of it.

29 January 1991; Colleen's Journal: "All was well with the release until I heard heavy breathing. Moose? No, too rapid. Coyote? Fisher? Then I realized it was a dog. It had no collar and was eating the meat like it was starved. Then, another one without a collar. I grab the fir sapling that is acting as a door to my blind as a weapon and figure I will use it as a lance in case these guys are wild. I shout and clap. The dogs bark. I burst from the blind and scare one dog, but the second bares her teeth and growls. Fortunately at that moment her owner called and off she scampered. I told the owner her dog would probably be ill this evening, and then returned to the ravens."

Colleen released our second five-pack on February 21. They stayed around the whole deer we offered each of the next two days, fighting unsuccessfully with the Hills Pond pair. Colleen shared the blind with chickadees and shrews. One of the released birds froze her in the blind with a cold stare from mere inches. We were totally imbedded in the scene—part of the environment —we're a perch, a patch, a home for furred and feathered beast. As our new group stayed by their discovery, two previously radio-tagged birds were roosting with others on the edge of Lake Webb, several miles away as the raven flies. YW was still sending radio signals from the Weld dump. On February 23, the subordinate radio-tagged discoverer roosted near the food while the dominant bird roosted near Weld. We saw no soaring. The next morning, the subordinate and a few others who roosted nearby were at the food by 6:13. I heard the

Hills Pond pair quorking, ready to stiffen their defense. Seven minutes later the cavalry arrived. In the lead was the dominant radio-tagged bird. Waves of new birds dampened any hope the Hills Pond pair had of securing this scene. By 7:00 a.m., in the clear −2°F air, I counted forty ravens where yesterday there had been only six or seven.

Suddenly, the ravens were anxious. I heard clucking and *aaargh* sounds from beyond the food pile. The birds were aggressively scolding—mobbing— and moving closer. I had seen a fisher earlier in the winter and wondered if it was afoot. I was not eager to share my blind with that overgrown weasel. Or perhaps it was a bobcat. The winter ecology class had a glimpse of one last month. Or the dog pack Colleen had previously challenged. The unknown stood the hair up on the back of my neck. I saw the black mob and finally a white coyote trotted up for his share of the feast. He was huge and only a few feet from me. He quickly caught my scent and was off. I was convinced it was a wolf. Our friends suggested it was a coydog—the hybrid product of a male coyote and female dog. We later learned that Maine coyotes are larger than those of the western United States, in part because they have a close and hybrid history with Canadian wolves, not dogs. Whatever it was, it was gorgeous![2]

I snuck out of the blind, because the coyote had scared off the ravens for a moment. I checked on the other radio birds and discovered YW with another radio-tagged bird at the Weld dump. Soon I was in the hut watching the aviary birds and scanning for radio movements when the two birds from the dump seemed to be coming my way. The radio signals indicated they had crossed over York Hill and were in the general direction of the food I was watching earlier in the morning. Indeed, I confirmed their discovery of the new food on my way home. Information not only flowed from the food to the roost to the naïve, it also flowed directly to the naïve, something seabird biologists have long suspected to be important to the formation of bird flocks tracking fish. This phenomenon is called "local enhancement," the attraction of naïve animals to foods by the commotion of the scene. We have witnessed this often as wild birds flock to our aviary, and now we know how it plays into group formation in the wild. Raven groups assemble by a combination of recruitment from the roost and local enhancement.[3]

This night, everyone was soaring. The birds locally attracted from the dump soared as did those leading and following from roosts. Colleen and I witnessed three separate roosts emerge from the soaring party: a small bivouac at the food and two more distant roosts—one on York Hill by Camp Kaflunk and the other on Grahams' farm. All four radio-tagged birds were bedded in the distant roosts. On February 2, the party really kicked off. I observed fourteen tagged birds and all four radio-tagged ravens amidst a group of over fifty that cleaned up the once-mighty food pile. The coyote got his share as well, pushing ravens like erupting black lava from the feast. This festival was complete, and we knew the mechanics that derive from individual raven movements to produce the simple pattern of discovery, buildup, and departure of ravens from a discovery that so enthralled Bernd when he first watched ravens eat moose five years ago.

Ravens clearly preferred wild game to domestic fare. It had been over two weeks since we laboriously hauled another dead draft horse up Alder Brook Road and introduced it to five tagged ravens. Our discoverers attracted a small group of locals, but eventually they followed other leads and drifted away. The horse was rediscovered in mid-March, and as I watched thirty ravens eat in earnest a huge shadow sent them scattering. I heard an eagle calling, a comically musical cry from such a deadly force, but could not see the bird. We had never had this mighty predator join our ravens, so I craned around in the blind hoping for a glimpse. Bald Eagles were rare in New England at this time, still greatly suppressed by our species' careless overuse of poisons, notably DDT. Just over an hour after I entered the dark blind, a fully adult eagle rewarded my patience. In eagles, females are the larger, dominant sex, and I guessed this huge bird was a female. Her head and tail were radiant—such a contrast to the raven's black. She was perched right above the horse in a large, dead tree. The ravens were unwilling to feed below her, but they were intent on resuming their feast. An agile, stud raven swooped at the eagle three times and landed next to her. The raven gave the choking "air call" display and snapped his bill defiantly. The eagle could have cared less. Another raven perched a yard above the predator and was pounding furiously at the skeleton of the tree. Bark was flying, and twigs rained down on the eagle for a full two minutes. The eagle looked up slowly, and, as one of the wooden missiles drilled her in the back, she left. The stud raven was in hot pursuit, diving and screaming clucking alarms. The other ravens were more practical and quickly resumed dining on frozen horse.[4]

The struggle between raven and eagle—two species honed by nature into superb scavengers—revealed another benefit of raven sociality. A single raven could do little to dislodge an eagle, but a group—by luck, teamwork, or collective brainpower—was able to succeed. The raven that confronted the eagle from above, indirectly pelting it with debris, may have been a feathered Einstein, or just a lucky clown. But the chances that such fortunate actions will happen increase with each additional raven in attendance. I like to think I witnessed a purposeful tool use by a brilliant bird, but even if it was accidental, it offered a teaching moment to the frustrated raven pounding at the dead tree and perhaps to others watching. Making a connection between sitting above a predator, dropping sticks, and dislodging the threat would seem simple for a bird whose brain relative to its body size is on par with monkeys. I had read about researchers in the western United States climbing to raven nests only to have rocks tossed at them by irate ravens perched atop the natal cliff. I was relieved our birds had not yet fully grasped this notion but thrilled at seeing them well along the way.[5]

The days were getting longer, the ravens ranged widely, and our experiments were winding down. Colleen released our final group of discoverers across the highway from the Donkey Landing trap site during the last week of March with Bernd's help while I was at an interview in North Dakota, still hoping to land a coveted academic post. Apparently the birds had more options than a postdoc. They dispersed from the release area over the next few days rather than joining local roosts where they might recruit help. Their hurried exit caused Bernd to conclude the experiment was a failure and head back to Vermont. Unfortunately, he didn't communicate to Colleen that he had written off this experiment and opened the nearby trap. Colleen spent several frustrating mornings in the blind at the release site with no ravens in sight before finally discovering a group assembling outside the trap. Tempted, we planned for a final catch. It was April Fool's Day as I waited in the blind, ready to pull the trigger. My heart raced, just as it did every time I felt lucky enough to fool a raven. They were heading into the trap, and I was not greedy. I slammed the door on thirteen birds! Three were recaptures from our previous tagging efforts. One was an original survivor from our first aviary group. Colleen and I tagged and released them all as a parting gift to future raven researchers. Five of the birds were black-mouthed adults that might remain and breed nearby. We spent our last day in the hut on April 9, and released the final aviary group the next day. Our captive pair had a fresh nest and brood of young, so they remained in the aviary to be cared for by friends until Bernd moved back to York Hill, where he would spend the next year on sabbatical and recruit the next flock of raven researchers to follow up our discoveries. We were content to know that our efforts to capture, tag, and release more than 350 ravens would fuel more scientific dreams.

John's job searching had put him behind; he didn't have time to train for the final race. I started going out alone on training runs. One run was so icy that I turned around early fearing I would injure a dog if it slipped. I should have thought of myself. When I was loading the dogs into the truck, I slipped and knocked my head behind the ear on the door of the back compartment of the dog box. I saw stars. When my head cleared, I looked over at Buster, who gave me a quizzical look with his piercing blue eyes as if to say, "What are you doing on the ground?" Somewhat embarrassed and thankful that my audience was only four-legged and unable to tell of my clumsiness, I finished packing up and headed home. I told John about it when I stopped by the tree he had climbed to watch the roost. He asked to see my injury when he got home. He turned pale when he looked at it and told me to go to the hospital. I thought he was kidding. It was just a scrape. He took me to Zetta's to have her look at it and she said, "GO!" I fed the dogs, scooped the poop, and finally drove myself to the emergency room. I had an interesting story to tell while they reattached the backside of my ear with six stitches. The worst part was the bruising that went all the way down my neck.

The bruises were still fresh when we went to our final Maine sled race. John got some funny looks after they saw me. He played along with our sledding friends. We had a strong connection with so many now. I tried to hide the bruise with a turtleneck and hat, but I couldn't hide it all. To top it off, the weather was horrible in Greenville. The freezing rain turned quietly to rain. The race was called at the end of Saturday.

The Rangeley race usually ended the season for most mushers, but we decided not to run in it this year. I had committed to watching Hilary compete in the Miss Maine Teen Pageant. What a multitalented kid! The pageant judges had clearly studied her background materials. They asked her about being involved in dog mushing. I proudly listened to her describe raising a sled dog pup and racing a team of huskies. Her unique answers resonated with the judges. She was named most photogenic and second runner-up.

26 March 1991; Colleen's Journal: "We took the dogs for their last run, the snow was melting fast."

In early March we said farewell to our heavy oak sled and the awkward training cart Josh had named the "Death Mobile." The family that bought them also bought the Garden Way cart that had replaced the junker wheelbarrow used for hauling carcasses. We were starting to lighten our load in preparation for our move. Our destination was not settled: we waited for word from Fargo, Boise, and Anchorage.

eleven

Moving On

The roller coaster that all postdocs ride as they dream of permanent jobs and awake to rejection was slowing. An academic life in Montana, New Mexico, or North Dakota would not happen. None of my applications to colleges and universities, even those where I was invited to interview, resulted in the offer of a professorship. A bid to join an environmental firm in Alaska also fell flat. The word from Boise was more promising. During my interview with a consulting firm there, I met an energetic team of young scientists and technicians developing new ways to catch, track, and watch Golden Eagles and Prairie Falcons. They were passionate about the birds and devoted to their conservation. We bumped along thin roads in a vast plain of sagebrush, saltbush, and shadscale. We stood atop sheer cliffs of basalt, burned dark by now-dormant volcanoes, and peered into a canyon carved by one of the West's great rivers, the Snake. All around were birds of prey and their scavenging colleagues: coyotes, magpies, and ravens. This was my sort of place—vistas framed by sharp, snowy mountains; cattle guards straddling gravel roads, ground squirrels, jackrabbits, and tumbleweeds caught in barbed-wire fences. Shortly after returning to Maine, the phone call I had long imagined came through. The terms of the offer were generous: my salary would be boosted, our modest moving expenses would be covered, and I could take 15 percent of my time to study ravens in the shrub steppe of southwestern Idaho.

Because I had always seen myself in an academic job, deciding to become a consultant made me uneasy. Biological consultants are often viewed as consumers, not producers, of science. At best, they are seen as applying the scientific method to real-world problems. At worst, some have a reputation of doing or saying anything the client demands. Up to this point in my career, I had done only academic science, most of it basic research motivated only by interest in the truth about how nature worked. The insular quality of the academic world gave me freedom to discover as I pleased, and I feared I would lose this pleasure as a consultant. In the balance was the opportunity to conduct research that might help conserve the natural resources I so enjoyed. The deeper I looked into the Boise job, the more the balance shifted. I knew the principal investigator at the firm and his graduate research advisor, and I admired them both and the basic research they had published. The science of the current project also seemed sound. The firm was cooperating with federal agencies, universities, and nongovernmental organizations in a five-year study of falcon and eagle responses to military training. Funding was sufficient for sampling an unprecedented number of raptors and engaging the diverse team needed to understand predators, their prey, and the ecosystem within which they interacted. The overall project coordinator was a highly regarded professor from the University of California, Riverside. Everything I saw told me this was a solid research opportunity with basic and applied potential. In addition, Boise State University would host me as an adjunct professor of biology, allowing me to keep my foot in the academic door, teaching, advising, and supporting students as time and funding allowed. This wasn't the tenure track I desired but it was darn close.[1]

With few other real options, Colleen and I decided in late January to accept the offer and planned a move for late April 1991. We would have to leave Maine a few months earlier than planned, but our experiments were finished, and we had been working with an undergraduate student at the University of Maine, Farmington, who could track our birds as they dispersed through the spring thaw. The last bits of data would roll in as we headed west. Bernd was preparing for a year living on York Hill. It was time to focus on analysis and writing. It was time to move.[2]

In most academic relationships there comes a time when the student hungers to leave the mentor. Ten years of post-graduate schooling had given me enough confidence to crave independence. I wanted to define my own scientific path and settle into a more predictable lifestyle with Colleen. Bernd was rightfully defining his identity by the project and place he had invited us to share. Certainly I could have learned more by staying with Bernd: how to read nature, see her important questions, and reflect my knowledge with humble eloquence and wonder. Perhaps I should have. But tension was high. Bernd had paid with a failed marriage for his early investments in the project. I could never fully repay my debt to him for his early work, nor would I share evenly in the rewards our combined investments were now yielding. My relationship with Bernd was stretched but far from broken. We respected and admired each other, and we saw each other's weaknesses. Like the young ravens that matured from pink-mouthed beggars to black-mouthed yellers, I was ready to form new alliances and strut with my peers.

In our gamble to move to Maine we hit the jackpot. Colleen and I had lived a grand adventure in a new land. We had made strong connections with new people and their rural culture. We felt absolutely at home. And we knew other species—dogs and ravens—as few others could ever hope. Our relationship with each other was enriched by the challenges and discoveries we shared living, working, and playing together. At this young stage as a couple, complete immersion in each other's lives gave us a solid shared foundation to which we could always return.

I was content with our scientific accomplishments in Maine. Our proposal had been ambitious, but we had addressed each of our many objectives with a mixture of observation and experimentation. Bernd and I expected some leads to pay dividends and others to fizzle, and that was what happened. Our abilities to catch and tag hundreds of wild ravens and monitor their use of communal roosts, wild meals, and human refuse enabled us to clarify the role of social status, kinship, and gender to raven behavior. We better understood the alliances that formed between young male and female ravens and their immediate functions. And we knew something about the importance of these alliances and social status to pair formation and mate choice. Definitive tests of this important process remained, but we had opened the door. We had gained unplanned insights into the development of diet and vocal repertoires in the birds we raised and in those raised by wild and captive parents. It was clear to us that raven associations were structured by rules of dominance and sex, not by kinship. Ravens were selfish, doing what was best for each individual. Selfishness often gave the false appearance of generosity or reciprocity, but we learned that ravens were uniquely selfish cooperators. Successful ravens did not reciprocally share meals with unfortunate foragers at the roost, as did vampire bats. Nor did they behave like honeybees and communicate with hive mates the location of far-away foods. Their cooperation seemed less dependent on relationships between individuals and more dependent on the consequences of individual actions.[3]

We also had some failures. We were unable to observe individual ravens in wild roosts, as we had proposed. We learned a lot about how roosts worked, where they formed, and the benefits of joining a roost. But we did not decode the postures or calls that young ravens use to recruit the associates they so clearly needed for life among their territorial superiors. We were not surprised to fail in nature, but our inability to decode the secret of captive raven roosts was disappointing to us and I am sure frustrating to Bernd. To our eyes, the private actions of knowledgeable and naïve ravens remained unobservable. We had glimpses of excited knocking calls by some birds after they discovered food, and we heard the honking of ravens leaving a roost—but we never nailed a consistent recruitment signal, if indeed one exists.

Maybe if we had observed more, saw more clearly in the dark roost, focused rather than broadened our efforts, we would have found the mechanism of raven recruitment. But Bernd taught us to mine what was working and follow where nature was leading. The proposal we wrote together was a general guide, not a specific route. We had been blazing a trail, and as such we needed to be strategic, flexible, and adaptive to succeed. In the end, our creativity and luck at finding and chasing a few productive leads was enough. We were able to boil our years of research down into the simple but unprecedented claim that raven roosts were information centers. Six findings, which were the central propositions we made to the National Science Foundation, proved this claim. First, roosts consisted of both knowledgeable and naïve foragers. Second, ravens departed roosts each morning as highly synchronized groups, typically heading in a single direction. Third, this departure direction varied from day to day as the birds tracked new discoveries. Fourth, naïve birds followed roost mates to unknown feeding locations while naïve birds that we released outside of roosts were unable to do so. Fifth, birds we released at new feeding locations occasionally led roost mates back to these discoveries. Sixth, some of the same birds were both leaders and followers, suggesting that at least in a loose sense, good deeds were reciprocated.[4]

It made perfect sense from a Darwinian perspective that roosts should be information centers. Those that shared information, as well as those that followed, clearly benefited. Neither could feed effectively alone at foods defended fiercely by adult ravens, but by sharing information, they could all eat. Our findings were unique in proving that information centers could be mobile, forming near newly discovered foods and later at traditional sites when a feast was done. Soaring around a roost was an effective signal of roost movement, but the actual whisperings that went on in the roost about the location of the feast remain a puzzle. Nature did not fully reveal her secrets, but we were pleased to remove some of the mysterious cloak that had long darkened raven nights.

7 April 1991; Colleen's Journal: "We're giving ourselves a going away party today. A P.O.W. or 'piss on winter' party."

The party was a thank-you farewell. We invited all the people whom we had met through raven research and dogsledding, and we had a great turnout! About twenty-five braved the cool temperatures and sat on the deck of our one-room cabin and enjoyed a picnic supper. Ed drove up from Boston to say good-bye to us and the Maine family. Butch videotaped most of the party as a good-bye present. Everyone had a story to share about us, the ravens, or the dogs. The stories turned into long good-byes as the day got colder and darker. It was good to see how we had touched those who had been so good to us. Bill told of being frightened at first by the screaming and begging baby ravens he was raising with us. His fear quickly transitioned to wonder and a lifelong interest in birds. Ron Gerrish had to put the season's sap boiling on hold to join us, but the syrup was getting "daahk" as a raven. Lee brought a special pecan pie for John, which got Tom, Bill, and Butch wondering about their pies. There was a strong bond among these four boys, with obvious love and respect for each other and their biological or cultural mother, Lee. The dogs howled and barked throughout the party. They seemed to know something was up and wanted to add their stories and opinions. John and Bill planned a last fishing outing—they would troll for togue and salmon in the morning. We went to bed with full stomachs and enriched by the friendships that had warmly carried us through three cold Maine winters. I felt it was not good-bye but "until we meet again."

The people of Maine had forever embedded themselves in my heart. Living in Maine, I had acquired a deep psychological sense of belonging to the place and its people. If John had had an opportunity to stay, albeit not working with Bernd, I would have jumped for joy. John thought he was taking me home to the West, to the desert with sagebrush. Geographically and habitat-wise, yes, the West was home. But I had fallen in love with the Maine way of life, and I was not eager to leave. But a change was needed, as was a job, so reluctantly I waved farewell to our little cabin and friends, and we rode off to another chapter in our lives.

31 January 1991; Colleen's Journal: "John got an offer from Boise today. It'll be a change to a dry desert environment, but we're ready for a change."

The move was challenging. We had arrived with all our possessions fitting into a trailer pulled by our 4Runner. Now we had more stuff, more dogs, and two cars. We rented a fifteen-foot Ryder truck with a trailer for the 4Runner. John drove the Ryder with Sitka riding high as his copilot, and I drove the dog truck. Topper was my copilot while Kenai, Granite, and Buster rode in their boxes in the dog truck. The hardest thing to leave behind was Sky; she sat down and howled as we pulled out at 6:00 a.m. without her. I'm sure she thought her team was leaving for a run. Little did she know they wouldn't return. Tears blurred my vision as we headed toward Rumford and points farther west.[5]

Our trip back across the country again depended on friends and family. We drove through New York, north through Canada, and dropped down into Michigan to stay with my brother and his wife. We continued to Illinois to my aunt and uncle's farmhouse, then into Kansas to John's parents' house to pick up our belongings, stored in their basement for three years.

Along the way we learned that Siberian Huskies, particularly motivated ones like Buster and Granite, can escape from almost anything. Both managed to pull up a grounded cable at one stop and chew their way out of the dog box at another break. We had some interesting chases as well as some weird looks from bystanders. Kenai was content to stay put. Her usual car-sickness was cured by the second day of the trip; the tedium of a long ride seemed the proper medicine. Eventually Buster and Granite identified the dog truck as "home" and settled into a routine on the move.

From Kansas we drove west to Colorado, where we endured tornado sirens. Our six-person tent whipped in the wind overnight as five dogs and two people struggled to sleep, hoping we wouldn't end up back in the real Land of Oz.

April weather in the Rocky Mountains is unpredictable. As we drove into

Wyoming, we hit a snowstorm. John struggled with the windshield wipers on the Ryder as I tried to keep the two-wheel-drive dog truck on the road. We decided to stop in Rawlins, Wyoming. Camping was not an option because of eight inches of snow and ice, so we found a warm motel. We regretted that our sled was inaccessibly packed in the Ryder, or we would have done some urban mushing to ease our nerves.

We slipped and sloshed our way to Boise, but when we arrived at our temporary housing there was no place to put the dogs: the falconers with whom John would be working had used the promised dog kennels as hawk houses. As John settled into his position as assistant principal investigator, I used my expertise with wire and built a temporary dog kennel and went house hunting.

My role as technician had ended, and I was phasing into the supportive spouse role until we were well settled and I could look for a job. I still had to keep our dogs happy and healthy. Luckily, our shared interest and enthusiasm for dogsledding continued. John didn't have as much flexibility with his time as he had in Maine, but many weekends were devoted to the dogs.

Much of my experience in Maine centered on the bridges the ravens and dogs allowed me to build to supportive and fun people. With those bridges broken, I was lonely in Idaho. I was not directly involved with John's new job, so while he was chasing eagles and ravens I was trying to find people who were interested in sledding or Siberian Huskies. Because no active dogsledding groups existed, I started teaching a dogsledding class. My circle of friends interested in dogs had enhanced my experience in Maine, and now I set out to create new bonds with like-minded dog owners. During the six years we lived in Idaho I met many wonderful people through this venue. We drove farther to races than in Maine, yet we could train nearby on cold, flat desert roads. In some cases, we did demonstrations that led to races. Our experiences in Maine carried us through the newest chapter of life in Idaho. Our knowledge of a common bird allowed us to take the research with us and test our hypotheses in a new environment as well as transplant our expertise in dog-sledding to a new place.[6]

Before we left Maine, we made an agreement with Bernd that I would give priority to writing up our roosting results for publication. My new job and spare time would allow me to complete this chapter in our lives. This blending of the old and new is typical for young scientists: because we must accept one job before the previous one is fully completed, we are often writing up the results from a past project as we start new investigations. We discussed the authorship issues and all agreed that I would be the lead author on the paper and that Colleen would be a trailing author.

Bernd helped shape the paper from afar. Our working relationship im-proved with distance. We rewrote the paper three times before it was finally accepted for publication in *Animal Behaviour*. Each time we reorganized, rethought, and refined our presentation. We had struggled to get every bit of data we could, and now we had to crunch three years of notes into fifteen magazine pages. The variation that intrigued me had to be distilled into a general, comprehensible message. Doing so was like weeding a garden—the end result was pretty, but the work was numbing and tedious. For me, it also seemed endless. But persistence paid off. Even though our work did not see print until five years later, it remains my most significant paper, although not the least controversial. Five years after the paper was published, Bernd and I had to defend it against written challenges. Our critics suggested we rushed to conclude that ravens shared information. Years of cold mornings and critical experiments were not in our definition of "rush," so we reiterated our findings and efforts (and in so doing published a second paper emphasizing and expanding upon our findings). I am thrilled when my current students read about our work in their textbooks, but the greatest reward came seven years after our initial paper. In 2003, researchers in the United Kingdom reported that Welsh ravens also soared to share information at mobile roosts. Our hard work had been replicated, and independent confirmation is science's gold standard.[7]

In fact, the behaviors we knew from Maine play out regularly where ravens gather in the wintry forests of the Northern Hemisphere. From Maine to Iceland, England to Poland, Alaska to Minnesota, researchers have made observations consistent with our findings. Whenever large predators or harsh conditions kill native ungulates like deer, elk, and moose, ravens exploit the spoils using a combination of local attraction and distant recruitment from roosts. Our move to Idaho, however, had taken me far from this ecological stage.

In the frozen shrublands, ravens were different. We often passed road-killed deer in the snowy mountains where we now went to run the dogs, and in mid-December 1991, I was itching to watch a dead deer. I slipped one in the truck under the dog box and later dropped it in the desert shrubs near our new home. Two hundred and thirty ravens flew over the deer, but over the next four days only fifteen to twenty ravens dined. Thinking deer might be rare in this western rangeland, I tossed a sheep in the brush. That more typical offering was shunned for sixty days before the first raven tore wool. Clearly the Idaho ravens that now commanded my attention had not read our early papers. But could the exceptions I was seeing in this new country help explain the biological rules we honed in Maine?

The shrub steppe of the Great Basin is a cold desert. In many ways, it cannot be more distinct from the hardwood forests of Maine. Trees are scarce in the sage flats, and a raven perched low on an old cattle fence can see for miles. Sounds carry unimpeded through the dry, treeless western air. Death is as common here as in Maine, but the victims are small—mostly jackrabbits, snakes, and ground squirrels proffered to scavengers by eagles, falcons, and speeding cars. Agriculture—alfalfa, sugar beets, and a few grains—is irrigated into verdant patches that diversify and subsidize what a dry nature offers ravens. Cows and their stinking by-products piled high in feedlots and slaughterhouses choked us while we were in the field, but they also provided a rich and reliable bounty for the local ravens.

Contrasting scenery. The wide openness of Idaho, shown here, may be part of the reason its ravens do not need to share information at roosts. An independent hunter can easily find foods or raid those found by others.

Ravens have adapted to the unique features of landscapes around the world. Natural selection wedges them into local scenes from the Himalayas to Death Valley by adjusting their actions and customs, and even their size. Here in Idaho I noticed that they seemed to have changed their foraging and roosting styles to harvest the conspicuous bounty of road and raptor kills, offal, and agriculture. Ravens were always present as I started my new raptor research, and when I began to write up the Maine results, I recruited James McKinley and a succession of seasonal field technicians into a parallel study of Idaho ravens that we could compare with our work from Maine. We didn't dare build another aviary, but we followed birds in the field. We found breeding pairs to be much more tightly packed together in Idaho. In the stretch of Maine from Wilton to Weld we knew of five breeding pairs of ravens, but in the same size area in Idaho I counted twenty-five breeding pairs. Despite this abundance, ravens continued to be rare at the carcasses we provided. A typical group of ravens eating at the foods we placed in the Maine woods peaked at forty-four birds. But in Idaho the typical peak was only nine ravens. Even at deer I never saw more than thirty birds at a single time.[8]

Ravens accumulated at carcasses with a different tempo in Idaho relative to Maine. We had a few glimpses of recruitment from Idaho roosts, most dramatically as thirty came in one morning to a deer where the day before only three had fed. But the vast majority of the buildups we documented occurred during a single day. Dave Schuetze, a New Englander learning about Idaho, and I watched the typical progression of ravens at a road-killed jackrabbit. At dawn, a single raven flew over, followed by a few others, who circled but moved on. An hour later three ravens circled the warming hare and the party began. Five ravens landed on the road and began to move in. Bolder, faster, hungrier magpies rushed ahead and got the first bites. Ravens waited and pirated food from the magpies. A Rough-legged Hawk was attracted and tried to take the entire rabbit with one swoop. Trucks sped by, causing all the birds to flush wildly, but for only a short time. Eight ravens eventually assembled and along with the darting magpies they finished the rabbit within six hours of the discovery. The same story played out repeatedly another morning—on our way into the field we saw six jackrabbits on the road, and when we returned all had been consumed. In the land of dead jackrabbits, the finding is easy and recruitment irrelevant. Information about the location of a flat jack is too short-lived to be exchanged at night. We quickly proved that local enhancement is the primary mode by which ravens find carcasses. Although ravens also used this mode in Maine, it was responsible for far less of the eventual buildup of birds. Because the Idaho fare did not favor recruitment from the roost, the average group size of ravens at any given carcass remained much below that which we witnessed in Maine. In fact, it was similar to the small groups we watched assemble in Maine for the first few days after defended foods were discovered.

The facility with which ravens can use local or more distant sources of information impressed me. Clearly, social strategy is adapted to the local environment. If I was reading this story correctly, then behaviors should be much different at an Idaho roost. Wow, were they ever. In Maine, we rarely saw more than a hundred ravens roost together, but in Idaho records were set each night. On a crisp evening during my first winter I was treated to the first of many great shows. The sunset reflected off the basalt outcroppings. As the sage and grass flats turned to ink, the glassy insulators of a huge, 500-kilovolt power line literally glowed. Ravens flocked to the massive girders and wires that towered above the desert. The birds, who naturally would roost on cliffs and even in the stunted sage, now sat high on the wires shoulder to shoulder. They spilled into the steel supports and hunkered above the insulators. Their collective crap was so thick that it occasionally shut down the flow of juice from the Snake River dams to Las Vegas. But what really impressed me was that ravens actually came into Idaho roosts in synchronized groups from one or a few directions and left less synchronized in many directions. This pattern was directly opposite what we found in Maine. We confirmed it with a month of autumn observations at two Idaho roosts: Idaho and Maine ravens employed completely different roosting strategies.[9]

By watching ravens scavenge small, regularly available meals in the new visual and acoustic environment of Idaho, I could see how feeding strategies influenced roosting behavior. Roosts function as information centers where foods are long lasting and local cues cannot lead a raven to a sure meal. In Maine, adults defended food bonanzas because a controlled moose or deer might feed them for weeks or months. Faced with defense, nonterritorial birds had to attract and join others if they were to feed. Defense was noisy, and this noise was attractive to ravens, but in Maine it was insufficient at attracting enough ravens to dissuade the adults and enable those attracted to eat. The low density of ravens or the dampening of voices by a thick forest may explain why local cues were not effective in Maine. In Idaho, defense of carcasses was rare, and with many ravens in the area and little to muffle the noise or obscure the movements around a feast, groups could quickly and easily assemble by simply homing to the scene. And because most carcasses were small, and the scavenging community large and diverse, finds were rapidly consumed and irrelevant the day after discovery.

Roost size mirrored these local environmental conditions. Maine raven roosts were small because the information shared within must benefit all. These roosts contained enough ravens to search widely for rare dead animals and muster an effective army of recruits, but they were not so large that competition among the troops negated the benefits of reducing adult defense. Free from the need to function as information centers, raven roosts in Idaho could evolve in response to other pressures. Roosting together for safety, warmth, and social benefits not related to foraging swelled roost size.

Because raven roosts in Idaho rarely functioned as information centers, I had a new look at the recruitment signal that so eluded us in Maine. What Idaho roosts lacked must be part of the signal. They lacked dispersed arrivals, shifting locations, soaring displays, and uniformly synchronized departures of honkers. Ravens arrived at Maine roosts from many independent directions— this was how information was carried into the roost. In Idaho, ravens arrived mostly together, from a few places where they had foraged together. They did not bring information relevant to tomorrow's feast. Few if any birds needed to know where to go tomorrow. Each was well informed by the day's activities at feedlots, fields, and roadside kills. Without discoveries to report, roost sites did not need to shift location. In Idaho, ravens did not bivouac, and birds roosting at traditional sites did not soar. Soaring informed roosting ravens that a new discovery demanded a bivouac, but this information was not needed in Idaho. A few distinct stretches of power line were traditionally used for roosting, probably to cut commuting costs. Idaho ravens soared, often in large groups on thermals or updrafts along steep cliffs, usually well before making a beeline to roosts. In Idaho, soaring was more free-form, like a playful dance as birds chase and undulate on stiff winds or rise on hot desert air like a kettle of vultures above the African plain. The coordinating and gathering of independent hunters that we saw in Maine was not evident in the soaring flights of

Idaho. And finally, the honking we suspected was part of the actual recruit-ment mechanism may in fact be so. It was hard to hear distinct voices as thousands of ravens left the Idaho roosts. They flew from their high wires loudly, in confusing balls or strung out like geese. But these information-free departures were more gradual and less coordinated than those we watched in Maine. They sounded like ravens going to a roost or awakening from a bivouac near food. I never heard the honking and excited ringing calls coming from a tight-knit flock that first impressed me on the frozen spine of Taylor Hill. Honking ravens are sharing secrets.

Konrad Lorenz, who with Niko Tinbergen and Karl von Frisch founded the modern study of animal behavior, emphasized the importance of compara-tive study. By noting behavioral differences among species or between loca-tions, he said we could better understand the general rules that governed an animal's actions. The sagebrush ravens provided the comparison that Lorenz extolled. Idaho's ravens showed me what was so special about the ravens we knew so well from Maine. Sometimes to see the obvious, you need to look away. As tough as it was to leave Maine, the view from the West put my research and my life in better perspective. It was good to move.[10]

twelve

Twenty Years Later

A raven quorks from high above Hills Pond as we stroll Alder Brook Road. It is late August 2008. The curves of gravel are familiar, as are the camps along the way. The bridge is as we remembered. Just across it, Raymond Macomber, who built his cabin here in 1950 pokes his head out to say hello and recall the ravens. He is part of this land. The village of Weld also seems the same; the general store is tended by the same owners. The trail to Bernd's cabin remains unimproved, and the cabin itself has aged considerably and a replacement is planned. A new, open-air outhouse sits a few yards from its predecessor, which is now used for storage. The pair of loons on Hills Pond has produced but a single chick.

But there are changes. There are more side roads into the once-remote forest; there is a proposed and bladed subdivision on the summit of the Houghton Ledges; Farmington has a Walmart store; and the dumps that were so heavily used by ravens are now gone. We suspect raven numbers are down or at least more volatile in response. It was two decades ago when we settled into the small cabin in Tom and Zetta's backyard. Today, as visitors, we wouldn't think of staying anywhere else. We are introducing our two daughters to the land that so shaped our lives. They crave the warm sun, enjoy the quiet, and mostly like being able to try driving on the desolate gravel road.

As we walk, we are drawn off the road. Seemingly without thought John homes to the lookout spruce that he spent so many nights atop, scanning for ravens. It is easy to find. A wooden step that regularly boosted him into the branches still clings fast to the lower trunk, but just above the milled insult the tree has toppled. A strong wind, heavy snow, or normal decadence felled the conifer, and today it is on its way to returning to the soil. Our actions have changed this piece of Maine, but the actions of Maine changed us much more substantially.

We knew our time in New England had an endpoint, as had our graduate student years in Arizona. But when we crossed the Lemon Fair River long ago, we never expected to have the attachments to this place that pull us even today. We had been fully adopted into a family and melted into a living landscape. Maine gave us a cultural and geographic sense of place where we felt more deeply rooted than in Arizona before or Idaho after. Those roots are still strong. Tom and Zetta spread the word that we were returning for a visit, and in short order the entire family is on their back porch. Lee passed away shortly after we headed west, but Henry, Bill and Lili, Butch and Nancy, and Jimmy are all here. Their kids, toddlers and teens when last seen, are adults with children of their own. They are all glad to see us and meet our daughters. There are no dogs, and time has grayed us into a middle-aged sort of settled look, but we pick up conversations right where we had left them at our P.O.W. party decades earlier and a backyard away.

We caught up on their lives. Henry had retired at age sixty-three from International Paper. The company had busted the strike that so defined the part of Henry's life we had shared. Workers in the southern mills had refused to strike, and without solidarity across state lines, corporate America defeated the Maine worker. Jobs are still scarce up here. Butch now works in the mill for a reincarnated International Paper. Billy went back to school to study social work after most of the shoe factories in Maine closed. Even the sprawling Bass shoe company of Wilton was gone. Now Billy pursues his music career.

We had new tales to tell. We had learned much more about the mythical and natural raven. We added dogs over the years and had two wonderful daughters. Our joke was that we would add a dog or a child for every year of marriage. We got to thirteen. We raced faster and longer, but life soon overwhelmed our hobby. Now we live among Border Collies not sled dogs. Brodie and Topper would approve.[1]

As we retraced familiar walks, we were transported back to training runs, races, experiments, and good times. Like labor pains, the challenges were mostly forgotten. Controversy was blurred. As parents and mentors of students and postdocs of our own, we now saw our time in Maine more as Bernd had seen it then. Having students of our own working on our raven projects, we know better the investments that were needed to make a project successful. But we also saw the importance of a motivated and capable colleague. With invested students and invested mentors, conflict is inevitable; both want success and few motivated people see the same path to a goal. Scientists in particular may consciously avoid one path simply to blaze a new one. Today this is obvious; twenty years ago it was at times frustrating.

John finally got the academic job he wanted. By luck, the research initiated in Idaho spread to include studies of jays, crows, and ravens in Washington, and when a professorship at the University of Washington was announced, John was in the right place at the right time to land it. We are still accumulating experiences and learning from each new place, but we can honestly tell the young scientists whom we have the pleasure to work with that what may seem like hell today will surely be heaven tomorrow. The freedom of a postdoc more than compensates for its uncertainty and insecurity. Embrace it and know there is a job waiting. Let no person dim your passion.

Today Bill and Lili tell us how difficult it is to keep the passion for science in young people. Aaron, their son who often helped us catch and tag ravens, joins in the discussion about his high school science project. He prepared a vignette on ravens complete with a miniature, working trap and spruce observation blind. It wasn't accepted, however, because "animal projects" were no longer sanctioned. An agenda, driven by important and real concerns for animal welfare, has missed its mark in this case. Rather than instilling a respect for life it has dimmed the flame of curiosity.

Writing was a way for us to relive, relearn, and reflect on our past. Our notes, journals, and letters sometimes stung, but mostly they put us right back in the woods. We could hear ravens, feel the cold, and get steamed over terse communiqués. The risks we took, the people we lived among, the dogs we tended, and the ravens we studied all shaped us. Confronting the past has been unexpectedly cathartic. It has strengthened our relationship with Bernd and made us aware of the need to confide, trust, and talk openly with students and colleagues. But mostly it provided a perspective that we had been too busy to fully appreciate. Today as we sit among old friends and rekindle strong bonds we feel even more a part of Maine. We learn that Hills Pond is for sale and wonder if we should think more seriously about retirement. We have come full circle.

Appendices

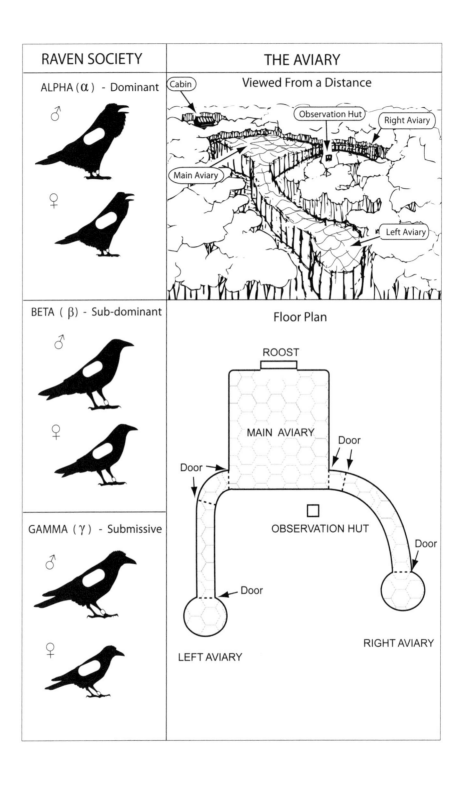

RAVEN SOCIETY	THE AVIARY

RAVEN SOCIETY

ALPHA (α) - Dominant

♂

♀

BETA (β) - Sub-dominant

♂

♀

GAMMA (γ) - Submissive

♂

♀

THE AVIARY

Viewed From a Distance

Cabin

Observation Hut

Right Aviary

Main Aviary

Left Aviary

Floor Plan

ROOST

MAIN AVIARY

Door

Door

Door

OBSERVATION HUT

Door

LEFT AVIARY

RIGHT AVIARY

A Schematic Chronology of Our Aviary Research

Over the course of our three-year research project we captured and released more than 300 ravens. Many of these were housed for various lengths of time in our aviary complex. We have described the general knowledge we gained from our time with these briefly captive wild creatures, and here we illustrate and summarize the main flows of ravens from captivity or birth into the aviary and back into the wild. Individual ravens to which we have referred in the text are signified by their wing tags. The gender (males larger and with shaggier throats) and social status (alpha nonbreeders and breeding adults with ears up and pants down; beta nonbreeders with sleek heads; and gamma subordinates with fuzzy heads) of central characters are indicated by icons arranged to the left of each diagram. The aviary and observation hut are drawn to scale and viewed from above. Please see the drawing by Jack DeLap on the facing page to understand how the completed aviary fit into the topography of York Hill,

facing page: Orientation for the summary of our aviary research. Ravens are illustrated to show their gender (relative size) and social status (dominant birds are shown with ears up and pants down, subdominants with sleek heads, and less dominant individuals with submissive, fuzzy heads). The identity of ravens featured in the text is indicated by abbreviated color combinations on their wing tags (here they are blank). The aviary complex is drawn to scale and shown from a distance on the actual topography of York Hill, behind Bernd's cabin. The scaled floor plan of the aviary is referenced to the distant view and includes the position of the six doors we manipulated for various experiments, main and satellite aviaries, roosting shed, and observation hut.

how we rendered this in two dimensions, and how the gender and status of important ravens are illustrated.

Our first challenge in conducting research with wild ravens in our experimental setting was to demonstrate that behavior was uncompromised by captivity. Bernd and I ran this experiment from February 16 to 27, 1988, with our first aviary group. At this time we had just completed the main portion of the aviary and the observation hut. We stocked the aviary with twenty ravens (sixteen juveniles and four adults) caught hours earlier in the meadow beside Bernd's cabin. We were buoyed by the natural behavior of these pioneers. They fed together, displayed their status to each other, wrestled, played, and called, just as did the birds we watched in the wild. Each night they tussled and gathered in the sleeping shed we constructed, and as darkness fell they roosted as a communal group. Our feasibility test was a success, which figured prominently in our proposals to the National Science Foundation for further research.

In late 1988, Colleen and I filled a now fully built aviary complex with a new research flock. Our goals were to replicate in fine detail the social interactions Bernd and I had observed among our first group of juvenile ravens as they fed and roosted together. Most important were the experiments we would devise to observe variously sized groups of juveniles interact with territorial adults. On December 29, 1988, we placed twenty juveniles in the main aviary and an adult pair in one of the satellite aviaries. Our juveniles were identified by the color sequences (RYR = red yellow red) on their wing tags. By opening the doors that stopped the juveniles from exploring the tunneled arms of the aviary complex, we could allow our captive nonbreeders to encounter, on their own volition, either foods that were undefended in the left arm and satellite aviary, or foods that were defended by the adult pair that resided in the right aviary. From the tiny observation hut, we recorded the communication and interactions among our captive juveniles, between the juveniles and the adults, and even between our captive ravens and wild ravens that were attracted to the commotion in the aviary. We released the captive juveniles from October to December 1989 and observed their interactions with wild birds at roosts and communal feasts over the next several years.

We augmented our captive stock by catching some of the wild ravens that visited the aviary. We built a small corral to funnel visitors to the aviary into a dead-end trap.

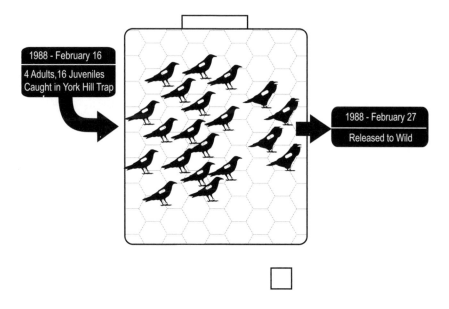

1988 - February 16

4 Adults,16 Juveniles
Caught in York Hill Trap

1988 - February 27

Released to Wild

Our first captive raven group and the aviary as it stood during our first test season. Only the main aviary, its roosting shed, and the observation hut were completed at this time. This group was held captive only for twelve days in February 1988.

During the first year, we caught an additional eleven ravens in this trap and held them at our house aviary for a few days before releasing them into wild roosts and at garbage dumps in the region. These birds, tags sporting the prefix "NV," were described in chapter 8 as they helped us test the information center hypothesis.

We restocked the aviary complex from January to February 1990 with thirty-one juveniles caught from the wild. We typically housed only twenty birds at a time in the main aviary, but as we were interested in how new recruits were treated by an established flock, we constantly mixed up the birds we introduced during the second

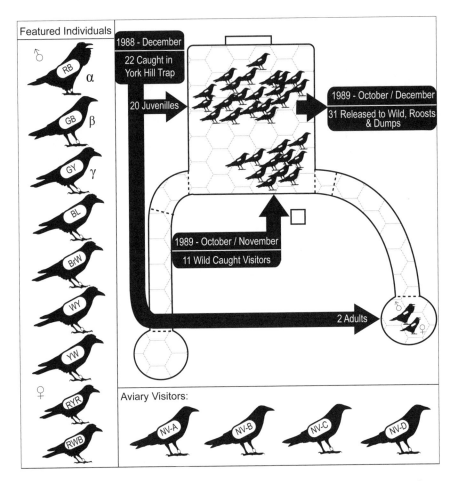

Featured Individuals

♂
RB α
GB β
GY γ
BL
BrW
WY
YW
♀
RYR
RWB

1988 - December
22 Caught in York Hill Trap

20 Juvenilles

1989 - October / December
31 Released to Wild, Roosts & Dumps

1989 - October / November
11 Wild Caught Visitors

2 Adults

Aviary Visitors:
NV-A   NV-B   NV-C   NV-D

A completed aviary complex now houses our second group of ravens and a pair of territorial adults. Eleven wild birds who visited the aviary during 1989 were captured and held briefly prior to release at roosts and landfills.

winter of aviary work. We stashed birds briefly at our home aviary and secluded them for various lengths of time in the unoccupied left aviary. We also introduced our hand-reared baby ravens (sporting yellow [Y] or red [R] tags) from Vermont to the wild juveniles in the aviary complex at this time. We continued to replicate our observations to determine how juveniles accessed food defended by the territorial adults, and we contrasted their behavior toward adults with their behavior toward one another. As we finished our observations, we released the juveniles individually from January to April 1990, often outfitting them prior to departure with a radio transmitter. We tracked these released birds daily to learn how they used communal roosts, followed knowledgeable peers, and interacted with others after their return to the wild. Our first experiments designed to observe free-living ravens moving between feeding locations that they had discovered and communal roosts featured B70 and B71. Our first suggestion that such experiments might actually work involved B90, who appeared to lead roost mates back to the food we had planted for him to discover.

We continued to replicate our feeding experiments with a fourth group of ravens throughout the summer and autumn of 1990. In April, we captured eleven juveniles at Donkey Flats and housed them until September to October in the aviary complex. In addition to our standard observations of their interactions with the defensive adults, we experimented with mate choice among these birds. By housing them in various combinations, we reduced the status of dominant males (RG, WBr, BrGr) and elevated that of the subordinates (Br). We then observed females (GBG, RW) adjust their interest with the males, noting that some pumped-up subordinates were now more attractive to females and that some deflated dominants were accordingly less attractive.

Much of our attention during this summer was focused on the adults as they nested in their aviary. We observed them care for and then disperse their young (YA4, YA5) from the natal territory. The aviary complex afforded us novel views of the formation and dissolution of familial bonds because we could see every move the family made, especially around dispersal time. We documented parts of the raven life cycle that were rarely seen in the wild—their mating, nurturing of young by parents, observational learning by growing offspring, and dispersal from the safety of home to the uncertainty of life with new and immediately aggressive peers.

From September to October 1990, our captive wild and parent-reared ravens were released as part of our new field experiments. These birds were outfitted with radio tags and released from small pet carriers at large animal carcasses we placed in the field. We tracked the movements and behavior of each released bird to document how it used and conveyed information at its nightly roosting aggregations about distant feeding opportunities. YW, a prodigal son from the second group, rejoined the aviary group and was used in a release experiment.

Our fifth aviary group included thirteen wild juveniles that we captured individu-

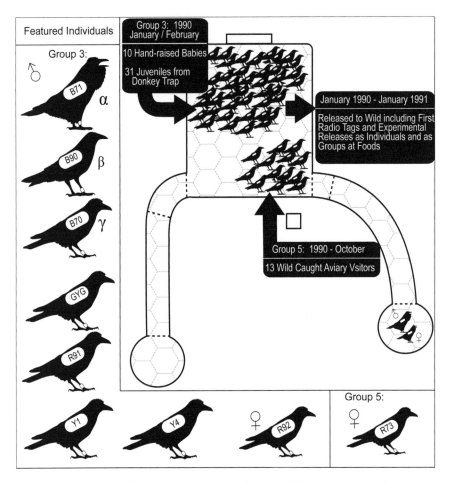

In our second year of research we observed three different groups of ravens in the aviary. Groups 3 and 5, which included mixes of wild and hand-reared ravens are illustrated (figure on opposite page shows Group 4). Many of these birds were held only briefly before being returned to the wild to test the central predictions of the information center hypothesis.

ally as they visited the aviary. We used this small group to replicate our experiments on the foraging of nonbreeding ravens in the presence and absence of territorial adults. We began these experiments in October 1990 and released the juveniles from November 1990 to January 1991. These birds are illustrated with the other groups we used principally for replication in 1990. Again we used these releases as additional experiments, radio-tagging birds before release and letting them "discover" food

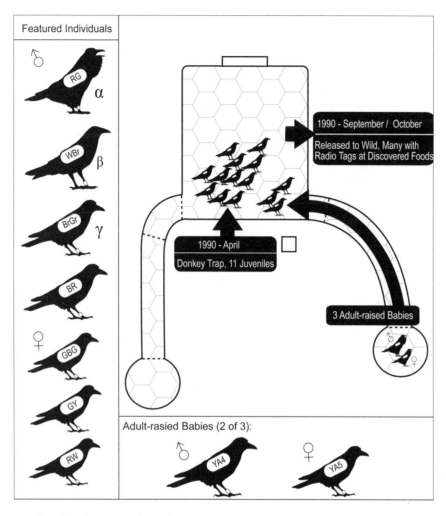

Our fourth group of captive ravens was used to understand mate choice
and the raising of young by the adult pair.

bonanzas as they rejoined wild raven society. R73 was especially instructive in showing us that knowledgeable ravens recruit naïve ones from the roost.

   While we learned much from each group of ravens in the aviary, to the statistician
in us each group was but a single sample. To improve the generality of our results, we
needed large samples, which meant we needed less detailed but key observations on
more groups. We did this work from January to April 1991 by catching three groups of

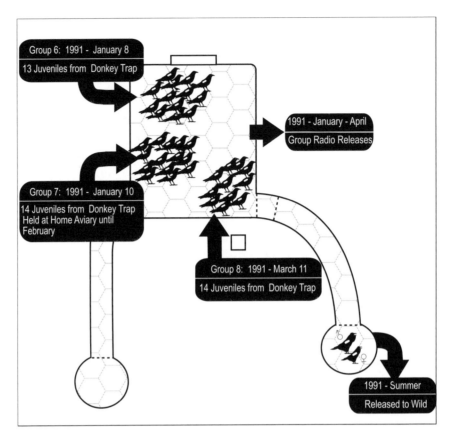

The final three groups of ravens that we studied to replicate our findings on social interactions and group foraging dynamics. Bernd released the adult pair in summer 1991, and they then remained around York Hill, where they established a territory and lived freely.

juveniles and housing them for about one month each in the aviary complex. During their time in the aviary we documented their dominance hierarchy and measured their feeding, fighting, and vocal behavior with and without the influence of the adult pair. We radio-tagged them and released them as groups of discoverers at carcasses of domestic or wild animals that we had seeded into the snowy Maine forests. As we prepared to move west, we completed experiments and released the eighth juvenile group to live within the aviary. Bernd opened the adult aviary in the summer of 1991, and the pair that had taught us so much about territoriality and parenting style slowly expanded their defended turf. They raised a second brood of young in the aviary nest and eventually roosted near Bernd's cabin. The next year, and for many years thereafter, they bred as free-living wild birds in the nearby conifer forest.

The capturing and housing of wild ravens for our aviary experiments had been scientifically productive if naturally disruptive. But now all was right. Wild ravens, many of whom were in our grasp at some point in their lives, searched for food, played in the snow, rocketed from the windy sky, squabbled and challenged each other, and even raised their offspring on York Hill.

The Natural Histories of Dogs
and Ravens

Our understanding of animals has been greatly expanded as researchers from different disciplines can now instantly share their findings and regularly do so. Old approaches of inquiry merge with fascinating new genetic, physiological, and behavioral approaches to paint an increasingly complete picture of the history and inner world of many species. Dogs and ravens have become especially well known in the few decades since they first caught our attention. To provide a broader perspective of those species, which figure so prominently in our story, we synthesize the growing knowledge about our central characters in the paragraphs that follow. Our information comes from the primary and secondary scientific literature listed in the notes and the bibliography. In addition to these sources, we suggest the following books for those who wish to know more:

On Dogs

Attla, G., with B. Levorsen. 1974. *Everything I Know about Training and Racing Sled Dogs.* New York: Arner Publications.

Brearley, J. M. 1974. *This Is the Siberian Husky.* Neptune City, NJ: T.F.H. Publications.

Cellura, D. 1990. *Travelers of the Cold: Sled Dogs of the Far North.* Anchorage: Alaska Northwest Books.

Coppinger, L. 1977. *The World of Sled Dogs: From Siberia to Sport Racing.* New York: Howell Book House.

Coppinger, R., and Coppinger, L. 2001. *Dogs: A New Understanding of Canine Origin, Behavior, and Evolution.* Chicago: University of Chicago Press.

Coren, S. 2004. *How Dogs Think: What the World Looks Like to Them and Why They Act the Way They Do.* New York: Free Press.

Handelman, B. 2008. *Canine Behavior: A Photo Illustrated Handbook.* Norwich, VT: Wolf and Word Press.

Horowitz, A. 2009. *Inside of a Dog: What Dogs See, Smell and Know.* New York: Scribner.

Levorsen, B., ed. 1976. *MUSH! A Beginner's Manual of Sled Dog Training.* New York: Arner Publications.

Lorenz, K. 1954. *Man Meets Dog.* London: Methuen.

Miklósi, Á. 2007. *Dog Behaviour, Evolution, and Cognition.* Oxford: Oxford University Press.

Salisbury, G., and L. Salisbury. 2003. *The Cruelest Miles: The Heroic Story of Dogs and Men in a Race against an Epidemic.* New York: W. W. Norton.

Schwartz, M. 1997. *A History of Dogs in the Early Americas.* New Haven: Yale University Press.

Stuck, H. 1914. *Ten Thousand Miles with a Dog Sled: A Narrative of Winter Travel in Interior Alaska.* 1988 reprint. Prescott, AZ: Wolfe Publishing.

Thompson, R. n.d. *Seppala's Saga of the Sled Dog.* Volume 1. Self-published.

Thompson, R. n.d. *Seppala's Saga of the Sled Dog.* Volume 2. N.p.: R.T.C.I. Press.

Willett, D.W. 1986. *The Seppala Siberian.* Viola, ID: Heritage North Press.

Zimen, E. 1981. *The Wolf: His Place in the Natural World.* London: Souvenir Press.

On Ravens

Boarman, W. I., and B. Heinrich. 1999. Common Raven (*Corvus corax*). The Birds of North America, No. 476, ed. A. Poole and F. Gill. Philadelphia: Birds of North America.

dos Anjos, L., S. Debus, S. Madge, and J. M. Marzluff. 2009. *Handbook of Birds of the World,* vol. 14. Barcelona: Lynx Edicions.

Glandt, D. 2008. *Der Kolkrabe. 2. Auflage.* Wiebelsheim: AULA-Verlag.

Heinrich, B. 1999. *Mind of the Raven: Investigations and Adventures with Wolf-Birds.* New York: Cliff Street Books.

Kilham, L. 1989. *The American Crow and the Common Raven.* College Station: Texas A&M University Press.

Marzluff, J. M., and T. Angell. 2005. *In the Company of Crows and Ravens.* New Haven: Yale University Press.

Ratcliffe, D. 1977. *The Raven.* London: T&AD Poyser.

Sax, B. 2003. *Crow.* London: Reaktion Books.

Zawadska, D. 2006. *Kruk.* Świebodzon, Poland: Wydawnictwo Klubu Przyrodników.

The Domestic Dog

Evolution and Domestication

All dogs (*Canis familiaris*) share a single common ancestor, one that is genetically distinct from but closely related to the modern gray wolf (*Canis lupus*). Wolves evolved about 1 million years ago, and dogs were derived from wolves after that time. Despite their common ancestry, today dog and wolf are each pursuing a distinct evolutionary trajectory. We know the evolutionary history of many plants and animals, dogs and ravens included, because biologists today have unprecedented views of the actual formation of species, afforded from a battery of readily available genetic techniques. This new view often complicates our ability to say when two forms of an animal are actually distinct "species," traditionally defined as two organisms that do not interbreed, but it greatly improves our ability to describe the history and likely future of related organisms. By looking at pieces of the full genetic complement of a species throughout its geographic range, or by comparing genes among closely related species, we can see if forms are becoming more or less genetically similar. Because dogs and wolves are distinct and becoming more so, we consider them to be different species even though they can interbreed. The close ancestry of dogs and wolves is indicated by their membership in the same genus (*Canis*). Their biological family (Canidae) includes all wild dogs, foxes, coyotes, and wolves. They are in the order Carnivora, which also includes bears, weasels, seals, lions, and tigers.[1]

There is no doubt that dogs evolved from gray wolves, but the timing, location, and degree to which humans or wolves initiated the process are not entirely clear. Recent analyses of dog and wolf genes, coupled with archeological finds, have narrowed the range of possibilities and together suggest that domestication was ancient and included repeated mixing of wolf and dog genes through purposeful or accidental interbreeding.

Dogs were likely derived from wolves between 14,000 and 31,000 years ago. Earlier claims based on mitochondrial DNA, which suggested that this split may have occurred more than 100,000 years ago, are less well supported. (Mitochondrial DNA is a sequence of genes that occurs within the mitochondria of an animal's cells. It is often used by evolutionary geneticists to infer the timing at which related forms diverged because this DNA is not mixed up during sexual reproduction but is passed intact from mother to offspring and is rapidly and regularly changed by mutation.) Dogs have a common ancestor, derived from Middle Eastern wolves, but it appears that early dogs began to diverge by different husbandry practices, including selection for small size by agrarian peoples and backcrossing ancestral dogs with wolves in some Asian and European regions. Around 12,000 years ago, the Levant peoples of the Fertile Crescent apparently favored small, smart, and social dogs, which fit nicely into their agrarian lifestyles. These people were keen on domestication; they are credited with developing cereals, cats, and goats. In contrast, in northern Europe and Russia, Ice Age hunters favored large dogs. These Paleolithic people had dogs at least 31,000 years ago, as indicated by a skull found in the Goyet cave along the Samson River of Belgium and an intermixed track of footprints from a child and a large canid in France's Chauvet cave. In fact, the dog is the oldest known domestic species. Perhaps hunting and scavenging Neanderthal people were coevolving with wolves. Ice Age hunters may have favored large, wolf-like dogs to help them track, kill, and transport large game, especially reindeer and mammoths. Early dogs may have also been play objects, hot water bottles, babysitters and child substitutes, diapers, and true trusted companions. It seems certain early dogs were valued as collaborators and protectors, and they may also have been a source of food for humans.[2]

The dog is "a remarkable social invention, both for protection and as an aid to hunting." We know that once people associated with wolves, they could selectively breed the animals they valued and selectively cull those they did not. The Sioux, for example, valued large dogs for hunting, protection, and spiritual food. Their large, wolf-like dogs were produced by killing all the puppies in a bitch's first litter and keeping only the largest few puppies of her second litter. What we do not know is if or how humans began the domestication process.[3]

There are at least three viable alternative explanations for how humans and wolves interacted during the process of domestication. Some suggest that wolves were drawn to hunting communities, where people captured and raised submissive or placid puppies that then imprinted on people as their pack members. These wolves perhaps helped humans capture large mammals and provided protection. Ancient peoples may have bred imprinted wolves for desired characters, thus beginning the process of domestication. Under this scenario, dogs owe humans for their existence. At the start of the twenty-first century, researchers provided a second, alternate hypothesis, suggesting that wolves actually started the process of association by scavenging from early human villages, dumps, and foraging sites. Natural selection favored wolves that could tolerate people. This process predisposed wolves to further taming, breeding, and domestication. As the tamer wolves encountered people more directly, perhaps their utility to humans in other venues became more apparent. In this way, our early ancestors may have survived in part because of their ability to domesticate the wolf into a versatile and useful partner. Building on these ideas, a third theory has been put forth: some have suggested that it is best to view changes in both humans and wolves as a simultaneous process of coevolution. This latest theory posits that both wolves and people benefited from their early associations during the Ice Age as they hunted and herded large ungulates, mainly reindeer, on the northern steppe. The social nature of wolves, which includes sharing, obeying, and gaining approval from dominant animals in the pack, made them ideal associates for early people. We may even have co-opted some wolf morality, as wolves provided a model social system to survive on the riches of the Pleistocene. As we "tamed" the wolf, so too did the wolf tame early humans. Perhaps all three theories, and even more, are correct. In some places, early peoples coevolved with wolves. In others, they captured and tamed wolves. And in still other, more permanent settlements, natural selection favored the wolf that became a dog and lived among us.[4]

The Siberian Husky and other ancient breeds are useful vantage points from which to further investigate the early course of domestication. The incredible phenotypic diversity seen among our modern dog breeds is segmented into the "ancient" and the "modern" breeds. The Siberian Husky is one of thirteen ancients (along with Basenji, Afghan Hound, Samoyed, Saluki, Canaan Dog, New Guinea Singing Dog, Dingo, Chow Chow, Chinese Shar-Pei, Akita, Alaskan Malamute, and American Eskimo Dog). Malamutes, Siberian Huskies, Samoyeds, and Eskimo Dogs are all northern breeds with genetic links to Middle Eastern and European wolves. They represent either an ancient mixing of Paleolithic and Levant dogs or a backcrossing of Levant dogs with wolves during the last few thousand years. Breeds not considered ancient were derived from Middle Eastern wolf stock with clear connection to the Levant culture. These modern dog breeds arose mostly from controlled breeding during the Victorian era (1830–1900). They were selected for a great variety of functions useful to humans, including defense, herding, retrieving, hunting, speed, companionship, and novelty.[5]

During the formative coevolution of people and wolves that produced dogs, ravens also were important players. As efficient scavengers, ravens favored increasingly large wolf and human societies. The need to defend food from hungry ravens may have favored distinct roles within bands of early people—searchers, collectors, defenders, and the like. The ability of early humans to track wolves may also have been partly due to the conspicuous flocks of ravens that shadowed wolves and advertised the locations of kills with loud calls and excited flights.[6]

Regardless of how domestication began, the results of it are splendid. Selection for diverse functions has produced 173 breeds recognized in 2010 by the American Kennel Club (AKC), the governing body of purebred dog sport in the United States. Worldwide, over 400 breeds are recognized. Dogs vary from the four-pound Chihuahuas to massive Great Danes; from Mexican Hairless Dogs to poodles, whose curls never stop growing. All colors are represented except green. Each breed owes its existence to a selective force by humans for work, sport, or companionship. The strength and consistency of human selection for breeds is remarkable; all but the 13 ancient breeds were crafted in the last few hundred years.[7]

History of Sled Dogs and the Siberian Husky

Ancient rock paintings in central Siberia reveal that humans first used dogsleds at least 4,000 years ago. Dog-assisted locomotion allowed hunters to search extensively with less effort, which would have certainly been useful in the expansive Arctic.[8]

As early European explorers pushed into the northern regions of the world, they encountered native peoples who used dogs and sleds for transportation. Explorers adopted this form of transportation to further investigate previously unreachable places. Lieutenant Ferdinand Petrovich Von Wrangell explored the north coast of Siberia in the 1820s using local sled dogs that would later be known as Siberian

Huskies. In the mid-1860s, the Russo-American Telegraph expedition utilized teams of Siberian Huskies to transport equipment and supplies to work crews forced to install telegraph poles throughout the winter. Without these robust dogs, work could have been done only in the brief summer of the far north.

Many men would not have survived the 1898 Alaskan gold rush without sled dogs, although many of these dogs were not northern breeds. As more people poured into Alaska, they adopted dogs for transport, especially for freighting goods and mail. With so many exceptional dogs around, wagers were sometimes made about the best or strongest sled dog. Informal races were born. Soon these became formalized, and in April 1908, the All Alaska Sweepstakes began.

In 1909, a team of smaller dogs brought from Russia by William Goosak and driven by Louis Thrustrup demonstrated that even though these dogs were small and were what some called "Siberian rats," they seemed to have more endurance than the Malamute mixes kept by most people in the Arctic region. In addition, the small dogs from Siberia required little food for the amount of work that they achieved. "Fox" Maule Ramsey decided he needed some of these Siberians so that he could win the sweepstakes race. He chartered a cargo ship and sailed for Russia, where he acquired sixty Siberian Huskies at Markovo on the edge of the Anadyr River. In 1910, some of these dogs were in the team driven by John "Iron Man" Johnson, the first time an all-Siberian team won the All Alaska Sweepstakes. In 1913, Norwegian Leonhard Seppala began training Siberian Huskies for his employer, the Pioneer Mining Company, which had collected the dogs from Siberia for Roald Amundsen's aborted expedition to the North Pole. Seppala won his first sled race (the forty-two-mile Moose Burden Handicap) with these dogs; he attributed his win to a raven that flew in front of his team and stayed just ahead of the lead dogs for four miles, giving them a needed turbo boost. From 1915 to 1917, Seppala would take all-Siberian teams to victories.

Seppala and his dogs became famous for their part in the Great Serum Run in 1925. They helped transport the serum needed to stem the diphtheria outbreak that threatened Nome. In 1927, Seppala went to New England with his now well-known serum team. He raced against local teams and won, breaking many records. Everyone wanted one of his little Siberians, and soon he established a kennel. Olaf Swenson imported seven more Siberians from Russia in 1929. Today's Siberian Huskies can trace their lineage back to Swenson's and Seppala's dogs. In 1930, the AKC officially recognized the Siberian Husky as a breed. Fairbanks Princess Chena, a bitch, was the first Siberian Husky in the AKC stud book. She was announced in December 1930. Although she was smaller than her ancestors, she was in fact quite similar to the oldest known Ice Age dogs.[9]

Morphology, Physiology, and Behavior of Sled Dogs

Although sled dogs are not wolves, the close and recent genetic legacy that binds these two members of the Canidae is evident through their many similarities. The entire genus *Canis* has a sixty-three-day gestation period. When born, pups are all of the same basic shape and all weigh about three-quarters of a pound (toy dog breeds are somewhat smaller on average). Dogs have the same number and kinds of teeth as wolves, coyotes, and jackals, but they are much smaller. The oblong cross-sectional shape of the canine teeth provide gripping strength far beyond other carnivores with more rounded teeth.[10]

There are also basic differences. Unlike a wolf, a dog can have two litters in a year if provided with the right food resources. Dog skin is thicker than wolf skin. Dog skulls are small, relative to body size, and dog brains are small relative to skull size compared to wolves, although both certainly have advanced cognitive abilities, including an ability to comprehend, or at least react to, others' intentions.[11]

The dog's morphology, physiology, and behavior are a blend of wolf heritage and human invention. Northern dog breeds have improved on the basic wolf design to work with people in extreme climatic conditions. Early sled dogs were bred for endurance and to run moderate speeds for great distances while carrying a light load. Wolves are neither faster nor stronger than sled dogs, nor do they have more endurance.[12]

Sled dogs balance the need to stay warm with the ability to not overheat. The moderate size of sled dogs enables them to efficiently shed the heat generated during work, while their short ears and ability to curl into a tight ball while resting and sleeping conserve heat when temperatures are low. In fact, the ratio of body surface area to weight in sled dogs allows for heat to radiate more easily than in bigger dogs. A thick, double coat insulates northern dogs and wolves from the cold. The outer layer is made of long coarse guard hairs that shield the body from water, snow, and sun. The inner layer, or undercoat, is a soft dense fur able to insulate against temperatures as extreme as $-80°$F. The long, thick tail protects the face from the cold; wolves and northern dogs curl up to sleep, even on ice. Their long legs enable quick and efficient movement, and they also act to conserve or shed heat from the body core. When heat is generated by exercise, blood flows to the feet, enabling cooling by radiation. But when heat needs to be conserved, the lower legs and feet of a husky approach the temperature of the environment, effectively shutting off radiation. To keep the feet near the freezing point, the arteries of the legs, with their warm blood, run right along the veins in an arrangement known as a countercurrent exchanger. By passive diffusion the warm arterial blood heats the cold venous blood as it returns from the toes. The feet of a husky thus remain cold and do not lose heat to the environment. But how do they not become frostbitten at extreme temperatures? In arctic-adapted canines (foxes, wolves, and seemingly huskies), special blood vessels go directly from the warm body core to the surface of the footpads, where they act like hand warmers, heating the extremities. When temperatures rise, dogs can sweat through their footpads, but wolves cannot. Both dogs and wolves also shed their dense undercoat to increase heat radiation during the long hot days of summer.[13]

Sled dogs are carnivores. Their digestive physiology is tuned to a steady diet of meat, with some minimal plant matter thrown in for variety. As with wolves, they eat a big meal by gorging and then digesting it. Because running a dog on a full stomach is risky, mushers typically feed their dogs late in the day, after their daily run. During a long race, the dogs are only snacked lightly. Racers in long-distance events like the Iditarod must take breaks to feed and rest their dogs. They take on a pace much like a hunting wolf pack.

The sensory world of dogs is more finely tuned to sound and smell than is ours. Dogs and wolves can hear at higher frequencies (47,000 to 65,000 cycles per second, hertz), have greater peripheral vision (240° to 270° versus 200°), and detect movement better than humans. These are likely adaptations to hunting that enable them to scan efficiently and to hear small prey. Prick ears aid in locating prey by rotating independently. This feature also allows sled dogs to keep one ear on the musher and the other on more interesting distractions. A dog's sense of smell is 1,000 to 10,000 times better than a human's, in part because dogs have much larger olfactory lobes in their brains, and they have a Jacobsen's organ (a special pouch of receptive cells located on the roof of the mouth with ducts in the mouth and nose that allow scent molecules to enter). Dogs do not see quite as well as humans do in bright light. To improve light "gathering," the dog eye has a tapetum behind the retina that reflects light. (The tapetum lucidum is a layer of cells that reflects light back through the retina so that it can be better absorbed by photoreceptive cells that enable vision in dim light.) Huskies, especially ones with blue eyes, may not have this structure, which may be an accident of selective breeding for other traits. In northern regions where snow naturally reflects light, the tapetum would not provide an advantage, and so this special structure may have been lost. Color vision in dogs is not as refined as it is in humans. Dogs see green, yellow, and orange as yellowish. They see violet and blue as blue. Blue-green appears gray to a dog, and red is very dark gray or black.[14]

The communicative world of dogs revolves around scents, sounds, and visual signals. An exceptional sense of smell allows dogs to leave messages for others by scent marking (urinating, defecating, and rubbing their anal glands in important places, notably territory boundaries or travel routes). Dogs check each other's anal glands and genitals directly to establish sex and age, as do wolves. Over moderate distances, dogs keep in communication by barking and howling. Individual wolves in a pack often have a characteristic howl. Howls bring a scattered pack together, advertise the location of individuals, and demark territory. Howling and barking are contagious. Dogs bark more than wolves and have developed a rich repertoire of barks with unique and graded meaning. Barks are individually distinct, and their pitch, tone, and duration tell of the dog's motivation or emotion. Low frequencies are used in threatening situations. Higher pitches are related to submission. Communicating at close range in dogs is achieved through a great range of postures. Bowing the head and wagging the tail signify willingness to play. Tucking the tail between the legs and possibly rolling over, or even licking the face of another, indicate submission. A tail raised to horizontal or higher mast signals dominant status. Ears laid back warn of fear or submission. Ears pricked forward reveal interest and excitement. Raising the upper lip into a snarl shows the canine weapons and indicates aggression. Tail postures also denote recognition. Dogs wag their tails mostly to the right when they see their owners, but if a dominant dog approaches them they wag mostly to the left.[15]

Sled dogs use all their powers of communication to organize their social lives. Dominant dogs are not always the largest, and males are not always dominant over females. Instead, a group of Siberian Huskies living together will form a social hierarchy often determined by age or how long they have each been together. New dogs invariably go to the bottom of the social ladder. Huskies will also pack with humans, accepting as their leader the person who tends them. Lone Siberian Huskies tend to get into trouble; they have a tendency to get bored because they need interaction with a pack.

The dog musher is constantly arranging his pack to be an efficient running group. Large males often are the wheel dogs, and they bear the brunt of the load. Females are often faster, and they can be the best team leaders. The leader in a dog team is not necessarily the dominant dog; in fact, the best leader is a smart dog that anticipates what a musher desires and does not fight with other dogs.

The Common Raven

The Common Raven was formally recognized as *Corvus corax* by Carolus Linnaeus in 1758, but this widely distributed species frequently interacted with humans throughout the Northern Hemisphere for thousands of years before this official designation. Its large size, including a large and remarkable brain, loquacious voice, tameness, and utility in finding food have endeared the raven to shamans and storytellers since the dawn of humanity. The raven—as trickster, creator, omen, and fellow being—has motivated Pleistocene cave dwellers, the Norse, Londoners, Northwest Indians, poets, moviemakers, sports teams, and rock bands. The mystique of the raven continues to shape our culture, and we theirs.[16]

Evolutionary History

The modern influence of the raven has a deep past, but one that is changing rapidly. If we assume that DNA not under the pull of natural selection changes in a regular and precise way, we can use it as a molecular clock to date when the modern raven emerged from its ancestors. In this work, ornithologists do not completely agree, but they are increasingly comfortable with molecular change of about 1–2 percent per million years. Using this gauge, four major raven lineages shared a common ancestor from 3.8 to 1.7 million years ago. A likely start to the adaptive radiation of ravens (3.8 to 2.3 million years ago) was in Africa and involved *C. albus* and other African ravens (e.g., *C. albicollis*) diverging from each other. Shortly thereafter (3.6 to 1.7 million years ago), Common Ravens and their African relatives (e.g., *C. albus*) diverged from each other. The Common Raven evolved in Eurasia and quickly and repeatedly colonized North America.[17]

The Common Raven is a poster child of genetic complexity and the processes by which species are made and lost. There appear today to be at least three independent evolutionary paths being followed by ravens. There is little if any interbreeding between Common Ravens of the Old World and those of the New World (although intensive sampling throughout Beringia—the area formerly bridging Siberia and Alaska—is lacking), which allows these two groups to maintain slight but distinctive genetic signatures. In addition, Common Ravens on the Canary Islands (samples from Fuerteventura Island only) are morphologically and genetically distinct from other old-world ravens, apparently having charted a unique evolutionary course after diverging from each other approximately 650,000 years ago. Thus, Common Ravens on the Canary Islands, elsewhere in the Old World, and in the New World appear sufficiently isolated today to evolve independently. Further analyses may yield additional significant evolutionary units within the Common Raven, because existing analyses suggest that these three independent evolutionary trajectories are but a portion of a more diverse past.

In the Old World, a variety of recognizable morphological forms have been described (see the descriptions of subspecies at end of this appendix). These may have been especially distinct 1 million years ago, but today they intergrade extensively and do not have unique mitochrondrial genes (other and more extensive analyses may reveal subtle genetic differences).[18]

In the New World, repeated past crossings of the Bering land bridge are eroding genetic diversity. Upon colonizing the New World, the Common Raven diverged into two clades. (Clades are genetically distinct groups within a species.) These two clades differ by 4.04 percent in their Cytochrome *b* gene and 5.02 percent in mitochrondrial control region DNA. That is a lot—more genetic divergence than is seen among many fully non-interbreeding species. (As with researchers investigating the timing at which dogs and wolves diverged, avian researchers also use mitochondrial DNA to infer when closely related birds diverged. Cytochrome *b* and the control region are specific genes in the mitochrondrial DNA that are often used in bird research because they are easily isolated, rapidly evolving, and change only in response to random but regularly occurring mutations.) The "California clade" is found throughout the western United States and represents most individuals in the Mojave Desert. The "Holarctic clade" occurs throughout the Old World and is the only clade identified from samples in northern North America (Alaska, Canada, Maine, and Greenland). Ravens from both clades coexist in roughly equal proportions in a large area of North America, including Washington and Idaho. Where mating patterns and clade identity are known (the temperate rainforests of the Olympic Peninsula of Washington state, where Bill Webb, Kevin Omland, and I have studied them), pairing between members of different clades is common, suggesting substantial gene flow between clades and a shared current evolutionary trajectory. This shared evolutionary present, despite a separate evolutionary past, is consistent with a lack of distinctive differences in behaviors and morphologies between the clades and suggests that calls to anoint the California clade of ravens as a distinct species are not justified at this time.

The existence of both clades in western North America suggests that ravens may have colonized North America at least twice. Initially, the California clade and the Holarctic clade diverged from each other approximately 2 million years ago (3.5 to 1.7), perhaps as dramatic glacial ice advances pushed the original Common Ravens of North America into southern, ice-free refugia. These distinct California clade ravens remained isolated from other Holarctic clade ravens for about 1 million years, during which time, their sister taxon, the Chihuahuan Raven (*Corvus cryptoleucus*) evolved. These taxa differ by 1.75 percent (all mitochondrial DNA) to 1.8 percent (Cytochrome *b* only), suggesting that they diverged between 1.1 and 0.6 million years ago, well after the two clades of Common Ravens diverged. Common Ravens of the Holarctic clade may have reinvaded North America across the Bering Strait in the last 15,000 years in the company of humans and wolves (or early dogs).[19]

Brains

The raven is the largest songbird (58–69 centimeters long with a mass of 600–2,000 grams; see data in section on subspecies that follows). Its brain size relative to its body size is more similar to primates than it is to other birds. This large brain is responsible for the raven's often-cited insightful behavior. Although ravens are not known to manufacture tools, like some corvids, they pull strings to retrieve out-of-reach foods, mimic human voice in appropriate contexts, lure small animals to their death, stand on light sensors so illumination and associated warmth can be used in arctic settings, work as teams, play, and deceive. The mentality of ravens in particular and corvids in general is increasingly seen on a par with monkeys and apes. Corvids understand causal connections and use these to solve problems; employ creative, innovative, and flexible behaviors appropriately in novel situations; use insight and experience to imagine appropriate strategies; and even imagine possible future events.[20]

Physique

The raven's long, broad wings enable frequent soaring or powerful directional flight. Its tail is especially long and often is spread to form a diamond shape, which helps distinguish it from other crows and ravens that overlap its range. The bases of a Common Raven's neck feathers are grayer than those of the Chihuahuan Raven (*C. cryptoleucus*). The throat feathers are long and sword-like, especially in males, and are erected during courtship and dominance displays. The large, black bill has prominent bristles that cover less than half of its length (another way to tell them from Chihuahuan Ravens). The legs and feet are black. The iris is light blue in hatchlings, gray in juveniles, and turns dark brown within the first two years of life. Juvenal plumage is looser, duller with less metallic sheen, and lacking in lanceolate throat plumes. The feathers of subordinate juveniles and yearlings often fade to brown and become worn and frayed, especially in extremely cold or desert climes. A young raven's first molt (June–October) replaces all body feathers and up to two inner, upper, greater wing-coverts, so that older juveniles and yearlings resemble adults in body sheen and throat plumes, but their wings and tails generally remain dull and often wear and fade to brown before the next molt. Adults molt their feathers annually, typically just as breeding is ending (May–October). The base of the bill gradually turns from yellowish to black during the first year and the tongue, gape, and palate turn from red to mottled gray/black to fully black during the first two years, depending on social status. Dominant birds attain a black mouth lining within a year, but subordinates may not obtain black lining for several years.[21]

Males and females are similar in plumage, but males are significantly larger. In all known cases, mated pairs include males that are noticeably larger than females. (For example, in twenty-six pairs of birds that my students and I captured and measured in western Washington, the males were 174±17.5 grams heavier, and 5.0±0.8 millimeters [bill length] or 13.4±2.8 millimeters [wing length] larger than their mates.)

Voice

Ravens have an extensive repertoire of calls, most of which we do not fully understand. There are at least twenty distinct calls of known function, seventy-nine call types distinguished spectrographically, many mimicked sounds, and numerous utterances of unknown meaning. At least some calls are learned socially from mates, and especially from nearby (within twelve kilometers) birds of the same sex. Adults kaw loudly and hoarsely when alone or in groups. This deep-pitched croaking may vary in pitch and intensity to convey the caller's motivation. Territorial adults quork often in sequence (*quork-quork*—pause—*quork-quork*) and frequently with wing-tucked barrel rolls and dives as they defend their territory. Mated pairs also frequently give loud, patterned knocking, like two wood blocks rapped together, that is audible for several kilometers and likely serves to defend territory from long range. Loud, harmonically rich hoots, yells, or honks are used by territorial adults to thwart intruding ravens. Adult females often give knocking calls in sequences of two, three, seven, or more syllables when excited. Very rapid knocking (rattling) by females often occurs during duets between mated birds after territorial defense or during courtship. The male and female often perch side by side, bend over, and as the female spreads her wings and rattles, the male opens his bill, fluffs his throat feathers, and moves his head in a choking motion uttering a quiet garble of clicks, hisses, and gurgles while flashing his nictitating membranes (air call). Around the world, pairs respond to predators, especially near their nest, with a series of staccato clucks given while flying excitedly with rapid and shallow wing beats. A somewhat similar *ku-uk-kuk* is given by one raven pursuing another raven in aerial chase. The attacking raven utters this call as it closes in or dives at the intruder. Adults give a large variety of bell-like, hiccup, dripping, woo-woo, and toot calls of unknown function that may be regionally, locally, or individually distinct. Growls, whines, and screams are common among jostling birds entering a communal roost and goose-like honks often are given by birds departing roosts in the morning. Juveniles and females beg in typical corvid fashion to be fed by their parents and mates. These change to distinct gurgling sounds as food is swallowed. The juvenile food-begging calls transition into the yells of immatures, which are given at the sight of defended food (*haa*) or as dominants approach food (*who*). Immatures in vagrant feeding assemblages cower and beg in submissive posture with fluffy plumage (not flapping wings) from aggressive adults or more dominant immatures. Two immatures trill in escalating vocal bouts that if not broken off will lead to physical fights. Soft, babbling renditions of the full repertoire of sounds are common, especially by lone immatures of those discovering new foods.[22]

Habitat

Ravens are extreme habitat generalists breeding throughout the forested (boreal, coniferous, and deciduous) and open (grassland and shrubland) coastal, steppe, mountain, desert, tundra, and cliff regions of the Northern Hemisphere, principally north of 35° N. In the more open habitat in southern (typically shrublands and deserts) and in northern (shrublands and tundra) portions of their range, they live where cliffs, sparse trees (including Joshua trees, *Yucca brevifolia,* in the Mojave Desert), and human structures afford nest locations. In coniferous and broadleaf forests in midlatitudes they nest in trees more often than on cliffs and outcrops. Ravens do not inhabit dense tropical rainforest but are abundant in temperate (coniferous) rainforests along the northern Pacific Coast of North America.[23]

Historically, ravens have been common in all human settlements within their range, but today they frequent human refuse tips (garbage dumps); patrol and scavenge from roadways and recreational sites (least so in northeastern United States); and inhabit rural farms and settlements, small towns, and a few large cities. In western North America, they are abundant in Anchorage, Alaska, and locally abundant in coastal and most natural habitats in the Los Angeles, Riverside, San Diego, and San Francisco, California, metropolitan areas (that is, they are rare in city centers but common in undeveloped coastal habitats and parks scattered around and throughout these cities). They are rare to absent from Boise, Idaho; Seattle, Washington; Phoenix, Arizona; and Vancouver, British Columbia, despite being common just outside these cities in wildland settings. They are also rare in large cities throughout the rest of their range. Some avoidance of urban areas may reflect unsuitable habitat (Boise, Mexico City), abundant competitors such as gulls and crows (Seattle, Vancouver), recent and extensive devastation (Warsaw, Berlin), and historical persecution (Oslo, London, Prague). Currently, ravens are expanding in middle and Western Europe and the eastern United States, in part because of restoration efforts. They are also expanding and increasing locally, often dramatically, in the western United States and northern Alaska in response to food (garbage, roadkill, agriculture), water (impoundments, fountains, and watered gardens), and nest site subsidies (power poles, and, increasingly, buildings and rigs associated with drilling for petroleum reserves).[24]

Food

The raven is an opportunistic scavenger closely associated historically with large carnivores (most notably wolves) and wasteful omnivores (notably humans). Despite social, vocal, mental, and morphological specializations allowing for efficient scavenging, the raven is a quintessential generalist and omnivore that eats a huge variety of animals and plants. It preys on adult and nestling birds, eggs, small mammals (regularly young, occasionally adult, rabbits and hares and newborn lambs), sick and dying larger mammals (including sheep), toads, snakes, juvenile turtles, fish, and invertebrates (notably grasshoppers, locusts, butterflies, beetles, crane flies, ants, slugs, scorpions, earthworms, snails and a diversity of marine invertebrates). Ravens scavenge garbage and slaughterhouse offal, dung (including that of sled dogs and wolves), and nearly any kind of carrion, including sheep and cow placentas, discarded entrails of hunted animals, dead fish and whales, and road-killed mammals, birds, and reptiles. They eat a variety of plant matter, including fruits, grains, berries, buds, and calcareous seaweed (*Corallina officinalis*). On some of the Canary Islands, fruit (especially *Opuntia* and *Ficus*) dominates the diet. Predatory behavior may result in significant, but local, reductions in the nesting success of colonial-nesting birds and particularly vulnerable and rare species such as desert tortoises (*Gopherus agassizii*).[25]

Ravens find food by sight, sound, and perhaps by olfaction at very close distances. They fly along roads and actively scan for carrion; investigate the locations of gunshots, wolf howls, and calling conspecifics; cue on foraging birds and mammals (including exploring areas where other species gaze, and attending herbivores who might flush insects and small mammals); actively hunt from perch, wing, or foot; and exchange information at nocturnal roosts. They are excessively cautious and wary around new foods. Where large animal carcasses are a primary food, and when carcasses are especially widely dispersed and ephemeral (for example, in snowy, northern regions), naïve ravens follow knowledgeable roost mates over many kilometers to newly discovered food bonanzas. Passive following and active recruitment during social soaring may facilitate information exchange over these long distances. Ravens also roost communally very close to semipermanent food resources (that is, garbage dumps or residences consistently offering food supplements). Most individuals in such roosts likely know where the food source is located, so food information may rarely be formally exchanged. Other benefits of communal roosting (such as sharing information about other resources, reducing risk of predation, reducing commuting costs) likely favor this behavior in these situations. In either case, vagrant nonbreeders are the most frequent participants in winter roosts and hence most apt to cooperate in the sharing of information regarding food and other resources. These temporary groups of mostly unrelated and often different birds benefit from sharing information because of increased food encounter rates and increased ability to procure foods defended by dominant breeding pairs. Breeding pairs often discover food on their territory before vagrants and effectively defend it from single or small groups of vagrants. Breeding pairs may occasionally roost communally with vagrants, especially near abundant foods.[26]

Ravens hide (or cache) a variety of foods, mostly on the ground, at all times of the year. Caching may be triggered by ephemeral or contested foods, because controlled experiments reveal ravens do not cache when food is continuously available. They do, however, cache food from landfills where it is continuously available, even if the quality is variable. Eggs may be cached whole and placed in microsites suitable for long-term storage (for example, near permafrost in arctic climes). Large or scattered food items may be prepared away from the cache site to reduce transportation costs (such as strips of meat and individual crackers are collected to make a single load that is then carried en masse to the cache site). Memory of cache locations may be relatively short lived, but no one has rigorously tested this notion. In captivity, caching ravens are sensitive to the presence of others, watching others cache and remembering these cache locations. They also combat cache raiders by sneaking out of view to cache, making false caches, and moving caches from locations they perceive others to know. For example, if a raven has cached in the presence of an observing raven and later is near this cache location, the caching raven will move the cache if the former observer is in the area, but will not move the cache when a naïve raven is in the area. These observations suggest that ravens have a theory of mind—that is, they know what others know. In this respect, they are on par with humans.[27]

Sociality

Ravens are found as pairs or in loose groups. Adults, but especially nonbreeding vagrants, may congregate at large animal kills (20 to 200 birds), cliffs with strong updrafts that enable communal soaring (10 to more than 100 birds), and at nocturnal communal roosts, especially during winter (50 to more than 2,000 birds).[28]

Adult ravens are socially monogamous and, in most situations, inhabit multipurpose home ranges throughout the year. Most monogamous pairs remain intact from year to year, likely for the life of an individual. The only insights into pair bond duration in the wild comes from western Washington, where Bill Webb and I found none of twenty-six marked pairs to divorce over one to four years of observation. Social monogamy may not secure genetic monogamy, because we observed five instances of extra-pair copulations in a dense population of ravens nesting in the open shrublands of southwestern Idaho. The copulations occurred as soon as territorial males left their egg-laying females unattended at the nest. We do not fully understand defended space within the home range, but it appears that actual territory and defense of it is restricted to the portion of the home range within one to five kilometers of the nest. Defense is manifested in vigorous chases of intruders by residents accompanied by quorking, honking, and trilling vocalizations. If a resident catches an intruder, it will attack strongly with bill and feet. Certainly, territory defense is greatest near the nest and during the breeding season. But the multipurpose nature of the territory appears to vary with location, reflecting the type of food base utilized. In most locations, ravens visit and remain on their home range and perhaps within their territory throughout the year, but where conditions are exceptionally harsh and winter food is limited (for example, Greenland, other arctic climes, and the Mojave Desert), breeding birds may spend considerable periods away from their home ranges at concentrated or reliable feeding locations (rubbish dumps, ungulate winter ranges).[29]

Breeding

Ravens breed early in the year when snow often blankets the ground. In late January to mid-April, males and females spend increasingly longer periods of time in their territory and break sticks (25–150 centimeters long, 0.5–3 centimeters in diameter), which they use to construct new nests or refurbish old ones. Both sexes procure nest material, but the female appears to complete most of the actual nest construction, especially shaping the nest bowl. Ravens locate their nests 3–30 meters high in the stout, lower branches of trees, 5 to more than 30 meters high on the upper third of steep cliffs, or up to 46 meters high on human structures such as utility poles. Nest trees often have few substantial branches below the nest, and cliff sites often are well protected beneath overhanging blocks or ledges, in cracks, or in small caves. Many anthropogenic nest sites are used, including buildings, signs, radio towers, abandoned vehicles, utility poles, oil derricks, bridges, irrigation pipes, and windmills. Responses of nesting adults to intruding humans are tempered by prior persecution. A large and bulky platform of sticks, as big as a laundry basket (40–153 centimeters in diameter × 20–61 centimeters tall), is lined with fine roots, grass, string and other bits of rubbish, and mammal fur to make an inner cup the size of a large salad bowl (22–30 centimeters in diameter × 13–15 centimeters deep). Nest construction takes one to three weeks.[30]

Females lay 1–8 (typically 4–6) green to blue, frequently blotched with green, brown, or purple, ovate (44.0–52.3 × 30.7–36.2 millimeters) eggs within a week of nest completion. Females incubate twenty to twenty-five days. Males occasionally sit on eggs, but only females have functional brood patches. Both parents brood and feed nestlings. Eggs hatch asynchronously, and nestlings fledge after four to seven weeks. One case of successfully rearing two broods in a single season is known from Riverside, California. Average brood sizes in most locales (Britain, Ireland, the Olympic Peninsula of Washington, California, and Idaho) vary from 2.5–3.6 young per nest, whereas slightly larger average broods of 3.8 and 4.2 have been recorded in Utah and Oregon. The lowest fledging success recorded is on the Olympic Peninsula, where thirty-five pairs fledged an average of 1.2±0.21 young per nest. Elsewhere in North America and Britain this fledging success ranges from 1.7 in Wyoming to 3.1 in Idaho. Fledglings remain with their parents for a few weeks to several months after leaving the nest and typically depart the natal territory by late summer. Survival during the first year of life varies from 38 percent in the Mojave Desert to 74 percent in western Washington, most probably because there are differences in vulnerability to mammalian predators shortly after fledging. Annual survival of breeders may be lower than expected based on body size. On the Olympic Peninsula, annual survival of forty-six radio-tagged adults averaged 68.2 percent, and survival of three-year-old ravens in the Mojave averaged 87 percent, both of which are significantly less than the much smaller American crow. In the western United States, the proximity of human-originated food sources appears to enhance adult and juvenile survival. The maximum recorded lifespan in the wild is thirteen years four months, but there are credible reports of captive ravens living forty to eighty years.[31]

Movements

Ravens, especially breeders, are relatively sedentary. Breeders may fly 10–30 kilometers from their nest to distant, predictable food sources and travel throughout their 12- to 1,950-square-kilometer home ranges. Adult home ranges vary widely among individuals and locations (averaging 1,211 hectares on the Olympic Peninsula, 2,730–19,500 hectares in Minnesota, and 30–440 hectares in coastal California). Non-breeders are less sedentary, ranging widely and nomadically over 1,200 to more than 1,900 square kilometers each winter among concentrated, but ephemeral, food sources. These birds may routinely travel 20–70 kilometers one way from their communal roosts to daily feeding locations. In the Mojave Desert, juveniles concentrate in urban and agricultural landscapes, which they assess throughout their home ranges of 142 (for males) to 188 square kilometers (for females). These estimates were based on observations of twenty-four males and fifteen females. In Britain and most of North America, ravens spend most of their lives within 50 kilometers of their birthplace. In Britain, only four birds, all nonbreeders in their first two years of life, traveled more than 200 kilometers from their natal territory. Maximum distances between birth and recovery sites include 551 kilometers in Britain and 480 kilometers in Oregon. Ravens in Greenland and other locales above 60° N (or at extreme altitudes) are considerably less sedentary. During winter, adult and juvenile ravens from interior Greenland travel over 150 kilometers one-way to the coast. One fledgling traveled 811 kilometers from Kangerlussuaq to the southern tip of Greenland in fewer than 146 days. Another raven from northern Greenland moved 1,120 kilometers to the south.[32]

Subspecies and Distribution

The Common Raven ranges from seasonally ice-free coasts and islands at ~77° N through nearly all forested, steppe, desert, mountain, cliff, and shrubland environments to ~12° N in Nicaragua. This wide latitudinal range also includes tremendous range in elevations (below sea level in Death Valley, California, to 6,400 meters on Mount Everest). Many subspecies have been described based on clines in morphology (larger birds occur in northern and high elevation portions of the range and the smallest forms occur in southern and desert portions of the range) and plumage (birds tend to be less bluish in gloss with less pronounced lanceolate throat plumes in southern and desert locations). There may today be only three groups within the Common Raven that are isolated in an evolutionary sense (Canary Island, other old-world, and all new-world forms), and so here we arrange eleven traditional subspecies into these three significant evolutionary units.[33]

1. CANARY ISLAND RAVENS *Corvus corax canariensis* is confined to the Canary Islands and morphologically similar to *C. c. tingitanus* (wing length: 370–405 millimeters; bill length: 69–75 millimeters, based on measurements of ten adults). At least ravens from the eastern Canary Island of Fuerteventura have distinct brownish plumage and mitochondrial DNA consistent with a long history of evolution independent of other old-world ravens. The DNA sequences of their mitochrondrial control regions average 3.39 percent divergent from a large sample of Holarctic clade ravens, indicating relatively independent evolution by these Canary Island ravens for approximately 650,000 years (assuming 5 percent divergence of control region DNA per million years). This is the most unique subspecies of Common Raven examined to date and its possible single common ancestor, divergent mitochrondrial DNA, and disagnosable appearance confirm the evolutionary significance of this subspecies. Pending more detailed analysis of other Holarctic clade ravens, especially *C. c. tingitanus* and *C. c. canariensis* from the western Canary Islands, which look like typical Holarctic birds, this form could be considered a distinct species (*Corvus canariensis*).[34]

2. OTHER OLD-WORLD RAVENS OF THE HOLARCTIC CLADE *Corvus corax corax* occurs throughout northwestern Europe from the British Isles, Ireland, and Scandinavia south through France where it grades into *C. c. laurencei* and east of the Yenisei

River in western Siberia where it grades into *C. c. kamtshaticus*. It also grades into *C. c. kamtshaticus* south from Siberia and western Russia to the Black Sea and Caucasus, northern Iran, and Kazakhstan. It is accidental to Svalbard (Spitsbergen) and Novaya Zemlya. This is a moderate-sized form (wing length: 375–442 millimeters; bill length: 68–84 millimeters, based on measurements of 24 adults). Analysis of the mitochrondrial control region suggests any past phylogenetic structuring that imparted unique morphology to *C. c. corax* may now be declining with extensive blending of phenotypes across the Old World.

Corvus corax hispanus occurs in Spain, Iberia, the Balearic Islands, and Sardinia and perhaps extends through Corsica and Italy. This form has relatively short wings and more of an arched bill than *C. c. corax*. Current genetic composition of the mitochondrial control region is not consistent with a unique evolutionary trajectory for Italian ravens. Instead, Italian ravens share genes with *C. c. corax* from Ireland, Russia, and Siberia (as well as an ancestral gene type also found in new-world ravens) indicating that past uniqueness may be in the process of being lost by intergradation with *C. c. corax* to the north and *C. c. kamtshaticus* to the east.

Corvus corax laurencei occurs east of *C. c. hispanus* from eastern Greece and Cyprus through the Middle East to eastern Kazakhstan, northern India, and western China. Ravens of this form are slightly larger than *C. c. corax* and similar to *Corvus ruficollis* in having worn, brown plumage on the nape, mantle, and throat.

Corvus corax tingitanus lives in the coastal regions of North Africa (Egypt to Morocco south to pre-Saharan Atlas). The plumage of these ravens is glossy and "oily" with short and less pronounced throat plumes. This form is small with a very short, stout bill (64–73 millimeters long, based on measurements of 22 adults), long wings (380–420 millimeters, based on measurements of 22 adults), and short tail. No genetic analysis of this form has been done.

Corvus corax varius is a large subspecies (wing length: 400–465 millimeters; bill length: 75–89 millimeters, based on measurements of 12 adults) from Iceland and the Faroe Islands. Genetic analyses are lacking, but geographic isolation (perhaps interrupted by Norwegian Vikings who explored Iceland and used *C. c. corax* as navigational aids) suggests this subspecies is evolving separately from other members of the Holarctic clade.

C. c. kamtshaticus occurs from Siberia to Kamchatka, the Commander Islands, and the coastal regions of the Sea of Okhotsk south to northern Mongolia, northern Manchuria, Sakhalin, the Kuriles, and Hokkaido, Japan. This form has a robust body (wing length: 400–450 millimeters; bill length: 72–86 millimeters, based on measurements of 30 adults), typical of animals living in the far north and intergrades extensively with *C. c. corax*. Further analysis of ravens from Beringia is needed to fully resolve the uniqueness of this subspecies and *C. c. principalis*.

C. c. tibetanus lives at high elevation in central Asia from Tien Shan and Pamirs to the Himalayas and Tibet. It is a very large form (wing length: 470–490 millimeters; bill length: 77–85 millimeters, based on measurements of 10 adults).

3. NEW-WORLD RAVENS *Corvus corax principalis* occurs from northern Alaska across the ice-free portions of northern Canada to the ice-free coasts of Greenland south through central and eastern Canada, northeastern United States, and the Appalachian Mountains to northern Georgia, then west across the northern United States and southern Canada to the Pacific Coast of Oregon, Washington, Canada, and Alaska. The size of *C. c. principalis* varies gradually from massive birds in the north (67° N at Kangerlussuaq, western Greenland, 248 adults averaged 1607±9.4 grams in mass and 429.8±3.7 millimeters in wing length) to relatively large birds in the northeastern (44°42′ N near Weld, Maine, 17 adults averaged 1316±29.7 grams mass; 33 adults averaged 85.4±0.68 millimeters in bill length) and northwestern (47°57′ N near Forks, Washington, 22 adult females averaged 1060±101 grams in mass, 78±3 millimeters in bill length, and 415±8 millimeters in wing length; 24 adult males averaged 1216±107 grams in mass, 82±4 millimeters in bill length, and 428±10 millimeters in wing length) continental United States. Members of this group carry the Holarctic clade haplotype, perhaps indicating a recent colonization of the New World by *C. c. kamtschaticus*. Holarctic clade ravens occur infrequently but consistently in all samples of ravens from the western United States, suggesting this form may be extending its range south.

Corvus corax sinuatus occurs in the Rocky Mountains of western North America south from British Columbia through Idaho, Montana, Utah, and Colorado through the Great Plains, Great Basin, and southwestern mountains of the United States to mainland Mexico and Nicaragua. This is a relatively small form (856–987 grams; except perhaps those farthest south) with short wings and tail, short and slender bill, and small feet and skull. The range of this subspecies includes a mix of Holarctic and California clade haplotypes, perhaps suggesting that past genetic uniqueness is now being reduced by gradation with *C. c. principalis.*

Corvus corax clarionensis occurs from northern California south through Baja California, Clarion Island, and east through the Mojave Desert. This is the smallest race in North America (151 adults averaged 793.4±6.0 grams in mass, 66.4±0.3 millimeters in bill length, and 407.4±1.3 millimeters in wing length) and the one most closely aligned with pure California clade haplotypes. The distinctiveness of this form may reflect an independent evolutionary trajectory during past glacial maxima that is today blending with more common and widespread forms that recolonized the New World using land bridges at the end of the Pleistocene.

Status and Conservation

The Common Raven occurs in widely distributed, low-density, and self-sustaining populations across most of its historic range. Variation on this theme often directly relates to past persecution or modern subsidizing by humans. In much of western North America raven populations are expanding, often at alarming rates, because human activities provide food, water, and nest sites that increase reproduction and survival (especially of juveniles) and allow territories to become established far from natural nest sites (especially in open tundra and shrublands). In some of these situations populations are locally extremely dense. Modeling efforts in 2005, however, suggest that some locally dense populations (West Mojave Desert) are maintained by immigration of nonbreeders to locally abundant food subsidies. West Mojave Desert populations outside of urban areas may not be demographically self-sustaining. In Western Europe, ravens were valued sanitary engineers in medieval cities but were widely persecuted from the mid-1600s to the mid-1900s or later. Wonder and appreciation were replaced with fear and apprehension as ravens were increasingly viewed as scavengers of the dead (including humans) and harbingers of evil. As a result, European raven populations were reduced, often to the point of creating "cultural gaps" in the species' distribution (throughout much of northern, middle Europe). Persecution has been greatly reduced in most parts of Europe today (but continues to be rewarded in Iceland and Greenland), and ravens are reclaiming their former haunts, even in highly developed portions of London, Moscow, Berlin, Vienna, and Warsaw. Active reintroduction efforts, in addition to reduced persecution and increased subsidization, have aided the return of ravens to Germany, the Netherlands, and the southeastern United States.[35]

Although general persecution of ravens has been reduced in recent times, their increasing populations in much of the western United States have led to conflict and targeted killing campaigns. Increasing populations often conspicuously congregate at garbage dumps, agricultural fields, desert water impoundments, and open-country petroleum development sites. This increase may bring ravens close to crops and sensitive wildlife species and convince resource managers and members of the public that raven control is necessary. To control ravens, managers are advised to first reduce subsidies, then use behavioral modification, and as a last resort, lethal removal. To date, little has been done to reduce subsidies—engrained human attitudes are difficult to change. Some landfills and artificial nest sites have been retrofitted to reduce raven use. Rather than removing subsidies, managers often simply opt to kill ravens. Large numbers of ravens have been shot and poisoned in California, Oregon, Utah, and Nevada with limited, local, and short-term benefits to pistachio nuts, Greater Sage Grouse (*Centrocercus urophasianus*), Least Terns (*Sterna antillarum browni*), Sandhill Cranes (*Grus canadensis*), desert tortoises, and Snowy Plovers (*Charadrius alexandrinus*). Lethal control may be ineffective because raven removal allows other generalist predators to increase, and wide-ranging ravens quickly recolonize areas when lethal control ends if food, water, and nest subsidies are not reduced. In addition, many lethal control efforts focus on concentrations of nonbreeding ravens, which leaves the breeding population intact to fuel continued population growth. Lethal control often is most effective at outraging the public rather than restoring endangered species.[36]

Notes

Chapter 1. Can You Make a Living from a Love of Natural Science?

1. Russ Balda's nutcracker research was summarized in Balda and Kamil (1989, 1992). John's graduate research with Russ was reported in their book, *The Pinyon Jay* (Marzluff and Balda 1992). Bernd's article on ravens that first alerted us to his new research was published in 1986 in *Audubon* magazine. The conference hosted at Northern Arizona University on social behavior in 1986 was published as Slobodchikoff (1988). It included early thoughts from Bernd about ravens and research from John and Russ Balda on jays.

2. *Ravens in Winter* (Heinrich 1989) detailed Bernd's early thinking about ravens sharing food. The discovery of the dancing language of bees was seminal to Carl von Frisch being awarded the Nobel Prize (with Konrad Lorenz and Niko Tinbergen) in 1973. Bees who find food return to the hive, and their actions—the pattern, speed, and orientation of their movement inside the hive—encode information about the location (how far, what direction) and quality of their find (von Frisch 1953, 1967, 1974).

3. Bernd's insect work was beautifully summarized in *Bumblebee Economics* (Heinrich 1979). His work on chickadee foraging cues appeared in the journal *Ecology* (Heinrich and Collins 1983).

4. Bernd's early life and attachment to York Hill and the Adams family was described in *In a Patch of Fireweed* (Heinrich 1984).

5. Social hierarchies were first described in the chicken (Schjelderup-Ebbe 1922).

This idea has been applied to studies on nearly any social species from insects to fish, birds, mammals, and people.

6. Evolving models of wolf pack social structure were described by Miklósi (2007).

7. Smith and Furguson (2005) described the reluctance of wolves to leave their pens in Yellowstone.

8. Moody was quoted in the *Anchorage Daily News,* March 1, 1993. The Coppingers summarized their insights into dogs, including the quote we reference, in Coppinger and Coppinger (2001).

9. The basics of training your dog to pull a sled and building the necessary equipment can be found in Levorsen (1976).

Chapter 2. Stocking the Aviary

1. See appendix 2 for specific data on masses of paired ravens. We reported changes in mouth lining with age (Heinrich and Marzluff 1992). We collected blood from each captured raven so that we could determine how closely related birds that shared food were. Working with Patty Parker Rabenold, a conservation geneticist, we fingerprinted the DNA within the blood of each bird (bird blood cells, unlike mammalian blood, is nucleated) and determined that few close relatives fed together. Most ravens that shared food were a random collection of individuals, not siblings, parents and young, or even more distant relatives (Parker et al. 1994).

2. Coppinger (1977) and Coppinger and Coppinger (2001) stated that dogs are just smart enough to know and dumb enough to do what people want.

3. D. Milne, How do ravens get dinner dates? It's costing you 50G to find out. *National Enquirer*, 1988.

Chapter 3. Torture in the Hut

1. We described raven hierarchies (Marzluff and Heinrich 1991). Smith and Ferguson (2005) speculated on the overthrow of an alpha wolf by subordinates.

2. A general discussion of grooming and social hierarchies can be found in Wittenberger (1981). Specific discussion of allopreening in birds and its role in dominance was from Harrison (1965).

3. Tinbergen's accomplishments resulted in a Nobel Prize (shared with von Frisch and Lorenz in 1973) and are reviewed by Kruuk (2003). Bernd's hypotheses were discussed in Heinrich (1988a).

4. Principle of antithesis from Darwin (1871).

5. We discussed why ravens yell in Heinrich and Marzluff (1991).

6. The advantages of group foraging by ravens were discussed in Marzluff and Heinrich (1991).

7. Sunbathing is common in corvids (Marzluff and Angell 2005a).

8. Eberhard Gwinner lived from 1938 to 2004. The obituary we quoted from was published in *Journal of Biological Rhythms* 19:463–464 (December 2004).

Chapter 4. Raven Nights

1. The information center hypothesis was proposed by Ward and Zahavi (1973) and some of the criticisms of it can be found in Mock et al. (1988) and Richner and Heeb (1995, 1996). Responses to criticisms can be found in Zahavi (1996) and Marzluff and Heinrich (2001). The dance language of bees was first described by von Frisch (1953, 1967, 1974).

2. Krebs (1974) suggested clumped heron departures supported the information center hypothesis. Van Vessem and Draulans (1987) claimed departures and arrivals to heron colonies were not consistent with the information center hypothesis. Greene (1987) demonstrated selective information exchange within osprey colonies.

3. Multiple functions of roosts were discussed by Weatherhead (1983). Information sharing was suggested by observations of vultures (Rabenold 1987) and hooded crows and ravens (Loman and Tamm 1980).

4. Vampire bat reciprocity was discovered by Wilkinson (1984).

5. Calls by ring-billed gulls coordinated synchronous departures from nesting colonies (Evans and Welham 1985).

6. Bub et al. (1995) illustrated the Swedish crow trap and other devices used to catch birds.

Chapter 5. Torment on the Trail

1. We summarize the history of dogsledding in appendix 2, as did Coppinger (1977), Willett (1986), Thompson (vol. 1 and vol. 2, n.d.), Brearley (1974), Cellura (1990), Coppinger and Coppinger (2001), and Salisbury and Salisbury (2003).

2. In modern sled racing, moose are a perennial challenge on the trail. For example, Susan Butcher had two of her dogs killed by moose in the 1985 Iditarod. Such challenges were summarized in the *Anchorage Daily News,* February 5, 2006, "Danger rides along the trail."

3. Moody's life was chronicled in the *New Hampshire Union Leader* (Manchester, NH) on September 30, 1994.

Chapter 6. Becoming Parents

1. Plumage and development of ravens was described by Boarman and Heinrich (1999).

2. Our subsequent research has shown the ability of crows to recognize individual human faces (Marzluff et al. 2010), almost certainly also done by ravens.

3. Our experiments on responses to novel foods were reported in Heinrich et al. (1995).

4. The influence of status on mouth color was from Heinrich and Marzluff (1992).

5. Our research into rearing and release techniques for crows, ravens, and magpies in support of endangered species recovery was reported in Whitmore and Marzluff (1998) and Valutis and Marzluff (1999).

Chapter 7. Dog Days

1. The dog days of summer are the sultry days from early July to early September. The term was derived from an ancient belief that the Dog Star, Sirius, was somehow responsible for the weather. The description of Siberian Huskies as "stubborn and easily bored" came from *Simon and Schuster's Guide to Dogs* (Pugnetti and Schuler 1980).

2. The entire Siberian Husky breed standard can be found at http://www.shca .org/.

3. Peggy Grant and the Marlytuk kennel were described in Brearley (1974). Leonard Seppala's role in bringing Siberian Huskies to North America was from Brearley (1974), Willett (1986), Thompson (vol. 1 and vol. 2, n.d.), and Salisbury and Salisbury (2003). Attla's book (Attla with Levorsen 1974) is a standard introduction to sledding.

4. The quote is from Lorenz (1954).

5. Coppinger and Coppinger (2001) discusses the marathon abilities of huskies.

6. Incomplete penetrance results in alleles blending their affect. Polygenic inheritance means that several genes codefine a trait's appearance. Both possibilities are common elsewhere in the mammalian genome.

Chapter 8. A Second Winter of Ravens

1. Our covered moose experiment was reported in Marzluff et al. (1996) and illustrated in Heinrich and Marzluff (1995).

2. Our release experiments were analyzed in Marzluff et al. (1996).

3. Group size and the roles of kinship and access control were reviewed by Waite and Field (2007). The speculation that ravens have influenced wolf social life and pack size was from Vucetich et al. (2004).

4. The costs and benefits of social foraging were detailed in Marzluff and Heinrich (1991). Optimal group size was discussed further in Marzluff et al. (1996).

Chapter 9. Dating and Mating

1. Hormonal control of breeding in birds was reviewed by Gill (2007).

2. Darwin discussed sexual selection (1871) and the chapters of Bateson (1983) reviewed a variety of theories and approaches to understanding mate choice.

3. Multiple cues that are simultaneously used to select mates was suggested by Burley (1981).

4. Pinyon Jay mate choice and pair bonding was from Marzluff and Balda (1988a, 1988b).

5. Lorenz (1954).

6. Gwinner's papers (in German) on breeding displays, molting, and play include (1964, 1965, 1966a, 1966b).

7. Raven nests are described in appendix 2 and in Boarman and Heinrich (1999) and Ratcliffe (1997).

8. Incubation by female and "courtship feeding" by male corvids is the rule (dos Anjos et al. 2009). A conspicuous exception is the Clark's Nutcracker, which breeds in late winter at high mountain elevations. Male and female nutcrackers are sustained by their protein-rich nut stores, and both sexes develop true brood patches and incubate.

9. Brood reduction, incubation, and general breeding behavior of birds are reviewed by Gill (2007).

10. Greenwood (1980) contrasts typical female-biased dispersal in birds with typical male-biased dispersal in mammals.

Chapter 10. Radio Waves

1. Tinbergen (1953).

2. Coyotes in Maine are larger, in part because of hybridization with wolves (Kays et al. 2010). The latest genetic evidence suggests that as coyotes colonized New England in the last century, they moved north and east above the Great Lakes and into the northern boreal forest where wolves were abundant. By 1940 coyotes were in New England, in part replacing extirpated wolves. The coyotes in this wolf-free area were of larger size, with broad well-muscled heads that were similar to wolves. Large size resulted from hybridization with wolves, not dogs, and it has enabled efficient hunting of deer by northeastern coyotes.

3. Local enhancement has been found to be important in assembling seabirds (Evans 1982; Evans and Welham 1985), raptors (Knight and Knight 1983), and our ravens (Heinrich et al. 1993) to visible, but distant, resources.

4. Bald Eagles have now recovered and are no longer on the list established by the U.S. Endangered Species Act, thanks to bans on the use of pollutants like DDT.

5. Janes (1976) reported ravens stoning would-be nest climbers. The relative brain size of ravens was discussed by Heinrich (1999) and Marzluff and Angell (2005a).

Chapter 11. Moving On

1. John Rotenberry was the overall project coordinator. Adjunct professors are not paid and do not participate in regular faculty doings. Such an affiliation, while

mostly voluntary, does help keep one connected to academic science. In my case it allowed me to develop and teach advanced classes in conservation biology and provided a home and financial support for my graduate students.

2. Jess Sproul tracked our birds.

3. The importance of status (Heinrich and Marzluff 1991; Marzluff and Heinrich 1991) was in contrast to the lack of kin structure in groups of ravens that forage together. Ravens that ate together were no more closely related than expected among random members of many different families (Parker et al. 1994).

4. These six findings were called for by Mock et al. (1988) as necessary to prove the existence of an information center. We summarized how our research fit these criteria in Marzluff et al. (1996).

5. This was the first time since we were married that Sitka regained her alpha female position in the front seat beside John.

6. One of Colleen's original sledding students (a teen at the time, Jaime Kinzer) is planning to run the 2012 Iditarod.

7. The results of Marzluff et al. (1996) were challenged by Danchin and Richner (2001), reasserted by Marzluff and Heinrich (2001), and independently confirmed by Wright et al. (2003).

8. Raven responses to carcasses in Idaho were from Marzluff and McKinley (1993).

9. Large communal roosts of ravens in Idaho were reported in Engel and Young (1992a).

10. Lorenz (1981) described the comparative methods in the study of animal behavior.

Chapter 12. Twenty Years Later

1. Granite had a litter of four pups on Mother's Day 1992. We kept two females (Wiley and Tuluquaq—"raven" in Greenlandic). One male (Rebel) went on to finish his show championship and sired several champions. One of Granite's great-great-granddaughters (owned by Susie Dillon, one of Colleen's students) not only finished the Iditarod in 2008, but led through the mountains for part of the race on Wayne Curtis's all–Siberian Husky team.

Appendix 2. The Natural Histories of Dogs and Ravens

1. The evolution of dogs from wolves was reported by von Holdt et al. (2010) and the timing of wolf evolution was provided in Schleidt and Shalter (2003).

2. Gray et al. (2010) estimated domestication by Levant 14,000 to 31,000 years ago. Vilá et al. (1997) estimated domestication occurred 100,000 or more years ago. The importance of ancestral Middle Eastern wolves was documented by von Holdt et al. (2010). Paleolithic people and their dogs were discussed by Germonpré et al. (2009). The role of dogs in Ice Age human cultures was discussed by Sablin and Khlopachev (2002), Schleidt and Shalter (2003), Germonpré et al. (2009).

3. Quote from Scott and Fuller (1965). Discussion of native interactions with dogs from Schwartz (1997) and Sablin and Khlopachev (2002).

4. Early suggestions of humans domesticating wolves were made by Lorenz (1954) and Clutton-Brock (1999). The suggestion that wolves initiated their relationship with people was made by Coppinger and Coppinger (2001). Most recently Schleidt and Shalter (2003) suggested wolves and people had a long and mutually reinforcing coevolutionary history that ended with domestication.

5. Von Holdt et al. (2010) document the variety and function of ancient and modern dog breeds.

6. Vucetich et al. (2004) described effects of ravens on wolves; Marzluff and Angell (2005a, 2005b) described effects of ravens on people.

7. Worldwide dog breed enumerated by Wilcox and Walkowicz (1995).

8. Rock paintings of dogsleds from Cellura (1990).

9. Early history of the Siberian Husky is from Thompson (vol. 1 and vol. 2, n.d.). Princess Chena is described by Brearley (1974). Comparison of Ice Age dogs to Siberian Husky by Sablin and Khlopachev (2002).

10. Basic similarities and differences between wolves and dogs from Coppinger and Coppinger (2001). Wolf teeth described by Smith and Ferguson (2005).

11. Recognition of intention of others by dogs was suggested by Schleidt and Shalter (2003), Udell and Wynne (2010), and challenged by van Rooijen (2010).

12. Brearley (1974) notes what function Siberian Huskies were bred to carry out. Coppinger and Coppinger (2001) refer to Zimen (1981) in comparing wolves and sled dogs.

13. The physiology of sled dogs was described by Coppinger and Coppinger (2001). Details on adaptations to the cold and countercurrent exchangers can be found in Irving (1966), Henshaw et al. (1972), and Schmidt-Nielsen (1981).

14. The sensory world of dogs is from Zimen (1981) and Coren (2004).

15. Communication in wolves is from Zimen (1981). Tail postures from Quaranta et al. (2007). Many of the postures used by dogs are shown in photographic form by Handelman (2008).

16. Interactions between ravens and people from Sax (2003); Ratcliffe (1997); Marzluff and Angell (2005a, 2005b).

17. Raven evolutionary history as revealed by genetic analysis from Feldman and Omland (2005). A molecular clock in birds is discussed by Fleischer et al. (1998) and Lovette (2004).

18. Continuing evolution of ravens from Omland et al. (2006) and Baker and Omland (2006).

19. Omland et al. (2000) discovered the Holarctic and California clades. Feldman and Omland (2005) refined the early history of ravens. Navarro-Siguenza and Peterson (2004) suggested the California clade should be considered distinct species.

20. Raven and corvid mentality are discussed by Heinrich (1999), Weir et al. (2002), Emery and Clayton (2004), and Marzluff and Angell (2005a, 2005b).

21. Basic raven physique is from Boarman and Heinrich (1999) and dos Anjos et al. (2009). Comparison of Common and Chihuahuan Ravens is from Bednarz and Raitt (2002).

22. Raven vocal communication was discussed by Conner (1985), Bruggers (1988), Heinrich and Marzluff (1991), and Enggist-Dueblin and Pfister (2002).

23. The habitat used by ravens was discussed generally by Boarman and Heinrich (1999), and specifically with respect to temperate rainforests by Marzluff and Neatherlin (2006).

24. Raven associations with people were discussed by Marzluff and Angell (2005a). The role of human subsidies fueling raven populations in western North America was discussed by Boarman (1993, 2003) and Bui et al. (2010).

25. Feeding habits of ravens were described by Ewins (1991), Heinrich (1999), Boarman and Heinrich (1999), Kristan and Boarman (2003), and Marzluff and Angell (2005a).

26. Foraging and hunting behavior of ravens was described by Harriman and Berger (1986), Harrington (1978), Heinrich (1988a, 1988b, 1989, 1995a, 1999), Heinrich and Marzluff (1991), Parker et al. (1994), Heinrich et al. (1995), Marzluff et al. (1996), Wright et al. (2003), Bugnyar et al. (2004), and White (2005).

27. Additional foraging observations, with a focus on caching by ravens were reported by Heinrich and Pepper (1998) and Boarman and Heinrich (1999).

28. The largest raven roosts were documented by Engel et al. (1992).

29. Pair bonding and social monogamy was discussed by Lorenz (1968). Mating outside the pair bond was documented by Marzluff and McKinley (1993).

30. General raven nesting behavior from Ratcliffe (1997), Boarman and Heinrich (1999). Specifics on raven use of cliffs, trees, and utility poles were provided from unpublished notes by Michael Kochert, Boise, Idaho. Raven nesting behavior on human objects was documented by Steenhof et al. (1993), Boarman (2003), Bui et al. (2010), and related to their defensive behavior by Knight (1984).

31. General breeding behavior was summarized by Boarman and Heinrich (1999). Parental care was observed by Steenhof and Kochert (1982). Variation in clutch size and nesting success was from Ratcliffe (1997), Webb and Ellstrand (2003), Marzluff and Neatherlin (2006), and Bill Webb's unpublished notes. The maximum lifespan of ravens in the wild is from Clapp et al. (1983) and Marzluff and Angell (2005a).

32. Variations in home range size and movements by ravens were reported by Bruggers (1988), Linz et al. (1992), Heinrich et al. 1994, Restani et al. (2001), Webb et al. (2004), and Marzluff and Neatherlin (2006).

33. The subspecies we recognize were described in Boarman and Heinrich (1999), updated by dos Anjos et al. (2009), and originally based on research by Miller and Griscom (1925), Vaurie (1954), and Omland et al. (2006). Measurements of old-world ravens are from Vaurie (1954), of Greenland ravens from Restani et al. (1996), of Maine ravens from our banding notes, of Washington ravens from unpublished banding records my students and I have taken, and of Mojave ravens from Bill Boarman's unpublished notes.

34. Extensive research on the unique Canary Island raven is reported by Glandt (2008, and personal communication), Baker and Omland (2006), and Omland et al. (2006).

35. Expanding raven populations have been studied by Boarman (1993), Marzluff

et al. (1994), Dunk et al. (1994), Sauer et al. (2000), Kristan et al. (2005), and Bui et al. (2010). Human attitudes toward ravens are discussed by Ratcliffe (1997), Sax (2003), and Marzluff and Angell (2005a). Persecution of ravens by people was reported by Schultz-Soltau (1962), Skarphédinsson et al. (1990), Restani et al. (2001), and Glandt (2008). Raven restoration was discussed by Renssen (1988).

36. Managing expanding populations of ravens was discussed by Larsen and Dietrich (1970), Boarman (1993, 2003), Luginbuhl et al. (2001), and Bui et al. (2010).

Bibliography

Attla, G., with B. Levorsen. 1974. *Everything I Know about Training and Racing Sled Dogs*. New York: Arner Publications.

Avery, M. L., D. L. Bergman, D. G. Decker, R. D. Flynt, and C. E. Knittle. 1993. *Evaluation of Aversive Conditioning for Reducing Raven Predation on Eggs of California Least Terns, Camp Pendleton, California—1992*. U.S. Department of Agriculture. Gainesville: Denver Wildlife Research Center, Florida Field Station.

Balda, R. P., and A. C. Kamil. 1989. A comparative study of cache recovery by three corvid species. *Animal Behaviour* 38:486–495.

——. 1992. Long-term spatial memory in Clark's nutcracker, *Nucifraga columbiana*. *Animal Behaviour* 44:761–769.

Baker, J. M., and K. E. Omland. 2006. Canary Island ravens *Corvus corax tingitanus* have distinct mtDNA. *Ibis* 148:174–178.

Bateson, P., ed. 1983. *Mate Choice*. Cambridge: Cambridge University Press.

Bednarz, J. C., and R. J. Raitt. 2002. Chihuahuan Raven (*Corvus cryptoleucus*). The Birds of North America, No. 606, ed. A. Poole and F. Gill. Philadelphia: Birds of North America.

Bent, A. C. 1946. *Life Histories of North American Jays, Crows and Titmice, Part 1*. U.S. National Museum Bulletin no. 191. Washington: Smithsonian Institution.

Boarman, W. I. 1993. When a native predator becomes a pest: a case study. Pp. 191–206 in *Conservation and Resource Management*, ed. S. K. Majumdar, E. W. Miller, D. E. Baker, E. K. Brown, J. R. Pratt, and R. F. Schmalz. Easton: Pennsylvania Academy of Science.

——. 2003. Managing a subsidized predator population: reducing common raven predation on desert tortoises. *Environmental Management* 32:205–217.

Boarman, W. I., and B. Heinrich. 1999. Common Raven (*Corvus corax*). The Birds of North America, No. 476, ed. A. Poole and F. Gill. Philadelphia: Birds of North America.

Brearley, J. M. 1974. *This Is the Siberian Husky.* Neptune City, NJ: T.F.H. Publications.

Brown, R. N. 1974. Aspects of vocal behavior of the raven (*Corvus corax* L.) in interior Alaska. MS thesis, University of Alaska, Fairbanks.

Bruggers, D. J. 1988. The behavior and ecology of the Common Raven in northeastern Minnesota. Ph.D. diss., University of Minnesota, Minneapolis.

Bub, H., E. Raddatz, F. Hamerstrom, and K. Wuertz-Schaefer. 1995. *Bird Trapping and Bird Banding: A Handbook for Trapping Methods All Over the World.* Ithaca: Cornell University Press.

Bugnyar, T., and K. Kotrschal. 2002. Observational learning and raiding of food caches in ravens, *Corvus corax:* is it "tactical" deception? *Animal Behaviour* 64:185–195.

Bugnyar, T., M. Stöwe, and B. Heinrich. 2004. Ravens, *Corvus corax,* follow gaze direction of humans around obstacles. *Proceedings of the Royal Society of London, B* 271:1331–1336.

Bui, T.-V. D., J. M. Marzluff, and B. Bedrosian. 2010. Common Raven activity in relation to land use in western Wyoming: implications for greater sage-grouse reproductive success. *Condor* 112:65–78.

Burley, N. 1981. Mate choice by multiple criteria in a monogamous species. *American Naturalist* 117:515–528.

Camp, R. J., R. L. Knight, H. A. L. Knight, M. W. Sherman, and J. Y. Kawashima. 1993. Food habits of the nesting common ravens in the eastern Mojave Desert. *Southwestern Naturalist* 38:163–165.

Cellura, D. 1990. *Travelers of the Cold: Sled Dogs of the Far North.* Anchorage: Alaska Northwest Books.

Cibois, A., and E. Pasquet. 1999. Molecular analysis of the phylogeny of 11 genera of the Corvidae. *Ibis* 141:297–306.

Clapp, R. B., M. K. Klimkiewicz, and A. G. Futcher. 1983. Longevity records of

North American birds: Columbidae through Paridae. *Journal of Field Ornithology* 54:123–137.

Clutton-Brock, J. 1999. *A Natural History of Domesticated Mammals.* Cambridge: Cambridge University Press.

Conner, R. N. 1985. Vocalizations of Common Ravens in Virginia. *Condor* 87:379–388.

———. 1988. Nest chronology of Common Ravens in Virginia. *Raven* 57:5–11.

Conner, R. N., and C. S. Adkisson. 1976. Concentration of foraging common ravens along the Trans-Canada Highway. *Canadian Field-Naturalist* 90:496–497.

Coombs, F. 1978. *The Crows.* London: B. T. Batsford.

Coppinger, L. 1977. *The World of Sled Dogs: From Siberia to Sport Racing.* New York: Howell Book House.

Coppinger, R., and L. Coppinger. 2001. *Dogs: A New Understanding of Canine Origin, Behavior, and Evolution.* Chicago: University of Chicago Press.

Coren, S. 2004. *How Dogs Think: What the World Looks Like to Them and Why They Act the Way They Do.* New York: Free Press.

Cramp, S., and C. M. Perrins. 1994. *Handbook of the Birds of Europe, the Middle East, and North America: The Birds of the Western Palearctic.* Vol. 8: *Crows to Finches.* Oxford: Oxford University Press.

Danchin, E., and H. Richner. 2001. Viable and unviable hypotheses for the evolution of raven roosts. *Animal Behaviour* 61:F7–F11.

Darwin, C. 1871. *The Descent of Man and Selection in Relation to Sex.* Vols. 1, 2. London: J. Murray.

Dorn, J. L. 1972. The common raven in Jackson Hole, Wyoming. MS thesis, University of Wyoming, Laramie.

dos Anjos, L., S. Debus, S. Madge, and J. M. Marzluff. 2009. Family Corvidae. Pp. 494–640 in *Handbook of Birds of the World,* vol. 14, ed. J. del Hoyo, A. Elliott, and D. Christie. Barcelona: Lynx Edicions.

Dunk, J. R., S. L. Cain, M. E. Reid, and R. N. Smith. 1994. A high breeding density of common ravens in northwestern Wyoming. *Northwestern Naturalist* 75:70–73.

Dunk, J. R., R. N. Smith, and S. L. Cain. 1997. Nest-site selection and reproductive success in Common Ravens. *Auk* 114:116–120.

Emery, N. J., and N. S. Clayton. 2004. The mentality of crows: convergent evolution of intelligence in corvids and apes. *Science* 306:1903–1907.

Engel, K. A., and L. S. Young. 1989. Spatial and temporal patterns in the diet of Common Ravens in southwestern Idaho. *Condor* 91:372–378.

——. 1992a. Movements and habitat use by Common Ravens from roost sites in southwestern Idaho. *Journal of Wildlife Management* 56:596–602.

——. 1992b. Daily and seasonal activity patterns of Common Ravens in southwestern Idaho. *Wilson Bulletin* 104:462–471.

Engel, K. A., L. S. Young, K. Steenhof, J. A. Roppe, and M. N. Kochert. 1992. Communal roosting of common ravens in southwestern Idaho. *Wilson Bulletin* 104:105–121.

Enggist-Dueblin, P., and U. Pfister. 2002. Cultural transmission of vocalizations in ravens. *Animal Behaviour* 64:831–841.

Evans, R. M. 1982. Foraging-flock recruitment at a Black-billed Gull colony: implications for the information center hypothesis. *Auk* 99:24–30.

Evans, R. M., and C. V. J. Welham. 1985. Aggregative mechanisms and behavior in ring-billed bulls departing from a colony. *Canadian Journal of Zoology* 63:2767–2774.

Ewins, P. J. 1991. Egg predation by corvids in gull colonies on Lake Huron. *Colonial Waterbirds* 14:186–189.

Feldman, C. R., and K. E. Omland. 2005. Phylogenetics of the common raven complex (Corvus: Corvidae) and the utility of ND4, COI and introl 7 of the b-fibrinogen gene in avian molecular systematics. *Zoologica Scripta* 34:145–156.

Fleischer, R. C., C. E. McIntosh, and C. L. Tarr. 1998. Evolution on a volcanic conveyor belt: using phylogeographic reconstructions and K-Ar-based ages of the Hawaiian Islands to estimate molecular evolutionary rates. *Molecular Ecology* 7:533–545.

Fritz, J., and K. Kotrschal. 1999. Social learning in common ravens, *Corvus corax*. *Animal Behaviour* 57:785–793.

Germonpré, M., M. V. Sablin, R. E. Stevens, R. E. M. Hedges, M. Horfreiter, M. Stiller, and V. R. Després. 2009. Fossil dogs and wolves from Palaeolithic sites in Belgium, the Ukraine and Russia: osteometry, ancient DNA and stable isotopes. *Journal of Archaeological Science* 36:473–490.

Gill, F. B. 2007. *Ornithology*, 3rd ed. New York: W. H. Freeman.

Glandt, D. 2008. *Der Kolkrabe*. Vol. 2: *Auflage*. Wiebelsheim: AULA-Verlag.

Gray, M. M., N. B. Sutter, E. A. Ostrander, and R. K. Wayne. 2010. The *IGF1* small dog haplotype is derived from Middle Eastern grey wolves. *BMC Biology* 8:1–13.

Greene, E. 1987. Individuals in an osprey colony discriminate between high and low quality information. *Nature* 329:239–241.

Greenwood, P. J. 1980. Mating systems, philopatry and dispersal in birds and mammals. *Animal Behaviour* 28:1140–1162.

Gwinner, E. 1964. Untersuchungen uber das Ausdrucks-und Sozialverhalten des Kolkraben (*Corvus corax corax* L.) *Zeitshrift für Tierpsychologie* 21:658–748.

———. 1965. Beobachtungen über Nestbau und Brutpflege des Kolkraben (*Corvus corax*) in Gefangenschaft. *Journal für Ornithologie* 103:146–177.

———. 1966a. Uber einige Bewegungsspiele des Kolkraben (*Corvus corax* L.). *Zeitshrift für Tierpsychologie* 23:28–36.

———. 1966b. Der zeitliche Ablauf der Handschwingenmauser des Kolkraben (*Corvus corax* L.) und seine funktionelle Bedeutung. *Die Vogelwelt* 87:129–133.

Handelman, B. 2008. *Canine Behavior: A Photo Illustrated Handbook*. Norwich, VT: Wolf and Word Press.

Harlow, R. C. 1922. The breeding habits of the northern raven in Pennsylvania. *Auk* 39:399–410.

Harlow, R. F., R. G. Hooper, D. R. Chamberlain, and H. S. Crawford. 1975. Some winter and nesting season foods of the Common Raven in Virginia. *Auk* 92:298–306.

Harriman, A. E., and R. H. Berger. 1986. Olfactory acuity in the common raven (*Corvus corax*). *Physiology and Behavior* 36:257–262.

Harrington, F. 1978. Ravens attracted to wolf howling. *Condor* 80:236–237.

Harrison, C. J. O. 1965. Allopreening as agonistic behaviour. *Behaviour* 24:161–209.

Heinrich, B. 1979. *Bumblebee Economics*. Cambridge: Harvard University Press.

———. 1984. *In a Patch of Fireweed*. Cambridge: Harvard University Press.

———. 1986. Ravens on my mind. *Audubon* 88:74–77.

———. 1988a. Winter foraging at carcasses by three sympatric corvids, with emphasis on recruitment by the raven, *Corvus corax. Behavioral Ecology and Sociobiology* 23:141–156.

——. 1988b. Why do ravens fear their food? *Condor* 90:950–952.

——. 1989. *Ravens in Winter.* New York: Summit Books.

——. 1995a. Neophilia and exploration in juvenile common ravens, *Corvus corax. Animal Behaviour* 50:695–704.

——. 1995b. An experimental investigation of insight in Common Ravens, *Corvus corax. Auk* 112:994–1003.

——. 1999. *Mind of the Raven: Investigations and Adventures with Wolf-Birds.* New York: Cliff Street Books.

Heinrich B., and S. L. Collins. 1983. Caterpillar leaf damage, and the game of hide-and-seek with birds. *Ecology* 64:592–602.

Heinrich, B., D. Kaye, T. Knight, and K. Schaumburg. 1994. Dispersal and association among Common Ravens. *Condor* 96:545–551.

Heinrich, B., and J. M. Marzluff. 1991. Do common ravens yell because they want to attract others? *Behavioral Ecology and Sociobiology* 28:13–22.

——. 1992. Age and mouth color in Common Ravens, *Corvus corax. Condor* 94:549–550.

——. 1995. Why ravens share. *American Scientist* 83:342–349.

Heinrich, B., J. Marzluff, and W. Adams. 1995. Fear and food recognition in naive Common Ravens. *Auk* 112:499–503.

Heinrich, B., J. M. Marzluff, and C. S. Marzluff. 1993. Ravens are attracted to the appeasement calls of food discoverers when attacked. *Auk* 110:247–254.

Heinrich, B., and J. Pepper. 1998. Influence of competitors on caching behaviour in the common raven, *Corvus corax. Animal Behaviour* 56:1083–1090.

Heinrich, B., and R. Smolker. 1998. Raven play. Pp. 27–44 in *Animal Play: Evolutionary, Comparative, and Ecological Aspects,* ed. M. Bekoff and J. A. Byers. Cambridge: Cambridge University Press.

Henshaw, R. E., L. S. Underwood, and T. M. Casey. 1972. Peripheral thermoregulation in two arctic canines. *Science* 175:988–990.

Hooper, R. G. 1977. Nesting habitat of Common Ravens in Virginia. *Wilson Bulletin* 89:233–242.

Horowitz, A. 2009. *Inside of a Dog: What Dogs See, Smell and Know.* New York: Scribner.

Houston, C. S. 1977. Changing patterns of Corvidae on the prairies. *Blue Jay* 35:149–156.

Howell, S. N., and G. S. Webb. 1995. *A Guide to the Birds of Mexico and Northern Central America.* New York: Oxford University Press.

Irving, L. 1966. Adaptations to the cold. *Scientific American* 214:94–101.

Janes, S. W. 1976. The apparent use of rocks by a raven in nest defense. *Condor* 78:409.

Kays, R., A. Curtis, and J. J. Kirchman. 2010. Rapid adaptive evolution of northeastern coyotes via hybridization with wolves. *Biology Letters* 6:89–93.

Kelcey, J. G., and G. Rheinwald, eds. 2005. *Birds in European Cities.* St. Katharinen, Germany: Ginster Verlag.

Kerttu, M. E. 1973. Aging techniques for the common raven (*Corvus corax principalis* Ridgeway). MS thesis, Michigan Technical University, Houghton.

Knight, R. L. 1984. Responses of nesting ravens to people in areas of different human densities. *Condor* 86:345–346.

Knight, R. L., D. P. Anderson, and N. V. Marr. 1991. Responses of an avian scavenging guild to anglers. *Biological Conservation* 56:195–205.

Knight, R. L., and J. Kawashima. 1993. Responses of raven and red-tailed hawk populations to linear right-of-ways. *Journal of Wildlife Management* 57:266–271.

Knight, R. L., H. L. Knight, and R. J. Camp. 1993. Raven populations and land-use patterns in the Mojave Desert, California. *Wildlife Society Bulletin* 21:469–471.

———. 1995. Common ravens and number and type of linear rights-of-way. *Biological Conservation* 74:65–67.

Knight, S. K., and R. L. Knight. 1983. Aspects of food finding by wintering Bald Eagles. *Auk* 100:477–484.

Krebs, J. R. 1974. Colonial nesting and social feeding as strategies for exploiting food resources in the great blue heron (*Ardea herodias*). *Behaviour* 51:99–134.

Kristan, W. B., and W. I. Boarman. 2003. Spatial pattern of risk of common raven predation on desert tortoises. *Ecology* 84:2432–2443.

Kristan, W. B., W. I. Boarman, and J. J. Crayon. 2004. Diet composition of common ravens across the urban-wildland interface of the West Mojave Desert. *Wildlife Society Bulletin* 32:244–253.

Kristan, W. B., W. I. Boarman, and W. C. Webb. 2005. *Stage-structured matrix models of common ravens (Corvus corax) in the West Mojave Desert, CA.* U.S. Geological Survey. Sacramento: Western Ecological Research Center.

Kruuk, H. 2003. *Niko's Nature.* Oxford: Oxford University Press.

Larsen, K. H., and J. H. Dietrich. 1970. Reduction of a raven population on lambing grounds with DRC-1339. *Journal of Wildlife Management* 34:200–204.

Levorsen, B., ed. 1976. *MUSH! A Beginner's Manual of Sled Dog Training.* New York: Arner Publications.

Linz, G. M., C. E. Knittle, and R. E. Johnson. 1992. Home range of breeding common ravens in coastal Southern California. *Southwestern Naturalist* 37:199–202.

Loman, J., and S. Tamm. 1980. Do roosts serve as "information centers" for crows and ravens? *American Naturalist* 115:285–289.

Lorenz, K. 1954. *Man Meets Dog.* London: Methuen.

———. 1968. Pair-formation in ravens. Pp. 17–36 in *Man and Animal: Studies in Behaviour,* ed. H. Friedrich, trans. M. Nawiasky. New York: St. Martin's Press.

———. 1981. *The Foundations of Ethology.* New York: Simon and Schuster.

Lovette, I. J. 2004. Mitochondrial dating and mixed support for the "2% rule" in birds. *Auk* 121:1–6.

Luginbuhl, J. M., J. M. Marzluff, J. E. Bradley, M. G. Raphael, and D. E. Varland. 2001. Corvid survey techniques and the relationship between corvid relative abundance and nest predation. *Journal of Field Ornithology* 72:556–572.

Mahringer, E. B. 1970. The population dynamics of the common raven (*Corvus corax principalis* Ridgway) on the Baraga Plains L'Anse, Michigan. MS thesis, Michigan Technical University, Houghton.

Marzluff, J. M., and T. Angell. 2005a. *In the Company of Crows and Ravens.* New Haven: Yale University Press.

———. 2005b. Cultural coevolution: how the human bond with crows and ravens extends theory and raises new questions. *Journal of Ecological Anthropology* 9:67–73.

Marzluff, J. M., and R. P. Balda. 1988a. Advantages of, and constraints forcing, mate fidelity in a Pinyon Jay society. *Auk* 105:286–295.

———. 1988b. Pairing patterns and fitness in free-ranging Pinyon Jays: What do they reveal about mate choice? *Condor* 90:201–213.

———. 1992. *The Pinyon Jay.* London: T & A D Poyser.

Marzluff, J. M., R. B. Boone, and G. W. Cox. 1994. Historical changes in populations and perceptions of native pest bird species in the West. *Studies in Avian Biology* 15:202–220.

Marzluff, J. M., and B. Heinrich. 1991. Foraging by common ravens in the presence and absence of territory holders: an experimental analysis of social foraging. *Animal Behaviour* 42:755–770.

———. 2001. Ravens roosts are still information centres. *Animal Behaviour* 61:F14–F15.

Marzluff, J. M., B. Heinrich, and C. S. Marzluff. 1996. Raven roosts are mobile information centres. *Animal Behaviour* 51:89–103.

Marzluff, J. M., and J. O. McKinley. 1993. Exploitation of carcasses and nesting behavior of common ravens in the Snake River Birds of Prey Area. Pp. 328–340 in *Snake River Birds of Prey Area Research and Monitoring Annual Report—1993,* ed. K. Steenhof. Boise, ID: U.S. Department of Interior, Bureau of Land Management.

Marzluff, J. M., and E. Neatherlin. 2006. Corvid response to human settlements and campgrounds: causes, consequences, and challenges for conservation. *Biological Conservation* 130:301–314.

Marzluff, J. M., J. Walls, H. N. Cornell, J. Withey, and D. P. Craig. 2010. Lasting recognition of threatening people by wild American crows. *Animal Behaviour* 79:699–707.

Miklósi, Á. 2007. *Dog Behaviour, Evolution, and Cognition.* Oxford: Oxford University Press.

Miller, W. D., and L. Griscom. 1925. Further notes on Central American birds, with descriptions of new forms. *American Museum Novitates* 184:1–16.

Mock, D. W., T. C. Lamey, and D. B. A. Thompson. 1988. Falsifiability and the information centre hypothesis. *Ornis Scandinavica* 19:231–248.

Navarro-Siguenza, A. G., and A. T. Peterson. 2004. An alternative species taxonomy of the birds of Mexico. *Biota Neotropica* 4 (2). Online at www.biotaneotropica .org.br.

Nogales, M., and E. C. Hernandez. 1994. Interinsular variations in the spring and summer diet of the raven *Corvus corax* in the Canary Islands. *Ibis* 136:441–447.

Omland, K. E., J. M. Baker, and J. L. Peters. 2006. Genetic signatures of intermediate divergence: population history of Old and New World Holarctic ravens (*Corvus corax*). *Molecular Ecology* 15:795–808.

Omland, K. E., C. L. Tarr, W. I. Boarman, J. M. Marzluff, and R. C. Fleischer. 2000. Cryptic genetic variation and paraphyly in ravens. *Proceedings of the Royal Society of London B* 267:2475–2482.

Parker, P. G., T. A. Waite, B. Heinrich, and J. M. Marzluff. 1994. Do common ravens share ephemeral food resources with kin? DNA fingerprinting evidence. *Animal Behaviour* 48:1085–1093.

Pugnetti, G., and E. M. Schuler. 1980. *Simon and Schuster's Guide to Dogs.* New York: Simon and Schuster.

Quaranta, A., M. Siniscalchi, and G. Vallortigara. 2007. Asymmetric tail-wagging responses by dogs to different emotive stimuli. *Current Biology* 17:199–201.

Rabenold, P. P. 1987. Recruitment to food in black vultures: evidence for following from communal roosts. *Animal Behaviour* 35:1775–1785.

Ratcliffe, D. 1997. *The Raven: A Natural History in Britain and Ireland.* London: T & A D Poyser.

Rea, A. M. 1986. *Corvus corax,* geographic variation. Pp. 65–66 in *The Known Birds of North and Middle America,* part 1. Denver: A. R. Phillips.

Rea, A. M., and D. Kanteena. 1968. Age determination of Corvidae. Pt. 2: Common and White-Necked Ravens. *Western Bird Bander* 43:6–9.

Renssen, T. A. 1988. Herintroductie van de raaf (*Corvus corax*) in Nederland. *Limosa* 61:137–144.

Restani, M., J. M. Marzluff, and R. E. Yates. 2001. Effects of anthropogenic food sources on movements, survivorship, and sociality of Common Ravens in the Arctic. *Condor* 103:399–404.

Restani, M., R. E. Yates, and J. M. Marzluff. 1996. Capturing Common Ravens *Corvus corax* in Greenland. *Dansk Ornitologisk Forenings Tidsskrift* 90:153–158.

Richner, H., and P. Heeb. 1995. Is the information center hypothesis a flop? *Advances in the Study of Behavior* 24:1–45.

——. 1996. Communal life: honest signaling and the recruitment center hypothesis. *Behavioral Ecology* 7:115–119.

Sablin, M. V., and G. A. Khlopachev. 2002. The earliest Ice Age dogs: evidence from Eliseevichi I. *Current Anthropology* 43:795–799.

Saiza, A. 1968. Age determination of Corvidae. Pt. 3: Juvenals. *Western Bird Bander* 43:20–23.

Salisbury, G., and L. Salisbury. 2003. *The Cruelest Miles: The Heroic Story of Dogs and Men in a Race against an Epidemic.* New York: W. W. Norton.

Sauer, J. R., J. E. Hines, I. Thomas, J. Fallon, and G. Gough. 2000. The North American Breeding Bird Survey, results and analysis. Version 98.1. Laurel, MD: Patuxent Wildlife Research Center. Online at http://www.mbr.nbs.gov/bbs/bbs.html.

Sax, B. 2003. *Crow.* London: Reaktion Books.

Schjelderup-Ebbe, T. 1922. Observation on the social psychology of domestic fowls. *Zeitshrift für Psychologie* 88:225–252.

Schleidt, W. M., and M. D. Shalter. 2003. Co-evolution of humans and canids: an alternative view of dog domestication: *Homo Homini Lupus? Evolution and Cognition* 9:57–72.

Schmidt-Nielsen, K. 1981. Countercurrent systems in animals. *Scientific American* 244:118–128.

Schultz-Soltau, J. 1962. Rückgang und Wiederausbreitung des Kolkraben (*Corvus corax* L.) im nördlichen Mitteleuropa, unter besonderer Berücksichtigung Niedersachsens. Abhandlungen und Verhandlungen des Naturwissenschaftlichen Vereins in Hamburg. *Neue Folge* 6:337–401.

Schwartz, M. 1997. *A History of Dogs in the Early Americas.* New Haven: Yale University Press.

Scott, J. P., and J. L. Fuller. 1965. *Genetics and the Social Behavior of the Dog.* Chicago: University of Chicago Press.

Skarphédinsson, K. H., Ó. K. Nielsen, S. Thórisson, S. Thorstensen, and S. A. Temple. 1990. *Breeding Biology, Movements, and Persecution of Ravens in Iceland.* ACTA Naturalia Islandica. Reykjavik: Icelandic Museum of Natural History.

Slobodchikoff, C. N., ed. 1988. *The Ecology of Social Behavior*. San Diego: Academic Press.

Smith, D. W., and G. Ferguson. 2005. *Decade of the Wolf, Returning the Wild to Yellowstone*. Guilford, CT: Lyons Press.

Steenhof, K., and M. N. Kochert. 1982. Nest attentiveness and feeding rates of Common Ravens in Idaho. *Murrelet* 63:30–32.

Steenhof, K., M. N. Kochert, and J. A. Roppe. 1993. Nesting by raptors and Common Ravens on electrical transmission line towers. *Journal of Wildlife Management* 57:271–281.

Stiehl, R. B. 1978. Aspects of the ecology of the Common Raven in Harney Basin, Oregon. Ph.D. diss., Portland State University, Portland OR.

Temple, S. A. 1974. Winter food habits of ravens on the arctic slope of Alaska. *Arctic* 27:41–46.

Thompson, R. n.d. *Seppala's Saga of the Sled Dog*, vol. 1. Self-published.

——. n.d. *Seppala's Saga of the Sled Dog*, vol. 2. R.T.C.I. Press.

Tinbergen, N. 1953. *Social Behaviour in Animals*. London: Methuen.

Udell, M. A. R., and C. D. L. Wynne. 2010. Ontogeny and phylogeny: both are essential to human-sensitive behaviour in the genus *Canis*. *Animal Behaviour* 79:E9–E14.

Valutis, L. L., and J. M. Marzluff. 1999. The appropriateness of puppet-rearing birds for reintroduction. *Conservation Biology* 13:584–591.

Van Rooijen, J. 2010. Do dogs and bees possess a "theory of mind"? *Animal Behaviour* 79:E7–E8.

Van Vessem, J., and D. Draulans. 1987. Patterns of arrival and departure of Grey Herons *Ardea cinerea* at two breeding colonies. *Ibis* 129:353–363.

Vaurie, C. 1954. Systematic notes on palearctic birds no. 5. Corvidae. *American Museum Novitates* 1668:1–23.

Vilà, C., P. Savolainen, J. E. Maldonado, I. R. Amorim, J. E. Rice, R. L. Honeycutt, K. A. Crandall, J. Lundeberg, and R. K. Wayne. 1997. Multiple and ancient origins of the domestic dog. *Science* 276:1687–1689.

von Frisch, K. 1953. *The Dancing Bees*. New York: Harcourt Brace Jovanovich.

——. 1967. *The Dance Language and Orientation of Bees*. Cambridge: Harvard University Press.

———. 1974. Decoding the language of the bee. *Science* 185:663–668.

von Holdt, B. M., J. P. Pollinger, K. E. Lohmueller, E. Han, H. G. Parker, P. Quignon, J. D. Degenhardt, A. R. Boyko, D. A. Earl, A. Auton, A. Reynolds, K. Bryc, A. Brisbin, J. C. Knowles, D. S. Mosher, T. C. Spady, A. Elkahloun, E. Geffen, M. Pilot, W. Jedrzejewski, C. Greco, E. Randi, D. Bannasch, A. Wilton, J. Shearman, M. Musiani, M. Cargill, P. G. Jones, Z. Qian, W. Huang, Z. Ding, Y. Zhang, C. D. Bustamante, E. A. Ostrander, J. Novembre, and R. K. Wayne. 2010. Genome-wide SNP and haplotype analyses reveal a rich history underlying dog domestication. *Nature* 464:898–902.

Vucetich, J. A., R. O. Peterson, and T. A. Waite. 2004. Raven scavenging favours group foraging in wolves. *Animal Behaviour* 67:1117–1126.

Waite, T. A., and K. L. Field. 2007. Foraging with others: games social foragers play. Pp. 331–362 in *Foraging*, ed. D. W. Stephens, J. S. Brown, and R. C. Ydenberg. Chicago: University of Chicago Press.

Ward, P., and A. Zahavi. 1973. The importance of certain assemblages of birds as "information-centres" for food-finding. *Ibis* 115:517–534.

Weatherhead, P. J. 1983. Two principal strategies in avian communal roosts. *American Naturalist* 121:237–243.

Webb, W. C., Jr., W. I. Boarman, and J. T. Rotenberry. 2004. Common Raven juvenile survival in a human-augmented landscape. *Condor* 106:517–528.

Webb, W. C., Jr., and N. C. Ellstrand. 2003. First record of Common Raven (*Corvus corax*) double brooding. *Western Birds* 33:258–261.

Weir, A. A., S. J. Chappell, and A. Kacelnik. 2002. Shaping of hooks in New Caledonian crows. *Science* 297:981.

White, C. 2005. Hunters ring dinner bell for ravens: experimental evidence of a unique foraging strategy. *Ecology* 86:1057–1060.

White, C. M., and M. Tanner-White. 1988. Use of interstate highway overpasses and billboards for nesting by the common raven (*Corvus corax*). *Great Basin Naturalist* 48:64–67.

Whitmore, K. D., and J. M. Marzluff. 1998. Hand-rearing corvids for reintroduction: importance of feeding regime, nestling growth, and dominance. *Journal of Wildlife Management* 62:1460–1479.

Wilcox, B., and C. Walkowicz. 1995. *The Atlas of Dog Breeds of the World,* 5th ed. Neptune, NJ: T.F.H. Publications.

Wilkinson, G. S. 1984. Reciprocal food sharing in the vampire bat. *Nature* 308:181–184.

Wittenberger, J. F. 1981. *Animal Social Behavior.* Belmont, CA: Wadsworth.

Willett, D. W. 1986. *The Seppala Siberian.* Viola, ID: Heritage North Press.

Wright, J., R. E. Stone, and N. Brown. 2003. Communal roosts as structured information centers in the raven, *Corvus corax. Journal of Animal Ecology* 72:1003–1014.

Zahavi, A. 1996. The evolution of communal roosts as information centers and the pitfall of group selection: a rejoinder to Richner and Heeb. *Behavioral Ecology* 7:118–119.

Zawadzka, D. 2006. *Kruk.* Świebodzin, Poland: Wydawnictwo Klubu Przyrodników.

Zimen, E. 1981. *The Wolf: His Place in the Natural World.* London: Souvenir Press.

Index

Page numbers in *italics* indicate illustrations.